APPALACHIAN ASPIRATIONS

APPALACHIAN
ASPIRATIONS

The Geography of Urbanization and Development in
the Upper Tennessee River Valley, 1865–1900

John Benhart Jr.

The University of Tennessee Press / Knoxville

Benhart, John E.
Appalachian aspirations : the geography of urbanization and development in the
Upper Tennessee River Valley, 1865–1900 / John Benhart Jr. – 1st ed.
      p. cm.
Includes bibliographical references and index.

ISBN-13: 978-1-57233-562-2 (hardcover : acid-free paper)
ISBN-10: 1-57233-562-9 (hardcover ; acid-free paper)

  1. Industrialization–Tennessee–Roane County–History–19th century.
  2. Industrialization–Tennessee–Loudon County–History–19th century.
  3. Tennessee River Valley–History–19th century.
  I. Title.
HC107.A135B46 2006
338.9768'84009034–dc22   2006023737

THIS ONE IS FOR THE HOME TEAM:

My wife Jacque, my daughter Carlee, and my son Jake—for unintentionally putting this project in perspective through the joy of our lives together

and

For my parents Jack and Patricia Benhart, my sister Cristen Breski, my grandmother Anne Wilk, my grandfather Edward Speck, and the memory of my brother Robert Francis Benhart

To love and be loved is to feel the sun from both sides.
—David Viscott

CONTENTS

FIGURES

MAPS

TABLES

ACKNOWLEDGMENTS

A large number of people have contributed to the completion of this work—I only hope that I give them the credit they deserve in these acknowledgments.

Employees at the Roane County (Tennessee) Heritage Commission in the early to mid-1990s, Jere Hall and Sarge, made it possible for me to find company records, literature, pictures, and other primary material. Later, in 2005, Robert Bailey at the Heritage Commission assisted me in obtaining digital copies of rare maps and photographs, which are significant to this work. The volunteers at the Roane County Heritage Commission have developed an excellent local historical collection, without which this book would be significantly different. I would also like to thank Danielle Wylie, a work-study student in the Department of Geography and Regional Planning at Indiana University of Pennsylvania, for her diligent work on "cleaning up" images of historical maps used in this book.

Important material was also found at several university and public libraries. In Knoxville, Tennessee, the staff at the University of Tennessee Special Collections and the McClung Historical Collection assisted in my sometimes aimless search for letters, documents, and records. At the Tennessee State Archives in Nashville, I was aided by several able and courteous staffpersons, who were particularly helpful in locating Sanborn maps. At the Virginia Polytechnic Institute's Newman Library, employees helped me find the material that I needed, even staying overtime as I pored over thousands of pages of East Tennessee, Virginia & Georgia Railway records.

I also have very much appreciated the opportunity to work with outstanding and generous instructors and colleagues in the completion of this project. During my appointment in the Department of Geography and Regional Planning at Indiana University of Pennsylvania, I have had the good fortune to work with outstanding and giving colleagues who are dedicated to academia. They each in their own way supported this project and made it possible through their approach to what we do. During my graduate studies at the University of Tennessee, Knoxville, my dissertation committee in the Department of Geography—Dr. Thomas Bell, Dr. Ronald Foresta, and Dr. Bruce Ralston—put a lot of time and effort reading my research and providing feedback that made the work better. Later, when I returned to Knoxville on sabbatical in the spring of 2004 as a visiting faculty member, they not only remembered the project, but were still interested in contributing to its evolution even as they had moved on to new and different facets of their own research. While at the University of Tennessee on sabbatical, I also enjoyed talking with Dr. John Rehder, who had good advice on the academic book publication process, and other faculty in the Department of Geography who welcomed me while I was there. I also would like to thank the reviewers of earlier versions of this manuscript—Paul Salstrom and Geoffery Buckley—for their constructive criticism and insightful comments. Their time and effort improved the book measurably.

My family has always been very important to me, and it is to them that I owe the largest debt of gratitude in the achievement of this work. My wife, Jacque, has been a constant supporter throughout this project. When I was working on my dissertation as a Ph.D. candidate, she was the one who always believed in what I was doing and made enough money for us to pay the bills. When I had the opportunity to take a sabbatical some years later to expand my research to write this book, Jacque was one hundred percent behind me, even though it meant that I would be spending time away from home, leaving her to care for our young children in my absence. I only hope that I can display the same degree of selflessness in helping her achieve her goals in life. My children, Carlee and Jake, are proof to me that God bestows great blessings. They don't know much about this book, but they had a lot of fun seeing the little apartment that Dad stayed in while he was doing research and picking flowers in Cades Cove when we visited Tennessee. I have learned more from being a father than from all the books that I have ever read, and I have Carlee and Jake to thank for that.

My parents, Jack and Pat Benhart, and my sister, Cristen, have always supported all of my endeavors and made me feel that I could succeed at them. My family always conveyed to my sister and me that we could accomplish anything if we put our minds to it and worked hard enough. Thanks, Mom and Dad, and thanks to all the members of my extended family for the many things I recall, and probably more for all the little things I don't that made all the difference along the way.

INTRODUCTION

Lenoir City will be . . . where the two streams of immigration and capital flowing southward—from the Eastern and Middle states . . . and from the valleys of the Ohio and Upper Mississippi rivers . . . will unite and build up a great industrial center.

—Prospectus of the Lenoir City Company, 1890

Locate your town where railroads are, or are bound to be, and where minerals are abundant close at hand, and you may build as many as you please.

—Prospectus of the East Tennessee
Land Company, 1890

Landscapes are substantial if intangible things. . . . They are . . . made within a context of well attested ideas and beliefs about how the world works, and how it might be improved.

—Edward Relph, *The Modern Urban
Landscape*, 1987

Unless you are from East Tennessee, or a historian with an interest in the production of freight rail cars during the early twentieth century, you have probably not heard of Lenoir City, Tennessee. Failure is a funny thing, in that most people are not nearly as interested in learning about it as they are success. Lenoir City, Tennessee, did not become a "great industrial center" as prophesied by the Lenoir City Company in 1890 (see the above quotation). Rather, it became a small regional city in East Tennessee that in the early twenty-first century seems no more or less remarkable than any other place (depending on your perspective). But Lenoir City and some of its neighboring

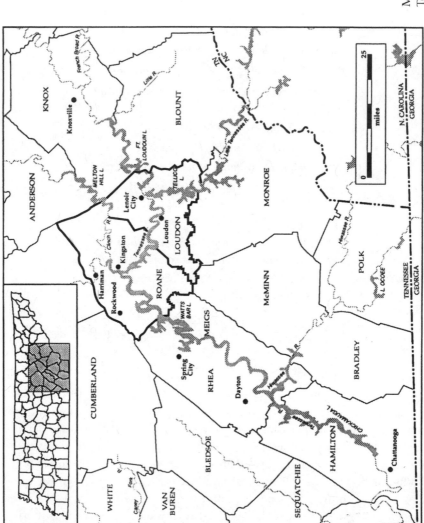

MAP 1. The Regional Context: East Tennessee.

settlements have a story to tell. The story in part is about failed aspirations: the failure to build great cities; the failure to implement new technologies; the failure to produce and export industrial commodities; and the failure (and the greatest sin for capitalists) to accrue profit. But this story is redeeming in that it provides an opportunity to clearly see the values, ideologies, ethics, and technologies of humans played out on the landscape of a particular region during a particular time period—the *Upper Tennessee River Valley* between 1865 and 1900. What we can learn from the Upper Tennessee River Valley has significant implications for understanding the inner workings and geographic implications of industrial and corporate capitalism in Southern Appalachia and indeed in many parts of the United States during this time period.

The Upper Tennessee River Valley encompasses present-day Roane and Loudon Counties, Tennessee. The region as I define it encompasses slightly over 589 square miles and lies approximately 50 miles southwest of Knoxville, Tennessee, and approximately 65 miles northeast of Chattanooga, Tennessee, in the southern portion of the Great Valley physiographic province. It is physically bounded by the southern extension of the Appalachian Mountains on the east, and the eastern edge of the Cumberland Plateau on the west, and is drained by the Clinch and Emory Rivers, which then contribute to the Tennessee River as it flows southwest down the valley.[1]

In its physical geography and preindustrial economy, the Upper Tennessee River Valley of 1865 was in many ways representative of Southern Appalachia as a whole. For much of the eighteenth and nineteenth centuries rugged topography limited in-migration of settlers and trade. The regional landscape dictated that sedentary agriculture took place on small to medium size farms. The ridges that defined the Tennessee Valley on the east and west, and intruded into it to form the Ridge and Valley Province, were densely forested and underlain by coal and iron ore. Settlers who migrated into the region via the Great Valley during the preindustrial period laid the foundation for the subsistence agriculture/mercantile economy that evolved in the region prior to the advent of industrial capitalism.[2] The Upper Tennessee River Valley, similar to much of Southern Appalachia, had hardly been touched by industrial capitalism before the Civil War. After the war, however, a combination of factors made many Southern Appalachian subregions attractive to capitalists who perceived new profit opportunities. The Upper Tennessee River Valley was one of these.

The Story

In the fall of 1865 Hiram Chamberlain and John Wilder rode on horseback from Knoxville, Tennessee, southwest into Roane County, Tennessee. Both men had been Union officers stationed in East Tennessee during the Civil War and had

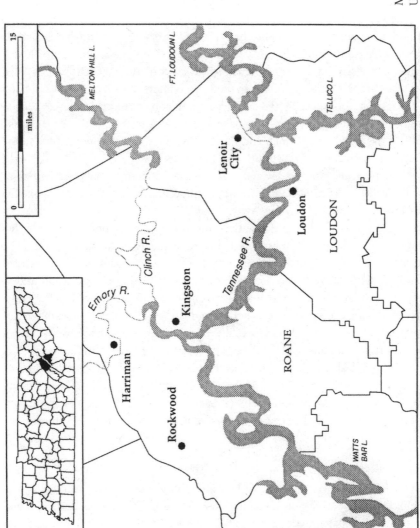

MAP 2. The Regional Context: The Upper Tennessee River Valley.

decided to stay in the South to pursue business careers. Wilder wanted to show Chamberlain an area where he had seen outcroppings of red iron ore, bituminous coal, and limestone in close proximity during a wartime operation. At the time of their trip, Chamberlain was a partner in a small rolling mill in Knoxville, and Wilder wanted his opinion on a site for a blast furnace to make pig iron.[3] After making a survey of the area, the two men agreed that it had access to all of the resources needed for iron production, and they proceeded to recruit business partners and buy mineral land. In late 1867 they and their business associates established the Roane Iron Company. By December of 1868, a blast furnace had been built with a production capacity of fifteen tons of pig iron per day. Less than a year later, the furnace employed enough workers to require permanent housing, and a town—Rockwood, Tennessee—was established.[4] This pattern would be repeated in many areas of Southern Appalachia in the post–Civil War period. The details about the dates and resources might differ, but the stories were the same—industrial capitalism came to Appalachia.

The 1865 ride with Wilder into the Tennessee countryside turned out to be an important trip personally for Hiram Chamberlain, as he remained involved with the industrial entity that he and Wilder established—the Roane Iron Company—for the next forty years. It also was important for the future of the Upper Tennessee River Valley. Chamberlain and his business associates proved to be agents of change for the region, as they worked to leverage its natural resources in production processes that would yield marketable industrial commodities.

In the late 1860s another East Tennessee businessman—Charles McClung McGhee—began working to improve the economic fortunes of the Upper Tennessee River Valley. McGhee was a native East Tennessean—born in Monroe County, Tennessee, and raised in Knoxville—who at this time was president of the People's Bank of Knoxville. In 1866 McGhee and a group of business associates orchestrated the merger of the East Tennessee & Georgia and the East Tennessee & Virginia Railroads by purchasing large blocks of stock in both companies. The resulting rail corridor connected Bristol, Virginia, to Dalton, Georgia, making the valley more accessible than it had ever been before and increasing its attractiveness to industrial capitalists. Charles McGhee served on the board of directors of the East Tennessee, Virginia & Georgia Railroad for the next twenty-five years; during that time the railroad expanded tremendously, and McGhee maintained close contact with friends and business associates in East Tennessee.

In 1882 McGhee became a member of the board of directors of the Roane Iron Company at the urging of Hiram Chamberlain. Chamberlain and McGhee had become business associates in Knoxville during the Civil War and were now working together to build Roane Iron. McGhee's involvement with Roane Iron was very important for the company, as he had two invaluable business connections—to the vast East Tennessee, Virginia, & Georgia Railroad system as a board member; and to the growing loan capital market of New York City as a result of his railroad dealings. McGhee, through his business connections and interest in economic development in East Tennessee, became one of the key players in introducing the business methods of corporate capitalism to the Upper Tennessee River Valley. For the next several years Chamberlain and McGhee would work to enable the Roane Iron Company to expand into steel production, the emerging industry standard material for railroad and manufacturing construction.

Some years later in the spring of 1890, an unknown author wrote of a town called Harriman, Tennessee, being built approximately ten miles northeast of where the Roane Iron Company built Rockwood in the Upper Tennessee River Valley: "This ideal site lay just outside the mouth of Emory Gap . . . at the junction of the Cincinnati Southern and the East Tennessee, Virginia and Georgia Railways. Coal was known to exist in Walden's Ridge . . . and iron ore was an accepted fact in the lesser ridges parallel, with limestone in rifle-shot of each."[5] The industrial capitalist logic in this description was so simple, so spatially obvious: the physical geography (the location of Emory Gap, mineral resources) and the human geography (rail infrastructure) dictated that Harriman had to be a success. The resources and infrastructure for industrial capitalism were in place just as they were at Rockwood—all that was needed was the addition of capital and labor. But there was more. Capitalism and capitalist strategies had changed since Wilder and Chamberlain took their horseback ride into Roane County in the mid-1860s. Harriman would have additional advantages relating to capital, the physical environment of the city, and the "social condition" of its population. The city of Harriman would be developed by a company called the East Tennessee Land Company (ETLC), a publicly owned corporation. Public ownership would allow the company to accumulate large amounts of capital to undertake development. Harriman would have an electricity plant, a waterworks, and a sewage system, and it would allow no saloons. It would be a perfect place to cultivate the labor force needed to manufacture goods efficiently and at the same time avoid the ills of contemporary cities that had been the product of unfettered industrialization—congestion, disease, and crime. In 1890 the East Tennessee Land Company wasn't just selling industrial capitalism, it was selling a combination of ideas about capital accumulation, economic development, and urban landscape as a form of ideology. The fact that many capitalists of the period embraced the "new" ideology, and backed their beliefs with their money, is telling as a reflection of the capitalist ethos of the period.

By 1895 things had changed dramatically in the Upper Tennessee River Valley. Observers were now offering a much different characterization of Harriman and its contemporaries. There had been a massive downturn in the American economy, often referred to as the Panic of 1893. Cardiff, Tennessee, was another "new" town in the Upper Tennessee River Valley, situated less than ten miles southwest of Harriman; a writer for the Chattanooga *Tradesman* painted this picture in 1895: "Today the town does not contain twenty people. The only signs of it that can be seen are a few deserted stores, rain-washed streets . . . and electric light poles which ornament the vacant fields."[6] Harriman and Lenoir City, the other new towns of the Upper Tennessee River Valley, did not disappear completely from the landscape, like Cardiff. Rather their development was halted and the pattern unintentionally preserved, like the imprint of a fossil in a stone. Cobb (1982), describes this period in northern Alabama in a similar fashion: "The expansion of the Alabama iron industry was accompanied by considerable boosterism and profiteering . . . often encouraging the development of new towns seemingly destined to become industrial centers. . . . By the mid-1890s, many of the once heralded metropolises had seen furnaces close, land sales fizzle, and their opportunistic boosters move on to areas with better opportunities."[7]

The emphasis of these accounts, regardless of time period, was the failure of land companies (capitalists) to accomplish what they had set out to do. To be sure, the attempts of the East Tennessee Land Company and its contemporaries to plan and build manufacturing complexes and model industrial cities in the Upper Tennessee River Valley had largely failed, leaving behind remnant landscapes. But for this story it is not the end result that matters so much. In telling the story of the Upper Tennessee River Valley, I take a different tack: that the strategies and methods of capitalists during particular time periods, and the geographic imprints that they leave behind on the earth's surface, can enhance our understanding of regional landscapes.

We can learn from the efforts of entrepreneurs who attempted to introduce industrial and corporate capitalism to the Upper Tennessee River Valley between 1865 and 1900. Although they did not succeed in achieving many of their goals in the region (producing steel or building large cities, for example), their stories illuminate some important aspects of regional geography and history, capitalist development strategies, and urban planning that were occurring throughout Appalachia and the United States during this period. A discussion of some important themes that run through the story of development in the Upper Tennessee River Valley between the end of the Civil War and the turn of the twentieth century are useful for context.

The Three Stages of Capitalism

Capitalism as an economic system has had a strong impact on the Upper Tennessee River Valley. There is a large body of literature that focuses on capitalism and how it has evolved over the last two centuries in the United States. This literature has covered a wide-ranging set of topics, from human value systems and regional trade regimes to changing profit strategies and geographic development patterns. Despite this broad range of perspectives on capitalism and its facets, there has been general agreement that regional economies in the United States between 1865 and 1900 manifested three stages of capitalism—*mercantile, industrial,* and *corporate*.[8]

Mercantile capitalism, the economic system under which the European settlement of the North American continent took place between 1650 and 1865, was involved in the buying and selling of various commodities but had little if any connection to their production.[9] Merchants bought cheap in order to sell high as they mediated among geographically dispersed producers and consumers. Their role within regional economies was to lower the cost and speed up the circulation of commodities (regional agricultural goods and imported manufactured products, for example) and capital by specializing in the marketing function. Profits resulted from the efficient performance of this role.[10]

The mercantile capitalist phase was dominant in the Upper Tennessee River Valley until the close of the Civil War in 1865. During the antebellum era, the Appalachian Mountains were a barrier to in-migration from the east. Settlers who traveled into the region via the Great Valley found limited availability of flat, fertile land and engaged in mixed-use agriculture on small valley farms. This agricultural economy was administered by a few important merchants in small towns such as Kingston and Loudon, Tennessee, on the banks of the region's three connected rivers—the Clinch, the Emory, and the Tennessee.

The early phases of the *industrial capitalism* that emerged out of the mercantile system in the United States after 1830 were marked by a sustained effort on the part of capitalists to control production and to buy labor in the same way they bought raw materials: as a specific quantity of work, measured by, and embodied in, the finished product.[11] The basic components of the industrial capitalist economic system were factories, mills, and workshops that provided employment to thousands of workers, and in doing so stimulated the urbanization process.

The industrial capitalist phase in the Upper Tennessee River Valley began with the activities of former Union soldiers, who initiated the first factory-scale industrial production in the region in 1867. These industrialists were motivated to invest in the region by the availability of coal and iron ore deposits in and around Walden's Ridge in Roane County, Tennessee. They constructed manufacturing facilities close to these mineral deposits and established communities in an effort to facilitate the production process.

Corporate capitalism evolved in response to the increased capital requirements of expanding business entities. Manufacturers in the most capital-intensive industries such as iron and steel, railroads, and textiles began to increase production capacity in order to achieve economies of scale. They also began to integrate resource acquisition, production facilities, and marketing within single business units in order to improve production and distribution. Forward integration by manufacturers took the form of expansion into the warehousing and sale of products. Backward integration was achieved by gaining control over the processes that preceded manufacturing, such as resource extraction and refining.[12] To fund these vertical integration activities, businesses began to reorganize into limited-liability ownership structures in which stock was sold to generate funds for business activities.

Railroads and land companies began the corporate capitalist phase in the Upper Tennessee River Valley in 1889. The entrepreneurs who established land companies were attracted by perceived profit opportunities and purchased hundreds of thousands of acres of land in the region as part of their development schemes. Each land company had access to large amounts of capital, and each initiated development projects that were *model real estate ventures* complete with plans for resource extraction, industrial production, and the establishment of cities.

The Role of Institutions and Individuals

The Upper Tennessee River Valley is a relatively small area, and its development pattern has been influenced by the same forces that have influenced Appalachia as a whole. Some of these forces—state government, the media, and railroads—are institutional in nature and have been cited as catalysts for regional development during the period between 1865 and 1900.

Southern Appalachia, in the post–Civil War period prior to the advent of industrial capitalism, has been characterized as largely isolated compared to many areas of the United States with respect to trade and transportation infrastructure.[13] In terms of local and regional economic structure, the region remained a frontier of sorts in the eastern United States. In much of Appalachia, subsistence agriculture predominated as regional farmers continued to rely on barter economies and adopted mechanization more slowly than farmers in other parts of the United States.[14] In the aftermath of the Civil War, then, much of Southern Appalachia was in a poorly developed stage of mercantile capitalism that hardly resembled the plantation-based economy of the lowland South.

The institutional and societal context for the arrival of industrial capitalism in Southern Appalachia emerged during the post–Civil War period, especially after Reconstruction. There has been debate about what forces brought about the institutional and societal changes that encouraged industrialization, urbanization, and the rise of the "New South." Some, most notably Woodward (1951), have suggested that an ascendant southern middle class was challenging the traditional economic dominance of the planter class in the aftermath of the war, while others, including Cash (1941), Wiener (1978), and Billings Jr. (1979), have argued that industrial capitalists worked cooperatively with (rather than struggling against) planters to ensure that agricultural and industrial pursuits did not impinge on each other within regional economies.[15] In any event, it is widely agreed that by 1870, a significant push was on to spur industrialization and the exploitation of resources in Southern Appalachia.

To what degree did institutions like state governments, railroads, and the media directly and indirectly encourage the spread of industrial and corporate capitalism in Appalachia? By the late 1860s many state governments were actively pursuing industrial investment. For example, in 1867 Tennessee established a state Board of Immigration, charged with encouraging immigration from northern states and Europe. The board, funded by state appropriations, produced literature and dispatched agents to northern and midwestern states touting the advantages of Tennessee and its resources.[16] During the same period, New South boosters such as Richard Edmonds (publisher of the periodical *Manufacturers' Record*), Henry Watterson (editor of the *Louisville Courier-Journal*), and Henry Grady (editor of the *Atlanta Constitution*) used their positions and their influence to convince both southern leaders and outside capitalists that the future of the New South (as opposed to the "old" agrarian order) lay with commercial and industrial development.[17]

Between 1870 and 1900 the railroads in Southern Appalachia expanded tremendously. Remote areas were now more accessible for resource extraction and industrialization, and their inhabitants were gaining exposure to the more advanced business practices of northern corporations and individual entrepreneurs. In the Upper Tennessee River Valley, these institutions played a large role in changing the character of the regional economy.

The Role of Business Entities in Creating Places

The urban settlements that were developed after 1865 in the Upper Tennessee River Valley were created by business entities. Before 1865, country merchant trade and agricultural marketing opportunities provided the impetus for the growth of small towns in the valley. But beginning in the late 1860s, companies such as the Roane Iron Company and the East Tennessee Land Company developed company towns and model industrial real estate projects as business ventures. How and why these businesses were compelled to build and plan towns and cities sheds light on the human and physical landscapes of these urban settlements in the past and present.

The role of business entities in creating and developing urban places has historically been determined by their business methods and profit strategies. Industrial businesses in the United States began to implement factory production between 1830 and 1870 because subcontracting and outsourcing systems of production were inefficient. Centralization of industrial employment allowed for the development and enforcement of regular hours of work, and the monitoring of worker efficiency and quality of the commodities produced.[18] In order for centralized production to be successful, a stable labor force was needed, preferably close to the production facility. In many cases, industrialists took matters into their own hands, recruiting workers and providing housing for them in isolated and often self-contained *company towns*. Industrial capitalists spent time and money to establish company towns because they believed their efforts would pay off in terms of more efficient industrial production and increased profit margins.[19]

Some industrialists even went so far as to invest in special types of urban settlements—*model company towns*—in the belief that certain types of physical environments would be conducive to increased production and profit. In model company towns, amenities such as water and sewer systems, public parks, libraries, sidewalks, and streetlights represented an effort to provide workers with a desirable place to live and raise their families. In the Upper Tennessee River Valley during the late nineteenth century, business entities created company towns and model industrial real estate ventures that reflected a spectrum of profit motives.

Industrialization, Urbanization, and Urban and Social Reform Movements

Industrial capitalism came to the Upper Tennessee River Valley in the form of mining, iron making, and large-scale railroad building beginning in the late 1860s. With industrialization came the inevitable problems and issues associated with significant numbers of people living in close proximity to one another and to industrial production facilities. Between 1865 and 1900, the style of urbanization that took place in the Upper Tennessee River Valley changed as reform movements emerged in response to the problems of urban industrial life. A comparison between the urban development patterns of Rockwood, Tennessee, and towns developed later, such as Harriman and Lenoir City, Tennessee, illustrates the impact of these social reform movements.

As they became part of the industrial labor force, workers were faced with the need for shelter near their workplaces. As industrialization progressed during the nineteenth century, in many instances the scale of production facilities increased, requiring larger numbers of workers. If independent developers could not, or would not, respond rapidly to the increased need for new housing, existing dwellings were forced to accommodate more people. In many American cities and towns, large boardinghouses and tenements were constructed by landowners and in some cases by laborers themselves to meet the demand.[20] This process created severe overcrowding and overwhelmed the capacity of the urban infrastructure, resulting in unsanitary and unhealthy living conditions.

Throughout the nineteenth century, a series of reform movements addressed urban problems through efforts to improve the living conditions in American cities, with the ultimate goal of making urban residents healthier and happier. Reformers believed that there was a causal relationship between the quality of environmental conditions and the level of human physical and mental health.[21] They addressed important urban issues of the era, such as sanitation and the need to expose urban dwellers to rural settings and the beauty of nature. The ideas of social reformers gradually filtered down to the public at large during the nineteenth century, and efforts were undertaken to address existing urban conditions through organized sanitary reform and urban parks movements.[22]

The social reformers' efforts to improve living conditions and the quality of life in American cities during the late nineteenth century placed heavy emphasis upon infrastructural solutions. As the ideas of reformers began to take hold within American society, they also influenced industrialists. Originally, manufacturers were most concerned with worker productivity and how it might be affected by the living conditions of the workers themselves. Some also began to believe that it was in their best interest to maintain a pool of healthy and loyal workers who were experienced and reliable. In some cases, manufacturers felt that the inability of independent developers to provide adequate housing for workers had a negative impact on labor stability and productivity. As a result, some decided to invest in the development of company-funded housing and communities for workers.

The first evidence of the influence of reform on urban development in the region appears with the activities of land companies. Each of the land companies that operated in the Upper Tennessee River Valley planned its city in advance and incorporated reform concepts such as urban parks, public sewer and water facilities, graded streets, and public lighting. In contrast to previous business entities, the land companies believed that incorporating principles of urban reform into the design of their cities was essential for success.

The Economic Development of an Appalachian Subregion

An understanding of capitalism and its different forms is important in examining and interpreting economic development patterns in the Upper Tennessee River Valley between 1865 and 1900. In particular, a focus on the stages of capitalism offers a reasonable strategy for analyzing the ways in which decisions impacting regional development were made in the United States in the mid- to late-nineteenth century. Having said this, it is important to note that capitalism doesn't evolve in isolation from other factors. Human decisions that lead to regional development aren't scripted. The industrial and corporate stages of capitalism had their inceptions at different times, with varying results throughout Southern Appalachia. Some areas were perceived to be advantageous and some were not—based on available technology, accessibility, and the presence or absence of particular resources. But what about the role of individuals in influencing regional development processes?

Burton Folsom, in the introduction to his book *Urban Capitalists,* discusses the debate within the social sciences regarding the impact of individuals versus general (nonhuman) forces on regional development. On one side of the debate (as Folsom frames it) is the idea put forward by many geographers and economists that environmental factors largely determine where particular types of development take place, as humans respond "rationally" to their context and make decisions accordingly. On the other side is the position espoused by many historians, emphasizing the importance of individuals in "making history" and offering as an example the role of entrepreneurs in taking risks, investing capital, and defining new markets. In his study of northeastern Pennsylvania, Folsom attempts to provide evidence of the latter—that "the quality of entrepreneurship . . . seems to explain urbanization more convincingly than the environmental determinism of so many social scientists."[23]

In telling the story of the development of the Upper Tennessee River Valley, I am not interested in advocating one side of the debate or the other. As a geographer, I believe that context matters quite a bit—that certain physical and human geographic prerequisites must exist for humans to consider particular courses of action as logical or feasible. For example, if iron and coal deposits exist in an area, and if railroads have already been built, the area would likely be perceived as highly advantageous for iron production—or at least more advantageous than someplace else. If these minerals and transportation infrastructure were *not* in place, it probably would not occur to most people to undertake those sorts of activities. As we will see, the capitalists who operated in the Upper Tennessee River Valley were keenly aware of the area's natural, technological, and financial resources and, in many cases, made very calculated decisions based on them.

However, people sometimes behave in ways that, based on context alone, we may not expect, and they do so for reasons we may not understand. The story of the Upper Tennessee River Valley provides many examples of this as well. An individual's affinity for a particular area, his or her values, or a person's desire to be close to friends and family could also play a major role in important decisions. Joseph Schumpeter, an economic historian, suggested that successful entrepreneurs have made "creative responses" to economic challenges, involving a variety of activities from accessing capital to manufacturing goods to building cities. He argued, for example, that the creative responses of certain capitalists "cannot be predicted" and can "shape[s] the whole course of subsequent events and their 'long run' outcome."[24]

This story about the Upper Tennessee River Valley employs a hybrid approach in analyzing regional development patterns between 1865 and 1900. It combines a thorough investigation of the geographic, economic, and technological contexts that existed in the region over time with a focus on the activities of key individual capitalists. During this period in the Upper Tennessee River Valley, some of the important contexts included physical geography (topography, hydrology, location of resources), iron- and steel-making technologies, transportation technologies, location of transportation infrastructure, organizational and capital structures of businesses, and the state of capital markets. The capitalists operating in the region during this era were important in bringing about regional development and the advent of more advanced modes of capitalism. Knowledge of these individuals—and their backgrounds, connections, and associations—offers insight into development patterns that would not make sense otherwise. In the Upper Tennessee River Valley, particular individuals were not only important in facilitating regional development, they were absolutely crucial in bringing about the advent of industrial and corporate capitalism in the region. These capitalists were conduits for the diffusion of new and different forms of capitalism into the Upper Tennessee River Valley.

In trying to understand regional development patterns, culture cannot be left out of the discussion. Just as the ideology of capitalism had a powerful influence on people's perceptions and decisions, we can assume that other ideologies and value systems also played significant roles. A large body of research documents the emergence of the urban/sanitary reform movement in the United States during the second half of the nineteenth century.[25] Schultz, in his book *Constructing Urban Culture,* details the emergence of a "new urban culture" in the United States during the nineteenth century, one that "arose from new attitudes about the relationship between the physical environment and bodily, mental, and moral health." In advocating the analysis of cities as cultural landscapes, he says: "Urban forms reveal what was and was not important to their builders and residents in any given moment."[26] Schultz's perspective suggests that in addition to capitalist imperatives, other human motivations also shaped the landscape when regional development occurred. In fact, corporate capitalists in the Upper Tennessee River Valley co-opted and integrated ideas of urban/sanitary reform with capitalist doctrine to formulate a regional development profit strategy in the late nineteenth century. Their profit strategy—which I call the *model industrial real estate venture*—was manifested in city plans drawn up and described in glowing terms in company literature. Granted, part of what these capitalists were doing was boosterism; however, it was boosterism designed to appeal to a particular market—the urban middle and upper class. In effect, they were selling a specific geographic and social vision of the industrial American city, one that they believed there was a market for.

Businesses in these areas had to operate within constraints imposed by such factors as levels of technology and capital availability. This leads to another question: Can understanding the development objectives of particular business organizations help us understand the qualities and characteristics of the places they created? If the answer to this question is yes (and I believe it is), another inherently geographic question presents itself: What kinds of places did capitalists create when they had the opportunity and resources to do so? The answer to this question is intriguing. Researchers such as Buder (1967), Francaviglia (1991), Garner (1984), Mosher (2004), and Shifflett (1991), among many others, have investigated in various regions and time periods the characteristics of communities (cultural, geographic, and social) established by business organizations. The Upper Tennessee River Valley saw a marked difference in the development objectives of business organizations established during the industrial capital period (prior to 1885) and those that began to operate during the emerging corporate stage (1885 and later). Understanding these development objectives is crucial to interpreting the geographic patterns of community development in the region.

In this book I examine the advent of industrial and corporate capitalism in the Upper Tennessee River Valley between 1865 and 1900. Rather than focusing on one stage of capitalism (for example, industrial capitalism) as it occurred throughout Southern Appalachia, the story focuses on a region and describes in detail how development took place over time. In this approach, the region is a constant, and the variables include factors such as the state of regional and national economies, capitalist strategies, technologies, relative location, and the decision-making processes of individuals. Like all stories, this is a story of specific people in a specific place; it focuses on the details of how economic development occurred in a fairly small region defined by the political boundaries of Roane and Loudon Counties, Tennessee. It is meant, however, to contribute in a broader way to understanding the evolution of capitalism and its regional impact in Southern Appalachia during this period.

CHAPTER 1

The Preindustrial Upper
Tennessee River Valley

*In Appalachia's preindustrial era . . . farming . . .
had to almost entirely provide the subsistence of
the families who were farming. No contradiction
existed between market farming and this necessary
subsistence farming, for Appalachia's most important
farm products . . . were just as suitable for supplying
outside markets as they were for home consumption*

—Paul Salstrom, *Appalachia's Path to
Dependency*, 1994

The physical geography of the Upper Tennessee River Valley prior to the advent of industrial capitalism was unique, but in some ways representative of Appalachia as a whole. It was representative in its relative geographic isolation in the Appalachian Mountains, an isolation heightened by the Muscle Shoals on the Tennessee River to the south. It was unique in that more arable land existed there than in most other subregions of Appalachia, as the deep soils of the Great Valley and the alluvial soils of the Tennessee River floodplain provided a fertile environment for subsistence farming.

The preindustrial Upper Tennessee River Valley was a sparsely settled region for much of the eighteenth century. The earliest European urban settlements were a product of settler struggle against the Cherokee Indians for land. The English, and later the Americans, built forts for protection from French and Indian attacks during the mid- to late 1700s. As native Indian groups were displaced over time by Europeans, these forts became the focus of economic activity. During the late eighteenth and early nineteenth centuries, roads began to be built through the region and an agricultural economy began to develop. River transport became significant, spurring the growth of towns such as Kingston, which became a break-of-bulk point for commodities moved by road and river. By the 1850s railroads appeared in the valley and played a key role in the development of the town of Loudon. Economic and settlement patterns created by subsistence and small-scale commercial agriculture and mercantile capitalism prevailed when industrial development of the region began in the post–Civil War era.

Indian and Early European Settlement Patterns

In the early eighteenth century, when Europeans first moved into the Upper Tennessee River Valley, the area was under the control of the Cherokee Indians, who had been living in the region since approximately A.D. 1000. They had developed a distinctive culture that included complicated mound burial rites, pottery making, a major commitment to maize agriculture, and a settlement pattern in which groups of permanent villages were satellites of larger communities with clearly defined ceremonial precincts.[1]

The area controlled by the Cherokees in the early 1700s was approximately forty thousand square miles, extending from the headwaters of the Tennessee River southward to approximately the southern edge of the foothills of the Appalachians, and east to west from the piedmont of the Carolinas and Georgia to the north-flowing Tennessee River in middle Tennessee.[2] The Cherokee population was distributed throughout approximately sixty to eighty towns in the early 1700s and was estimated to have numbered sixteen to seventeen thousand.

Cherokee towns were fairly permanent, located mostly along streams and rivers in valley areas. Agriculture was integral to their way of life. Corn was their main staple crop, but they also grew beans, gourds, and sunflowers as food crops. The Cherokee traveled over large areas in hunting parties in search of meat to supplement their diets. They had only a vague concept of landownership in the European sense. They knew what territory they controlled and could utilize for sustenance, but individuals did not claim land for themselves as property.[3]

The end of Cherokee control in the Tennessee Valley began with the arrival of Europeans in the early eighteenth century. Europeans settled East Tennessee late, compared to the coastal plain and piedmont areas of Georgia and North and South Carolina, with few incursions by individual trappers and traders. Until the early eighteenth century, the Appalachian Mountains were an imposing barrier to westward migration from English communities along the Atlantic coast. The French who had settled to the south and west were likewise dissuaded from moving into the Tennessee Valley by the impediment of the Muscle Shoals on the Tennessee River. The first major contact and negotiation that the English had with the Cherokee occurred in the South Carolina colony in 1721, when Indians ceded a tract of land in that colony.

The land of the Upper Tennessee River Valley was acquired through several treaties between the Cherokee and the United States government beginning in 1792.[4] The first of these was the Treaty of Holston, in which the Holston and Nolichucky River Valleys were acquired from the Cherokee for a $1,000 payment. The Holston Treaty was signed at White's Fort, later to become Knoxville, and was the groundbreaking agreement in opening the Tennessee Valley for Euro-American settlement. In fairly quick succession, further treaties were signed. Six years later, in 1798, the Treaties of Tellico were signed, in which lands in the French Broad and Clinch River Valleys were bought by the United States for $6,000. In the Third Treaty of Tellico of 1805, a large tract of land on the Cumberland Plateau, which formed the western boundary of the Tennessee River Valley, was purchased by the federal government for $14,000. The southern area of the Tennessee Valley remained under Cherokee control until 1819, when the renegade Chickamaugas finally gave in to federal government military superiority.[5] The final chapter of the Cherokee presence in East Tennessee was marked by the infamous Treaty of New Echota, which resulted in the cession of all Cherokee land east of the Mississippi River. The Treaty of New Echota was the basis for the forcible removal of the Cherokee to Arkansas and Oklahoma in 1838 by the federal government, known as the Trail of Tears.

Settler struggle against the Cherokee for land in the Tennessee Valley produced an initial settlement landscape that endured until the mid-nineteenth century. The English and Americans had built a network of forts for protection from French and Indian attacks during the mid to late 1700s. These forts often became the focus of economic activity during the mercantile capitalist stage in the region, emerging as the first urban settlements in the Upper Tennessee River Valley.

Forts were most often located at strategic points along river banks, where water transportation was available and movements of the enemy could be monitored and constrained. In East Tennessee, three major forts were established during the Indian period: Fort Loudon, Fort White, and Fort Southwest Point.

Fort Loudon, founded in 1756, was the oldest of these, and the first permanent European settlement in the Tennessee Valley. It was built on the banks of the Little Tennessee River during the French and Indian War as a defense for the English and their Cherokee allies against French attacks from the south and the west.[6] The other two forts were built in ensuing years as protection

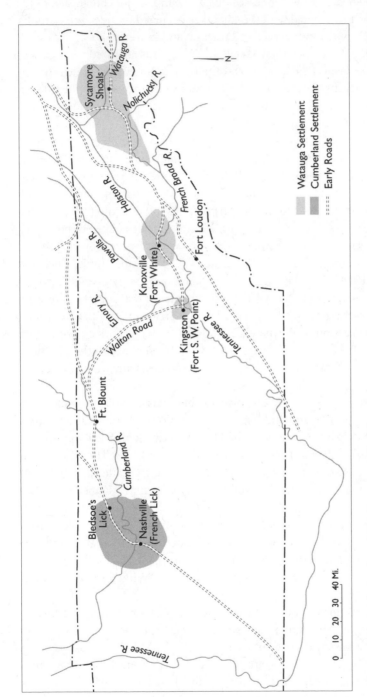

MAP 3. Early Major Roads and Fort Locations, East Tennessee.

for settlers against the Cherokee as larger-scale settlements were established in the valley.[7] Fort White was constructed in 1786 near the origin of the Tennessee River, on a well-fortified bluff site.[8] Fort Southwest Point was built in 1792 near the confluence of the Clinch, Emory, and Tennessee Rivers. Constructed by General John Sevier, it became a very important strategic site militarily as it served to cut off water travel and communication between the Upper and Lower Cherokee settlement groups.[9]

The Development of the Mercantile Capitalist Regional Economy

Prior to 1860, the Euro-American settlement pattern in the Upper Tennessee River Valley was shaped by subsistence and commercial agriculture, small-scale industry, and access to transportation (roads, rivers, and railroads). Settlements that had originated as trading posts and ferry crossings became marketing centers for agricultural products, and locations for mostly home-centered industry. Gristmills, tanneries, boot and shoe producers, hat makers, carriage makers, druggists, general store owners, and others relied on resources and customers from the surrounding hinterland. The evolution of the regional economy during this period was tied to the development of transportation infrastructure, which enabled both people and goods to move more quickly and easily over space.

Soon after Euro-American settlement began in the late eighteenth century, farming emerged as the dominant activity in the fertile lands of the Upper Tennessee River Valley. From its outset, agriculture in the region was dominated by corn, wheat, and oats. The limited availability of flat, fertile valley land dictated that these crops be grown on farms of small to medium size, generally between twenty and five hundred acres.[10] The region's farmers were not specialists; in addition to their staple crops, they also grew small amounts of many types of produce for their own consumption. This pattern of agriculture did not encourage the development of cash crops such as tobacco, cotton, or peanuts in the Upper Tennessee region. Consequently, the smaller-scale, mixed-use regional farms never used large amounts of slave labor as did their contemporaries in Middle and West Tennessee.[11]

By 1860 the agricultural economy of the Upper Tennessee River Valley had reached its highest level of organization and productivity. Approximately 365,000 acres of land,[12] worth $3,420,610, was in use for agriculture.[13] In the preceding decade, significant advances had been made in agricultural methods and organization, and a statewide movement to support agrarianism was in full swing. The Roane County Agricultural Society was formed as a local branch of the Tennessee State Agricultural Bureau. The Agricultural Society's mission was the improvement of farming methods on the county level. As part of this effort, the society organized annual countywide agricultural fairs during the 1850s, at which farming methods were demonstrated, various competitions held, and issues debated.[14] These fairs demonstrated the importance and prestige of agriculture in the state and the county in the pre–Civil War era.

The growth of the Upper Tennessee River Valley's agricultural economy became the impetus for the establishment of the first urban settlement in the region. The town of Kingston, which became the regional focus of commercial and political activity in the mercantile capitalist era, was established by an act of the state legislature in late 1799. Founded near the confluence of the Emory, Clinch, and Tennessee Rivers, Kingston began as a trading post for the federal government's military post at Fort Southwest Point (see maps 1, 2, and 3). Its functions expanded as the valley's population grew and as the political geography of East Tennessee began to take shape with the state legislature's establishment of new counties. By the turn of the nineteenth century, Kingston had become the marketing center for produce from the surrounding valley farms, mainly because of its access to river transportation. The town was named the county seat of Roane County in 1801.[15] Court facilities, law offices, mercantile establishments, and inns were established in Kingston to meet the needs of the rural hinterland for some sort of local government, as well as for basic goods and services.

Despite the steady flow of settlers into the valley during the late eighteenth and early nineteenth centuries, the growth of the area was hampered by inadequate transportation. The first settlers had floated down the Tennessee River or one of its tributaries on flatboats, or had followed poorly marked and hazardous game trails and Indian paths into the valley. The region remained without any improved routes of land travel until 1792, when the Treaty of Holston was signed, and provided for a road to be constructed westward from Knoxville to the new settlements of Middle Tennessee. The route chosen for the new road was from Knoxville to Kingston (Fort Southwest Point), where the Clinch River was crossed by ferry, west across Indian territory for one hundred miles to a ferry crossing of the Cumberland River (which became the town of Carthage), and on to Nashville via the settlement of Gallatin.

The road, which came to be known as Walton Road,[16] was completed in 1795 and improved in 1801 through state appropriations and the incorporation of the Cumberland Turnpike Company.[17] After 1800 the state of Tennessee increasingly encouraged the construction of roads into settlement areas.

In the early nineteenth century, Walton Road became the principal route of overland travel between East and Middle Tennessee. Kingston's location along Walton Road, and at the confluence of the Emory, Clinch, and Tennessee Rivers, cemented its primacy as the economic and commercial center of the region. Its access to water and land travel routes made it a natural break-of-bulk point[18] and a strategic site for the east-west transportation of both people and commodities. Many travelers on their way to Middle Tennessee and points west stopped in Kingston for rest and provisions. Would-be settlers also waited at Kingston for military escorts to accompany them on their journey west as protection from Indian attacks that occurred periodically in the territory between the Clinch and Cumberland Rivers.[19]

Until approximately 1830, road and unorganized river transportation dictated the pattern of commodity flows and the movement of people through the Upper Tennessee River Valley. As the region was settled, it became evident that the upper reaches of the Tennessee River contained natural obstacles that prevented the movement of larger boats between Knoxville and important southern ports such as Memphis and New Orleans. The most troublesome of these was Muscle Shoals in Alabama, a thirty-seven-mile stretch of rapids created by a cumulative vertical drop of 134 feet in the river. The shoals were located 260 miles upstream from the confluence of the Tennessee and Ohio Rivers. They could be traversed only during the high-water season and then only by boats small in comparison to those used on the Ohio and Mississippi Rivers. As a result, Muscle Shoals effectively cut East Tennessee off from the larger Deep South economy. By 1822 a regular steamboat line was in operation between New Orleans and the southern boundary of the Muscle Shoals, but the Upper Tennessee remained unserved.

In 1828 the steamboat era finally reached East Tennessee. During February and March of that year, the steamboat *Atlas* traveled from New Orleans up the Mississippi, Ohio, and Tennessee Rivers to Knoxville. The *Atlas* had crossed Muscle Shoals during a high-water period and arrived in Knoxville with much fanfare.[20] The city fathers of Knoxville looked forward to the arrival of steamboat transport and, in fact, gave the captain of the *Atlas* a $640 purse for successfully completing the journey. It would be another three years, however, before regular steamboat service began in the Tennessee Valley. This was a result of the successful plea of East Tennesseans to the state legislature in 1830 for $60,000 to improve conditions for water transport on the Tennessee River. The money was used to dredge a navigable channel between Knoxville and the Alabama state line.[21] The dredging made steamboat travel possible between Knoxville and Decatur, Alabama, at the head of Muscle Shoals from November until June.[22]

The advent of steamboat transportation brought significant growth to the economy of the Upper Tennessee River Valley, and the late 1830s and 1840s saw substantial growth in commerce on regional rivers. Agricultural products were brought down the Clinch and Tennessee Rivers in large quantities and were most often transported on to Chattanooga or Decatur, Alabama.[23] Kingston remained the focus of the emerging mercantile agricultural-steamboat-based economy, and its regional importance increased accordingly. Produce from the agricultural hinterland was assembled in the town, and its value was enhanced by reducing bulk and perishability. Corn, for example, was shelled and sacked, milled into cornmeal, or made into whiskey. A mill ground wheat into flour. Kingston's wharf was kept busy handling shipments of agricultural products and trade items. To accommodate passengers arriving by boat and overland stage, larger hotels and businesses were built during this period.

Kingston remained the sole urban settlement of any consequence in the region until the 1850s, when transportation innovation brought advantages to another site along the Tennessee River. The village of Blair's Ferry had been established in 1817 by the Blair family, some of the earliest settlers to the region. The family had come to an agreement with the Cherokee whereby they gained permission to operate a ferry across the Tennessee River.[24] Blair's Ferry remained a small river settlement for the next thirty years, growing only slightly with steamboat travel on the river. By the late 1840s the village consisted only of one general store, a steamboat landing, and a few houses. Blair's Ferry's fortunes changed, however, with the construction of the first railroad line into the region. The East Tennessee & Georgia Railroad ran from Dalton, Georgia, north to Blair's Ferry and was completed in 1852.[25] Within two years, Blair's Ferry became an important urban setting, due largely to its river and railroad connections.

The East Tennessee & Georgia Railroad was a revival of the Hiwassee Railroad, which had made an aborted effort to build a railroad from Dalton, Georgia, to Knoxville before its financial collapse in 1842. Following the termination of a civil suit against the Hiwassee by the state of Tennessee, the company was reorganized and obtained a new charter in 1848. Continuation of rail line construction north from Dalton was made possible through a loan of $350,000 backed by state bonds sold by the state of Tennessee.[26] By August of 1852 construction of the rail line had been completed from Dalton to Blair's Ferry and trains had begun operating. Blair's Ferry became the northern terminus of the East Tennessee & Georgia in 1852 mainly because funds were not available to build a railroad bridge across the Tennessee River at that time.

In the ensuing years, the economic advantages associated with the construction of the railroad brought rapid growth to Blair's Ferry. A larger town area was planned and platted in 1852, and the community was renamed Loudon, after the first English fort in the region. After completion of the railroad, a boomtown atmosphere existed, as Loudon became the only railroad-connected, break-of-bulk point in the valley. Produce in large quantities was brought from various locations on the river, transferred to the railroad, and shipped to points south. Traffic was so heavy during the harvest season that steamboats had to lay over several days to discharge cargo. Merchants began selling produce and dried goods in new stores, a flouring mill was built to refine corn and wheat, and a sawmill and foundry were established at the new transportation crossroads.[27] The population of Blair's Ferry/Loudon grew rapidly in the early rail period, propelling it from a small frontier settlement to an important regional town.

Loudon's boomtown era did not last long, however, as continued railroad expansion took away the town's locational advantage as quickly as it had conferred it. The East Tennessee & Georgia Railroad's problem with lack of construction funds was solved when the Tennessee legislature announced in 1854 that it would provide a loan for the extension of the line northward. The state provided $8,000 per mile of rail line on the condition that the line be completed to Knoxville. By June of 1855 the extension to Knoxville was completed, making it the northern terminus of the East Tennessee & Georgia. Less than three years later, Knoxville became the connection point between the East Tennessee & Georgia and the East Tennessee & Virginia Railroads, making it a strategic location on a rail network that stretched from Richmond to Atlanta.[28] Although Loudon's boomtown phase ended by 1855, it remained a locally important marketing center because of its river-rail connection.

The Civil War in the Upper Tennessee River Valley

The debate over states' rights and slavery came to Tennessee as it did other southern states in 1861. In June of that year, Tennessee held a referendum on seceding from the Union, which passed by more than a 50,000-vote majority statewide. The citizens of East Tennessee were largely against secession, as the agricultural economy of the region (unlike Middle and West Tennessee) was not dependent on slave labor. East Tennesseans varied in their moral objections to slavery, but collectively they did not identify with the large plantation owners of the deeper South who were benefiting to a much larger degree from it. The state legislature was aware of East Tennessee's antisecession sentiments, and in the summer of 1861 six Confederate regiments were sent to secure the region and the East Tennessee & Virginia (ET&V) and East Tennessee & Georgia (ET&G) Railroads, the principal rail transport route between the Confederate capital of Richmond and the lower South.[29]

The Upper Tennessee River Valley was controlled by occupying Confederate forces until the summer of 1863, when Federal forces began a campaign in East Tennessee. In August of 1863 General Ambrose Burnside directed his Federal Army of the Ohio to begin movement southward from Camp Nelson, Kentucky, into East Tennessee. Receiving advance notice of the movement of Federal forces, Confederate general Simon Buckner elected to abandon the Tennessee River Valley in the face of superior numbers. By September 1863, the region and its railroads were under Union control. Unfortunately, the fighting in the area would not end for over a year after this. The defeat of Federal forces under General William Rosecrans at Chickamauga to the south allowed Confederate cavalry to roam freely throughout East Tennessee. General Nathan Bedford Forrest in particular led raids into the region, inflicting heavy losses on crops and infrastructure. From the fall of 1863 until the end of the war, the Upper Tennessee River Valley endured several skirmishes between the two armies.

The agricultural mercantile economy of the Tennessee River Valley suffered during the Civil War. As a result of constant troop movements through the valley, the land was stripped of most of its foodstuffs. Businesses in towns such as Kingston and Loudon were not able to replenish their stocks because of the fighting, and many were forced out of business. Gold and silver had passed completely out of circulation so that any business transaction involved using paper money of questionable value. Many farmers were absent serving in the war, and their farms and property lay idle. By 1865 the prewar economy had regressed.[30]

One important result of the war that would have future ramifications for the region was the exposure of outside Union soldiers to the area and its resources. Union officers such as General John T. Wilder and Captain Hiram S. Chamberlain took notice of the large iron ore and coal deposits along the Cumberland Escarpment, which formed the western boundary of the valley. Although large-scale investment in the region would be delayed for a few years during the postwar recovery period, the interest of these entrepreneurs had been piqued, and it would soon play a large role in the valley's future.

As the Civil War came to a close, the Upper Tennessee River Valley continued to be dominated by agriculture. The war had taken its toll on the area, but the economic balance of agriculture and marketing remained, albeit on a smaller scale. The towns of Kingston and Loudon were the marketing centers for the mercantile economy, and they provided services for rural hinterland populations. The Upper Tennessee River Valley remained a relatively isolated area, with limited access to water transportation and its only railroad connection (the ET&G) running through the extreme eastern section of the region. The inception of industrial capitalism in the ensuing years, however, would modify the valley's character.

CHAPTER 2

The Introduction of Industrial Capitalism:
The Roane Iron Company and the Development
of Rockwood, Tennessee

Among a new generation of southern leaders . . .
the road to wealth seemed no longer to lead to the
plantation but rather to the coal and iron fields of
the Appalachians.

—Ronald Eller, Miners, *Millhands, and*
Mountaineers, 1982

Industrial Capitalism and Its Contexts

The early phases of the *industrial capitalism* that emerged out of the mercantile system in the United States after 1830 were marked by a sustained effort on the part of capitalists to control production and to buy labor in the same way in which raw materials were bought: as a specific quantity of work, completed and embodied in the finished product.[1] The basic components of the industrial capitalist economic system were factories and mills where tens, hundreds, or thousands of workers were employed, priming the pump of American urbanization.

Within the industrial capitalist system "proprietary-competitive" business entities were the predominant form of productive property organization. These were partnerships or proprietorships that owned *and* managed single production facilities. Successful competition between these enterprises depended upon the exploitation of labor and natural resources as productive inputs, the invention of increasingly efficient and profitable mass production technologies, and the development of products that would meet market demand.[2] The optimal balance of these components varied from one industry to another. While the production costs of some manufacturers were dominated by the costs of obtaining resources or labor, others required large amounts of investment capital to fund the construction of production facilities and technical innovation.

Manufacturers in the most capital-intensive industries such as iron and steel, railroads, and textiles began to increase production capacity in order to achieve economies of scale. They also began to integrate resource acquisition, production facilities, and marketing within single business entities in order to facilitate production and distribution. Forward integration by manufacturers took the form of expansion into the warehousing and sale of products. Backward integration was achieved by gaining control over the processes that preceded manufacturing, such as resource extraction and refining.[3]

During the postbellum period, circumstances led the way toward industrial capitalism in Southern Appalachia. States such as Kentucky, Tennessee, Virginia, and West Virginia launched campaigns designed to attract outside investment and immigration. In the late 1860s these states established boards to encourage immigration from northern states. In addition to such overt efforts to attract industrial investment capital and immigration, most state governments in Southern Appalachia provided less obvious, but probably more important, inducements to development, such as property ownership laws advantageous to mineral speculators, tax exemptions, and other special privileges.[4]

Simultaneously, speculators began coming to Southern Appalachia searching for resources and opportunities to be exploited. Some came specifically as a result of the work of boosters, but others had been exposed to the resources of the region through other avenues. Many of the early speculators were former Union or Confederate military officers who had served in Southern Appalachia during the war and had seen the potential value in the area's natural resources. Others were agents sent specifically by northern capitalists to explore the region and acquire rights to resources such as coal, iron, or timber. Eller describes the process of land acquisition by speculators in Southern Appalachia as one leading to "millions of acres of land and even greater quantities of timber and mineral rights pass[ing] into the control of absentee owners."[5]

The transition from mercantile to industrial capitalism during the period between 1830 and 1870 in the United States was spurred by the realization that less organized methods of early industrial activity were inherently inefficient. Irregularity of production, loss of materials in transit, slowness of manufacture, lack of uniformity, and unevenness in the quality of manufactured products were frequent problems. Factory production addressed these issues, as it allowed management to monitor employees' work hours and the quality of their production.[6]

In order for factory production to be efficient and profitable, a stable labor force was required. In established urban places, factory owners responded to workers' needs for housing by providing shelter that would appeal to the right mix of skilled workers for the factory's needs. In and around nineteenth century American cities, mill owners built a variety of housing types to be used by workers. In a typical urban situation, for instance, rows of small uniform structures were built on land adjacent to the mills. Larger houses were constructed for foremen at advantageous positions, from which the home activities of mill workers could be monitored and bosses could easily keep track of work attendance.[7] The result was distinct districts of company housing that were added to preexisting urban patterns.

The involvement of factory owners in providing housing was not limited to existing urban areas. Throughout the nineteenth century, manufacturers located their production facilities at rural sites near raw materials and power sources (such as Rockwood, Tennessee). In these situations, industrialists recruited workers and provided housing for them in *company towns*. Industrial capitalists established these types of settlements to facilitate factory production and increase profit margins.[8]

The Institutional Context for the Inception of Industrial Capitalism

After the Civil War, Tennessee was in a situation similar to that of many other southern states. Its prewar agricultural economy had been damaged, and its Reconstruction government officials were under federal mandate to rebuild the state's economy. These Reconstruction politicians formulated the first state policies and initiatives encouraging industrial development in Tennessee.

Technically, the state of Tennessee had been under Federal military rule since March of 1862 when Federal troops had forced the evacuation of Confederate forces from Nashville and Middle Tennessee. Andrew Johnson, an East Tennessean and a United States senator, was appointed military governor of Tennessee by President Lincoln at this time. Johnson's tenure as governor lasted until early 1865, when his duties as vice president of the United States required his presence in Washington, D.C. His last official act as governor of Tennessee was the authorization of elections to select officials for a civil state government. The election was held on March 4, 1865, and William G. Brownlow was elected governor by a large majority.[9]

Brownlow's Republican administration immediately undertook a program of sharp change from prewar policies. Prior to the Civil War, Tennesseans in general and the state government in particular held firmly to the doctrine of the superiority of agriculture to other economic activities. For example, in

1854 the Tennessee General Assembly, in the preamble of an act establishing a state agricultural bureau, explicitly designated agriculture as the source and foundation of all industry, declaring that the state must continue to rely upon it for its future prosperity.[10] Governor Brownlow's new direction was evident from his inaugural speech, in which he proclaimed that "the natural resources of the Southern States are being expatiated upon, in order that enterprising emigrants may be led to come among us and add to our capital and enterprise. Tennessee holds out inducements to wealthy and industrious emigrants that no other border state affords."[11] The new administration set about implementing a program of industrialization that would put the state in step with the industrial economy that was emerging north of the Mason-Dixon line.

The staple argument of Brownlow's pro-industrial Reconstruction government was the doctrine of state self-sufficiency. In 1868 a legislative committee reported that Tennesseans were spending more than $77,000,000 a year for imported manufactured goods. To remedy this situation, the state government established a State Board of Immigration in late 1867, charged with the encouragement of immigration from the northern states and Europe. The board was funded by state appropriations and was authorized to publish pamphlets, newspaper articles, and advertisements, as well as to send agents to northern and eastern states to tout Tennessee and its resources.[12] The theory behind this strategy was that changing from a predominantly agrarian to a diversified economy required the help of immigrants, skilled in machine labor and attuned to the factory system. This is evident in the preface of an immigration handbook published by the Board of Immigration. In it, author Hermann Bokum described the administration's desire to diversify Tennessee's economy: "Instead of an almost exclusive attention to agriculture, which has prevailed in the South for so many years, there is now a general desire that there should be a harmonious development of its resources. In consequence of it, immigration which was regarded with indifference or dislike, is now greatly desired."[13] During the late 1860s, various bills were introduced into the legislature explicitly inviting outside capital and industry to the state and establishing an association to encourage industry.

The favorable sentiment of Tennesseans toward industry during the postwar period was also encouraged by the sharp regression in agricultural prices beginning in the late 1860s. The price of cotton dropped from 23 cents a pound in 1868 to 15 cents in 1870 and 9 cents in 1878.[14] Wheat followed a similar downward spiral, dropping from $2.18 a bushel in 1868 to $1 in 1870, and bottoming out at 77 cents in 1878.[15] Largely as a result of these price decreases, many family farmers in Southern Appalachia were forced to look toward activities other than farming to make a living, further eroding their faith in agrarianism as the sole path to postwar prosperity. Industry was becoming more widely viewed not only as a feasible alternative for economic development by investors and policymakers, but also as a potential source of income and livelihood by ordinary southerners.

Radical Republican rule in Tennessee ended in 1869, when William Brownlow was elected to the United States Senate and resigned the governor's seat. The ensuing election resulted in the victory of the Radical-turned-Conservative DeWitt C. Senter in the governor's race, and Conservative majorities in both houses of the legislature.[16] Although the Conservatives made changes on many fronts during the "redemption" period following Reconstruction, they continued Tennessee's state policy of encouraging industrial development.[17] In fact, C. Vann Woodward has suggested that "redemption was not a return of an old system nor the restoration of an old ruling class. It was rather a phase of the revolutionary process begun in 1865."[18] The dominant element among the Conservatives who came to power on the heels of Reconstruction in the South were middle-class boosters, with a decidedly industrial, capitalistic outlook. In this respect, they broke with the old planter regime of the lowland South, believing that outside capital and industry should be at least part of the South's economic future.

An examination of two of Tennessee's early Conservative governors confirms Woodward's contentions. Former Confederate general John C. Brown took over the governorship of the state in 1870 from DeWitt Senter. Brown was an active industrialist who played a prominent role in Thomas A. Scott's ambitious schemes for a southern transcontinental railway, and he served as vice president of Scott's Texas & Pacific Company. Later he became president of the Bon Air Coal Company, and at the time of his death, he was serving as president of the expanding Tennessee Coal, Iron, and Railroad Company. His successor, James D. Porter, was also a Confederate veteran and industrialist. Porter served two full terms in office, after which he was elected president of the Nashville, Chattanooga & St. Louis Railroad. He also served on the board of directors of the Tennessee Coal, Iron, and Railroad Company, as well as several other financial enterprises in Nashville.[19] Brown and Porter were typical of the New South Conservatives who dominated Tennessee politics during the two decades following Reconstruction, mixing the mores of the Old South with a recognition that industrial capitalism was the wave of the future.

The pro-industrial policies of Reconstruction Radicals and "redemption" Conservatives contributed to growth in the manufacturing base of the state. By 1870, despite war damages and political turmoil, industry in Tennessee had surpassed its prewar proportions. The number of plants had more than doubled since 1860, from 2,500 to 5,300; the number of industrial workers had increased from 12,500 to 19,400; the value added in manufacturing had increased by $7 million to $15 million in 1870; and the value of industrial goods produced had almost doubled during the decade.[20] Leading the industrial emergence in Tennessee was the iron industry. Iron production in the state steadily increased between 1865 and 1870, fueling speculation that the iron ore and coal deposits of East Tennessee would serve as the basis for continued industrial expansion.

The Iron Industry in the Nineteenth Century

Between the late eighteenth century and the 1870s, iron production in the United States was carried out in small-scale facilities. Iron was the dominant metal-building material used during this period, as steelmaking was only in its infancy by 1870. Compared to the steel industry that would develop by the last decade of the nineteenth century, iron production in 1870 was a disconnected process performed by separate, unaffiliated companies.

The primary stage of ironmaking involved the smelting of iron ore in a blast furnace to remove impurities from the ore. The resulting product, pig iron, was often not refined enough to be worked into shapes without breaking; the metal required further purification. Skilled iron workers called puddlers performed this process—melting, stirring, and kneading pig iron ingots inside puddling furnaces until slag could be drained and the ingots fused to become a two-hundred-pound ball of wrought iron. This ball was sent through a squeezer and muck rolls, where remaining impurities were removed. The iron was then usually put through a secondary production stage in which it was reduced into blooms and then processed into finished products such as bars, rails, plates or sheets.[21]

Prior to the Civil War, almost all rolling mills were of the "two-high" type, in which iron was processed using two iron rolls or cylinders. After an initial pass, the hot wrought iron was lifted and carried manually over the top roll to be reinserted for another pass. With each successive pass, the pressure and width of the rolls were adjusted by workers who were called rollers. Through this process using manual labor and numerous reheatings, the iron was manipulated into rails, rods, bars, plates, and sheets.

Each of these stages of iron production required a specific set of locational attributes. Furnace operators, dependent upon a supply of bulky natural resources, located their furnaces in rural areas near hardwood forests and deposits of iron ore and limestone. Puddling furnaces were sometimes found in conjunction with blast furnaces, but more often they were associated with rolling-mill operations. Because of their greater labor requirements, their need for access to transportation facilities, and their large and constant demand for pig iron ingots, rolling mill owners most often located their production facilities at highly accessible transportation center—fairly large towns and cities.

Thus, prior to the 1870s, iron smelting, puddling, and rolling operations in the United States were carried out at dispersed locations. Few if any iron companies had access to the large amount of investment capital required to jointly operate a furnace, puddling department, and rolling mill. Because iron smelting was notoriously unpredictable—plagued by problems with furnaces, temporary labor shortages, and variable ore supplies—pig iron production rates were uncertain. Moreover, market demand for pig iron fluctuated as well. Rolling mills could also break down, rolled iron buyers sometimes canceled their orders, and for both furnace and rolling mill there was always the possibility of work stoppages because of labor problems. These fluctuations in supply and demand created a difficult situation for iron producers, and a need for an intermediary to match suppliers and buyers—the regional or urban merchant.[22]

The Establishment of the Roane Iron Company

In the late 1860s and early 1870s, a combination of factors favored the establishment of industrial enterprises in Tennessee. Government leaders were touting industry as the state's hope for economic development and recovery, and they instituted policies that encouraged industrial location within its borders. Union soldiers doing battle in Tennessee during the Civil War had seen industrial possibilities in its regions (East Tennessee in particular). After the war ended, large-scale industrial activity first came to the Upper Tennessee River Valley.

The Roane Iron Company was organized and incorporated in 1867, the brainchild of Union general John T. Wilder, a well-documented "economic carpetbagger" of the Reconstruction era. During the Civil War, as Wilder traveled through the region during military operations, he took note of the deposits of coal and iron ore present along the slopes of Walden's Ridge, and became intrigued with the possibility of a business enterprise in East Tennessee.

At the close of the Civil War, Wilder and another Union officer stationed in East Tennessee, Captain Hiram S. Chamberlain, set about establishing an iron production facility in the Upper Tennessee River Valley. Both men had previous experience in the iron industry. Wilder had served an apprenticeship at an iron foundry in Columbus, Ohio, during his formative years and in 1857 had moved west to Greensburg, Indiana, where he established his own foundry before the war.[23] Chamberlain had been the Union's chief quartermaster of East Tennessee and, while stationed in Knoxville, had operated a foundry that produced iron products for use by Federal forces.[24] Wilder and Chamberlain's initial step toward the establishment of an iron foundry was their purchase of 728 acres of Roane County land from local landowners in September of 1865.[25] The land was purchased from three different landowners at a uniform five dollars an acre. It wasn't until almost two years later, in June of 1867, that the

Roane Iron Company was officially organized as a branch company of the East Tennessee Union Petroleum, Coal, Iron & Salt Company (ETUPCI&S). The ETUPCI&S, controlled by important Knoxville business figures, had procured the land that Wilder had purchased in 1865, and the newly formed Roane Iron Company, with Wilder and Chamberlain as directors, reacquired it.[26] It is not immediately apparent why Wilder, Chamberlain, and the ETUPCI&S transferred the ownership of the Roane County land in this manner; however, the transfer does establish that at least a business connection existed between some of Knoxville's local business elite and the northern industrialists.

Wilder and Chamberlain were initially joined by five midwestern capitalists in the venture: W. O. Rockwood, Antrim R. Forsythe, David E. Rees, John M. Lord, and Henry C. Lord. These men were apparently associated with Wilder and Chamberlain either through wartime contacts or through business connections in Indiana or Ohio, and were well equipped to aid in the acquisition of start-up capital for the company. W. O. Rockwood was an Indiana native who had been a major in the Union Army and served under General Wilder in East Tennessee. Forsythe was an Indiana railroad promoter and banker; Rees was a banker in both Indianapolis and Chattanooga; John Lord was a wealthy Mexican War veteran from Indianapolis; and Henry Lord was a railroad promoter from Ohio.[27] In December of 1867 the Roane Iron Company was officially incorporated by the state of Tennessee with a stock capitalization of $100,000.[28] All of the stock declared at this time was owned by the original seven principals. Thus, although legally incorporated, the company was closely held and managed along proprietary lines.

Wilder and Chamberlain had chosen a site for Roane Iron that was close to the iron and coal deposits of Walden's Ridge, and within five miles of the Tennessee River. The company began activity in the region almost immediately in 1867. An additional one thousand acres of land were purchased in December of that year (by this time the purchase price of land had doubled to ten dollars an acre), and a contract was drawn up for the construction of a blast furnace to be completed by September 1, 1868. John Lord and W. O. Rockwood were to undertake the building of the furnace, and they agreed to build the furnace to the following specifications: a furnace to be powered by bituminous coal or coke, with an output capacity of at least 15 tons of pig iron per day.[29] These specifications are significant because charcoal was the dominant fuel nationally for iron production, and there were no pig iron facilities using mineral fuel in the South at this time.[30] They indicate that the managers of Roane Iron were intent on creating a state-of-the-art production facility on par with leading plants in the North.

Over the ensuing year and a half, the Roane Iron Company laid the groundwork for the efficient production and distribution of pig iron. Rights-of-way were secured for a rail line to the Tennessee River and for a road into coal extraction areas. The company continued its policy of obtaining local land for mineral extraction, either through outright purchase or mineral lease agreements. Also, a thirteen-acre tract was purchased on the Tennessee River to serve as a company landing.[31] In December of 1868, the Roane Iron Company's first blast furnace was "blown in," initiating the production of pig iron.

Laborers at the rural Roane Iron production site required housing, and in response to this need, the company established a settlement adjacent to the production facility. The community was named Rockwood in honor of W. O. Rockwood, the first president of the company.[32] The fact that the establishment of a town was not mentioned at early board of directors meetings suggests that the settlement was a spontaneous outgrowth associated with the needs of the nearby production facility. The first official mention of housing or lot subdivision came at a meeting in June of 1869, seven months after the start-up of production. In this instance, the plant superintendent (John Wilder) was authorized by the board of directors to subdivide company land in certain areas and to lease it with restrictions.[33]

The Early Years of Roane Iron

The Roane Iron Company's early years of operation in the Upper Tennessee River Valley were both innovative and tenuous. The use of mineral fuel at the production facility's resource-oriented location was the company's most significant early technological breakthrough. The coal found in this part of the Tennessee Valley was bituminous, typified by softness and high gas content. To be used effectively for iron production, bituminous coal had to go through a process that would expel its gases, leaving a denser product that more closely approximated pure carbon—*coke*. The coking process involved baking the coal in ovens in the absence of air to expel the gases and leave the carbon. Coke ovens were required to protect the coal-baking process from outside elements and to retain maximum heat for the operation. Coke had not been used as iron-furnace fuel in the South prior to the Civil War because of the high sulfur content of coal found there, which contaminated the iron made from it.[34] The Roane Iron Company was able to produce coke of high enough quality by 1868 to make acceptable pig iron, the first instance of this innovation in the former Confederacy. This enabled the company's facility at Rockwood to turn out from twelve to fifteen tons of pig iron per day, three times as much as charcoal furnaces could produce.[35]

Upon solving the coke fuel problem, Roane Iron built rows of coke ovens between its coal mines on Walden's Ridge and its iron furnaces to the east. Coal was brought on narrow gauge tracks from the mines to the ovens, and then in its coke form, it was taken to the iron furnaces for use as fuel. Iron ore was transported in the same manner from more dispersed areas of the company's holdings to the furnace. The pig iron produced was hauled on tracks five miles to the Tennessee River, initially by mules and later, after 1870, by a company-owned locomotive.

In the Roane Iron Company's early years of operation, the Tennessee River provided the only feasible means of transporting pig iron to demand points. Because in general the production of blast furnaces exceeded the demand of single iron refiners, Roane Iron required more than one steady consumer of its pig iron.[36] Early on, its principal consumers were rolling mills found upriver in Knoxville (the Knoxville Iron Company) and downriver in Chattanooga (the Southwestern Iron Company). The company struggled during this early period with production processes and unpredictable markets. Because the coke fuel method was new in the region, the company had to experiment with the intricacies of the process using Tennessee coal, causing irregularities in production. Also, the economy of the region was still recovering from the war, making demand for pig iron variable at best.

The Roane Iron Company survived this early period and, by 1870, began expanding its operations. From its inception, Roane Iron had been backwardly integrated, controlling most of its coal, iron, and limestone supplies through large landholdings in the Upper Tennessee River Valley. In 1870 the company made a move toward forward integration by purchasing the Chattanooga Rolling Mills, the property of a former customer, the Southwestern Iron Company. The purchase price was $225,000 in Roane Iron stock. In effect, the acquisition was a merger, making the principals in Southwestern Iron significant stockholders in the company.[37] This kind of transaction was typical of early industrial capitalism, in that closely held companies such as Roane Iron did not have the liquid capital to acquire competitors and often merged with them, an endowment of stock serving as compensation to stockholders in the acquired company.

The Chattanooga Rolling Mills facility had been constructed by the Construction Corps of the United States Military Railroads during the Civil War, after Federal forces had captured Chattanooga. The mission of the mill was to reroll tons of iron rails that had been damaged by retreating Confederate armies, so that they could be used for repairs on captured southern rail lines. In 1866, shortly after the war, the Southwestern Iron Company acquired ownership of the facility to use it as a rerolling operation for used iron rails. During the next three years, Southwestern Iron struggled to make the Chattanooga mill profitable in the postwar South. Southern railroads needed rails repaired and rerolled but did not have enough capital to pay for the service. Because of this, the supply of used iron rails was not steady, and the mill frequently had to operate at less than capacity. In 1869 Southwestern Iron remedied this problem by installing puddling furnaces at the Chattanooga facility, thereby allowing the production of rails from both old rails and pig iron.[38] This made the rolling mills much more versatile, and therefore attractive to a company such as Roane Iron, which was looking to expand its operations.

With the acquisition of the Chattanooga Rolling Mills by the Roane Iron Company, the original blast furnace operation at Rockwood became part of an integrated iron production system. Pig iron produced at Rockwood was shipped very cheaply down the Tennessee River by boat to Chattanooga, where it increasingly became the dominant component in the manufacture of rails. During the 1870s Roane Iron supplied iron rails to railroads that were beginning to expand lines into the South. The Louisville & Nashville Railroad, for example, was adding miles of rail lines to its existing system, as was the Cincinnati-Southern Railroad.[39] Roane Iron was able to compete successfully for iron rail contracts with northern producers because of its efficient integrated production system and its proximity to southern construction areas.

The creation of an integrated iron production system, along with the relatively steady demand for pig iron, necessitated further investment at the Rockwood furnace site. In late 1871, the stock capitalization of the company was increased to one million dollars, with proceeds from the issue dedicated to the construction of a second blast furnace at Rockwood.[40] The company apparently felt that with the favorable market for iron rails, larger supplies of pig iron would be needed at its Chattanooga operation in the future. In addition, negotiations were being carried on with the Cincinnati-Southern Railroad by 1872 for a right of way through Roane Iron landholdings in Roane County. The company desperately wanted the Cincinnati-Southern's Cincinnati-to-Chattanooga route to run through Rockwood, providing a transportation outlet for pig iron in addition to the Tennessee River. As a result of these negotiations, Roane Iron agreed to donate land, timber, and stone for construction through Roane County; land in Rockwood for depot and shop grounds; and right-of-way over company land in Chattanooga.[41]

By 1876 the Roane Iron Company was operating successfully in the southern iron rail market. It was employing approximately five hundred workers at the Chattanooga mill and three hundred in the two blast furnaces at Rockwood. These facilities had output capacities of 28,000 tons of rails per year and 24,000 tons of pig iron per year respectively at this time.[42] But unfortunately for Roane Iron, just as the company had begun to operate profitably in the southern iron market, technological innovation altered the preferences of rail consumers. Bessemer and open-hearth steelmaking had been gradually perfected in the United States during the late 1860s and early 1870s. In fact, as early as 1865, the first Bessemer steel rails were rolled in Chicago. This was followed by the founding of large Bessemer plants at Bethlehem, Pennsylvania, in 1868 (Bethlehem Iron Company); Johnstown, Pennsylvania, in 1871 (Cambria Iron); and Braddock, Pennsylvania in 1872 (Edgar Thompson Steel Works). The Trenton Iron Company at Trenton, New Jersey, was using the open-hearth method to make steel rails by 1868 and was supplying railroads in the northeastern United States by 1870.[43]

Steel rails were stronger and more durable than iron ones. Since the late seventeenth century, iron makers had known that blister steel, a material stronger than iron, could be made by heating wrought iron sheets until the impurities were burned away. But blister steel was of uneven quality and could only be produced in small amounts. Bessemer and Open Hearth innovations solved these problems, and made steel available for consumption in large amounts. Railroad managers realized that steel rails would allow the use of heavier and more powerful locomotives, larger freight trains, and permit more efficient overall operation. By the mid- to late 1870s, the purchase of steel rails as replacements for iron by railroads was common, limited only by capital availability and rail supply. This left the Roane Iron Company in a difficult position, as the railroads it used to supply switched to steel rails for new construction and replacement. In order to stay in the rail supply business, the company had to adapt.

Roane Iron Enters the Steel Rail Market

The Roane Iron Company made a determined effort to become the first enterprise to make steel in the South. The possibility of manufacturing steel rails was first discussed at a board of directors meeting in April of 1877, and the idea was accepted as a sound one. By July of 1877 Captain Chamberlain had traveled to steelworks in Cleveland, Ohio, and Harrisburg, Pennsylvania, investigating steel production methods. He had also met with Alexander Holley, a partner in the firm of Winslow, Griswold and Holley, which held Sir Henry Bessemer's American steelmaking patent and had built the first commercial Bessemer steel plant in the United States at Troy, New York.[44] Chamberlain apparently preferred the Siemans-Martin (open hearth) over the Bessemer process for steel production at Chattanooga, for by April 1878 construction of a Siemans-Martin works was underway.[45]

The Siemans-Martin production process was a variation of the open-hearth principle originally devised by Josiah Marshall Heath in 1845. It involved a regenerative furnace, which used the heat of combustion normally lost in hot chimney gases, in combination with the practice of charging scrap iron to dilute pig iron impurities.[46] The choice of the Siemans-Martin process was a logical one for the Roane Iron Company at this time. It did not require high-quality pig iron as did the Bessemer process. High-quality pig iron would have been prohibitively expensive, given the company's existing iron ore supplies. The quality of output could also be more effectively controlled with the Siemans-Martins process, in contrast to the uncertain quality of each Bessemer "cast."[47] One of the factors most important to Roane Iron was cost, and this also favored implementing the Siemans-Martin process. The company probably wanted to build a fairly small facility, and the minimum size of an efficient open-hearth plant was far smaller than that of a Bessemer plant.[48]

By early 1879 two Siemans ten-ton acid open-hearth furnaces and the associated equipment were installed at Chattanooga, and steel was being produced for the first time in the South. The inputs were pig iron from Rockwood, scrap iron, and a mixture of raw iron ore from Cranberry, North Carolina; Cartersville, Georgia; and Maryville, Tennessee.[49] This combination did not make for high-quality steel, however, and Roane Iron continued to experiment with the production process. The major problem was the high phosphorus content of the Rockwood pig iron, which contaminated the steel manufactured from it. The acid process that the company was using did not remove phosphorus in the course of refining the iron; the phosphorus simply would not combine with the acid lining in the refining vessel. In the years to come, experimentation revealed that the *basic* process (using a basic lining as opposed to acid) solved this problem by allowing phosphorus to combine with the lining and be carried off in the slag.[50] Unfortunately for Roane Iron, this innovation did not come soon enough, and the problem with phosphorus content continued to plague the operation at Chattanooga, eventually causing its demise. Although fifty thousand tons of steel rails were produced and sold over a four-year period by Roane Iron, the constant problems with steel quality in combination with increased competition caused the company to close its Chattanooga operation in January of 1883.[51]

This was not the end of the Roane Iron Company's efforts toward profitable steel production, however. Steel had yet to be produced anyplace else in the South on a consistent basis. The company apparently felt that the there was still a profit to be made in the steel rail market, and almost immediately after the Chattanooga shutdown in 1883, it began inquiring about the Bessemer steelmaking process.[52] By July of 1883 Roane Iron had obtained permission from the Bessemer Steel Company to use the basic Bessemer process for a royalty of one dollar per ton of finished steel.[53] The switch to the Bessemer process, however, would require several prerequisites, which the company did not have in place in 1883. The first of these was a supply of fairly pure iron ore from which to make low-phosphorus pig iron. It had become apparent during the company's experiment with the open-hearth process that the phosphorus content of iron ore found in Roane County was too high to make steel of consistent quality. Ore quality was even more important in the Bessemer process, and a new source would have to be found. The second was the availability of large-scale capital. A Bessemer converter was much more expensive than smaller-scale open-hearth equipment and would require larger amounts of capital than the company had ever before needed.

The decision to produce steel using the Bessemer process forced the Roane Iron Company for the first time to look outside of its closed capital structure for operating funds. The company realized that it could not obtain the large amount of capital it would need through its traditional means of offering new stock issues to its limited group of existing stockholders. Thus, it looked to the national finance market for the capital needed to retool the Chattanooga facility. At this time, however, the company did not have a nationally known business figure associated with it, and financial institutions did not generally loan large amounts of long-term capital to industrial enterprises. The Roane Iron Company needed a contact through which to gain access to finance capital.

Roane Iron found this contact in native East Tennessean Charles McClung McGhee. Charles McGhee had spent the majority of his adult life in Knoxville, Tennessee, and since the pre–Civil War period had been involved in railroad development in the South. The company's initial connection to McGhee was through Hiram Chamberlain. The two men had met during the Union Army's occupation of Knoxville, when Chamberlain was chief quartermaster and McGhee was one of the city's most prominent businessmen. They had business dealings during this period and apparently forged a profitable relationship, for they continued their association after the close of the war.[54] By the mid-1880s McGhee was a vice president of the East Tennessee, Virginia & Georgia Railroad (ETV&G), and was shuttling back and forth between Knoxville and New York City on business.[55] Through his railroad dealings, he was developing relationships with finance bankers that would prove valuable to Roane Iron.

McGhee became involved with the Roane Iron Company in the spring of 1882, when for the first time, he became a stockholder and member of the board of directors. This was shortly before the decision was made to produce Bessemer steel at Chattanooga.[56] For almost four years after the 1883 shutdown, the Chattanooga mill remained idle while Roane Iron made preparations and waited for the right time to reenter the steel rail market. By 1886 market prices had risen sufficiently to prompt the company to commit to production at Chattanooga. The board of directors voted in October of 1886 to raise $125,000 for the construction of the Bessemer works through the sale of bonds using the Chattanooga property as collateral. Chamberlain repeatedly requested, and received, McGhee's help in finding a lender to provide this capital.[57] The floating and sale of bonds was handled through the Central Trust Company of New York, one of the foremost financial institutions in the nation at this time.[58] McGhee lent invaluable assistance in the negotiations between Roane Iron and the Central Trust Company, as he had dealt with the trust company as a representative of the ETV&G Railroad.[59] McGhee's position on the Roane Iron board of directors from 1882 to 1889 and his role in allowing the company to access the New York capital market indicate his importance in facilitating industrial development in the Upper Tennessee River Valley.

In the ensuing year, Chamberlain and the Roane Iron Company attempted to build an efficient steel production facility at Chattanooga. There were still problems, however, with the quality of iron ore to which the company had access for steel manufacture. Roane Iron was forced to buy iron ore land in Carter County, Tennessee, and also to import pig iron from England for use in the Bessemer process. Chamberlain explained the situation to McGhee in a letter in the fall of 1887: "I find it necessary to make a rail perfectly satisfactory [sic] that it is much better to use some English pig. . . . I think it better that we have some foreign iron very low in phosphorus in our mixture. . . . we are making rails for the Cincinnati Southern and they are applying very serious drop tests to show the breaking or non breaking quality of the rail. To stand this test I think it better to use this English iron, or to use a small percentage of it."[60] McGhee did everything in his power to make Roane Iron's steel venture at Chattanooga a success, including providing business from the railroads with which he was involved. The ETV&G ordered steel rails from Roane Iron at McGhee's behest, as did the Memphis & Charleston Railroad, of which McGhee was president.[61] Roane Iron supplied these southern railroads during 1887 and 1888 but repeatedly ran into problems with the quality of rails made at the Chattanooga mill. In February of 1888, the ETV&G rejected a shipment of steel rails from Roane Iron because of imperfections.

The unreliable quality of rails produced at Chattanooga caused the demise of Roane Iron's steel operation. The company was operating on such a thin capital margin that any temporary work stoppage was enough to prevent the payment of monthly bills. When the ETV&G suspended rail purchases, the company's major buyer was gone, and the mill had to be shut down. Although McGhee intervened for Roane Iron with the ETV&G in this case, the incident is indicative of the problems the company had with the quality of its steel rails.

Eventually, Roane Iron's damaged reputation among the railroads and lower steel rail market prices dictated an end to steel production at Chattanooga. The company was operating at a loss during 1888 and 1889, and the board of directors recognized that the Chattanooga facility was the reason. A decision was made to attempt to sell the Chattanooga plant, and in late 1889 a group of buyers representing the Southern Iron Company became interested in the property. The sale of the mill was accomplished in October of 1889, for a price of $250,000.[62] The Roane Iron Company's attempt at finished steel production in the South ended, and the company retreated to the less risky production of pig iron at Rockwood.

During the same time period (1888), the Henderson Steel Manufacturing Company was successful in producing high-quality steel rails at another southern steel production site—Birmingham, Alabama.[63] Roane Iron's failure and Henderson Steel's success had wide-ranging implications—the former demonstrated to capitalists that sufficient-quality steel could not be made using the raw materials of the Upper Tennessee River Valley, while the latter offered a glimpse into the massive potential profits producing steel for southern railroads and urban markets. Chattanooga and Rockwood, Tennessee, the Roane Iron Company's integrated production locations, lost their initial advantage through this trial-and-error process. Birmingham, on the other hand, went on to become the largest steel production center in the South for the next century.

From 1867 to 1889 the Roane Iron Company was an innovative industrial enterprise, but with problems arising related to capital availability. Roane Iron's record as an industrial innovator during this period was impressive: it was the first iron manufacturer to use coke in the production of pig iron in the South (1868); the first company to produce steel of any type in the South (at Chattanooga in 1878); and the earliest enterprise to successfully manufacture Bessemer steel in the South (1887).[64] The company, however, was in a constant struggle to obtain the capital to continue development and achieve its objectives. In this respect, it was representative of proprietary-competitive industrial enterprises that had closed ownership structures and consequently had limited access to capital. Throughout this period in the company's history, attempts were made to obtain larger amounts of money for various purposes, mostly through the offering of new issues of stock to a small existing group of stockholders. For a while, this method worked, and Roane Iron managed to operate and innovate on a razor-thin margin. When the company decided to undertake the Bessemer venture, however, it needed a new approach. Existing stockholders did not have the resources to cover a new stock issue of that amount, and they were not about to relinquish control of the company. This is when Roane Iron enlisted the help of Charles McGhee and initiated its dealings with the Central Trust Company of New York. Throughout Roane Iron's growth and experimentation, its production facility at Rockwood remained open and continued to support the nearby community, but they too were affected by the company's shortage of capital.

Rockwood as Roane Iron's Company Town

The building of the Roane Iron Company's furnaces, and the establishment of Rockwood as a community, occurred in an initially isolated part of the Upper Tennessee River Valley. The existing settlements of Kingston and Loudon were more than twenty miles to the east, and the terrain in the western part of Roane County was rugged and constraining. The location had no connections to existing transportation routes, as no railroads or even wagon roads had been built through the area. Deposits of coal, iron ore, and limestone were abundant at and around the site, however, and the convenience of having access to these bulky resources at the production site guided Roane Iron's industrial development activities.

The Roane Iron Company's actions with respect to the early development of the town of Rockwood offer insight into its motives for building the community. The company did not sell any residential land in Rockwood but rather rented housing to workers who needed it.[65] In the beginning, worker housing was built as closely as possible to the furnaces, to minimize the distance employees would have to travel to work. Some of the earliest housing built by Roane Iron was a group of one-room structures known as Welsh Row, located adjacent to the furnaces.[66] During this early period the Roane Iron

Table 1
Inventory of the Roane Iron Company, May 20, 1870

Item	Capital Expended
Real Estate	$74,874.75
Houses	$52,198.50
Engines & Cars	$37,375.00
Mines	$13,670.00
Furnace	$61,845.00
Machine Shop	$2,289.41
Blacksmith Shop	$834.44
Foundry & Patterns	$1,541.05
Furnace Shop	$225.60
Sundries	$113,118.19
Do Supplies	$29,719.70
Accounts	$32,835.23
Total Assets	$428,702.86

SOURCE: Roane Iron Company, Board of Directors Minutes, May 20, 1870.

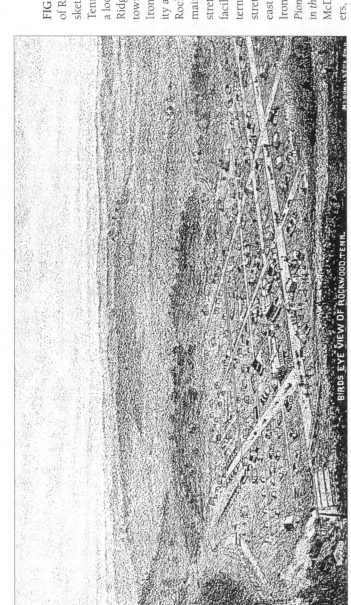

FIG. 1. Bird's-eye View of Rockwood, 1890. This sketch shows Rockwood, Tennessee, in 1890 from a location on Walden's Ridge, to the west of the town. Note the Roane Iron production facility at the bottom left, Rockwood Avenue (the main street in the town) stretching south from the facility, and the grid pattern of streets and houses stretching to the southeast. Source: The Roane Iron Company, *Rockwood: Pioneer Iron-Making Town in the South* (Cincinnati: McDonald & Eick Printers, 1890).

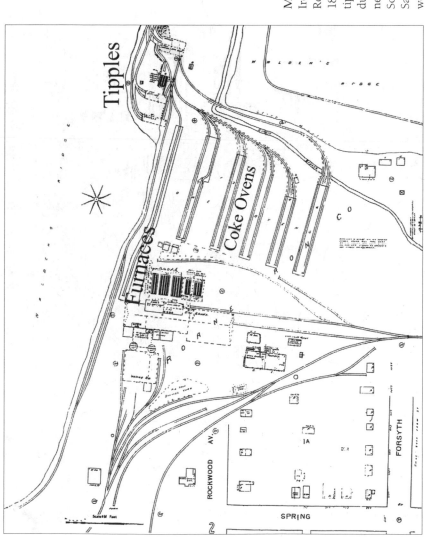

Map 4. Sanborn Map of the Roane Iron Company Production Facility, Rockwood, 1893. This map from 1893 shows the juxtaposition of coal tipples, coke ovens, and the iron production facility at Rockwood, Tennessee. Labels added by the author. Source: Sanborn Map Company, Sanborn Fire Insurance Maps, Rockwood, TN, 1893.

FIG. 2. Beehive Coke Ovens at Rockwood, Circa 1890. Source: The Roane Iron Company, *Rockwood: Pioneer Iron-Making Town in the South* (Cincinnati: McDonald & Eick Printers, 1890).

Company spent a significant amount of capital on the construction of housing—over $50,000 as indicated by an 1870 company inventory.[67]

The company's housing policy suggests that it wanted to provide housing for its workers while maintaining administrative control through landownership. The return that the company expected on the housing came in the form of reliable labor in the mines and at the iron production facility, and rent payments that could be drawn directly from employee wages.

Rental agreements included clauses forbidding the sale of dry goods. This tied in with another of the company's profit strategies, monopoly control of the sale of consumer goods at the company store. One of the earliest actions of the company was the founding of the company store in 1868, along with the authorization of funds to stock it with goods.[68] There were no other stores in the settlement during the company's first decade of operation. Thus, during the town's early years, the company effectively controlled employee trade through restrictive covenants and the establishment of the company store.

The Roane Iron Company did not draft a plan for the development of Rockwood during its early years of operation. The company built housing based on its need for workers. When the iron operation increased its production, more employee housing was needed and the company constructed more homes to be rented. Eventually, as construction continued over time,

Roane Iron Co's. Furnaces, Rockwood, Tenn.

FIG. 3. Roane Iron Company Blast Furnaces, Rockwood (date unknown). This photo shows the Roane Iron furnaces and their close proximity to Walden's Ridge in the background. Rockwood Avenue in the foreground came right to the facility's front gate. Source: Roane County Heritage Commission Photograph Collection, Kingston, TN.

this resulted in a symmetrical block town development pattern spreading out from the furnace area.

The production facility at Rockwood was typical of coke-burning blast furnace operations of the era. The facility site was located as far north as possible, abutting the formidable Walden's Ridge. Located adjacent to the ridge at mine openings were tipples,[69] in which coal was sorted and loaded into railroad cars. The coal was transported in the cars the short distance down the tracks to rows of beehive coke ovens where the coal was made into coke. The coke was then used as fuel for the smelting of the iron ore, also obtained from the company's mines, in sixty-five-foot-high blast furnaces (map 4).

Lime, which was needed as a flux to produce the desired chemical reaction, was also extracted and transported by rail from the company's kilns to the furnaces. The resulting product was pig iron, which was cast into ingots and stored in an adjacent yard until it could be transported to a buyer who would use it for the production of iron and steel implements.

This production system was geared toward a division of labor, for which the Roane Iron Company attempted to procure a corresponding workforce at the isolated Rockwood production site. In large part the manual work to be done around the coke ovens and blast furnaces required unskilled labor. Hiram Chamberlain expressed this during his 1883 testimony in front of the Senate Committee on Education and Labor, in which he described in general terms his assessment of the workforce required at Rockwood: "The labor employed there is of a cheaper class than that about rolling mills as a general thing, because there is more common labor employed directly about the furnace."[70] There were some functions that could only be performed by skilled labor at Rockwood, however, and Roane Iron had to attract skilled workers to the

Table 2
Occupational Breakdown of Rockwood, Tennessee, 1870, 1880

Occupational Class	1870	1880
Unskilled Blue-Collar	54.4%	69.0%
Skilled Blue-Collar	26.9%	22.5%
Low White-Collar	16.6%	7.9%
High White-Collar	2.0%	.6%
Total Number Employed	193	316

SOURCE: U.S. Department of Commerce, Bureau of the Census, Ninth Census, 1870: Population Manuscripts; Tenth Census, 1880: Population Manuscripts, Tennessee, Roane County.

The Introduction of Industrial Capitalism

isolated production site to operate successfully in the early years. In the late 1860s there were no significant pools of skilled, experienced iron-industry labor in Southern Appalachia; thus, as Chamberlain explained, "directly after the war all skilled labor in our line was, of course, brought down from the North. . . . it is true in this country, as in the North, that iron workers as a class, are foreigners—are not Americans. They are Englishmen, Welshmen, Irishmen, and other foreigners."[71]

Federal Manuscript census data show Chamberlain's descriptions of labor requirements at Rockwood to be accurate. Over 54 percent of workers residing in Rockwood in 1870 were unskilled blue-collar workers, while slightly less than 27 percent were skilled blue-collar workers.[72] Only a small percentage of residents were involved in white-collar occupations, and most of those were related to the company operations

The majority of employed persons in Rockwood in 1870 were born in the United States, but ethnic groups performed different roles within the industrial division of labor. The industrial occupations that required the most skill and experience (and which were the highest paying) were those in coal mining, and these jobs were dominated by foreign workers from the British Isles. The coal seams within Walden's Ridge were vertically tilted, and mining coal from them required a considerable level of expertise. In 1870, of thirty-two coal miners in Rockwood, over 65 percent were English, Scottish, or Welsh.

Table 3
Ethnic Breakdown of Selected Industrial Occupations, 1870, 1880

Population Group	Coal Mining		Ore Mining		Iron Furnace		Coke Ovens	
	1870	1880	1870	1880	1870	1880	1870	1880
Foreign-born	65.6	*	0.0	*	0.0	0.0	0.0	0.0
Native White	34.4	*	68.0	*	40.0	22.2	21.0	0.0
Native Black	0.0	*	31.8	*	60.0	77.8	78.9	100.0
Total Number Employed	32	*	22	*	17	27	19	5

*Coal and iron mining could not be distinguished in the 1880 census manuscript for Rockwood.

Source: U.S. Department of Commerce, Bureau of the Census, Ninth Census, 1870: Population Manuscripts; Tenth Census, 1880: Population Manuscripts, Tennessee, Roane County.

Table 4
Ethnic Breakdown (%) of Upper Tennessee River Valley Towns and Roane County, 1870, 1880

Population Group	Rockwood		Kingston		Loudon		Roane Co.	
	1870	1880	1870	1880	1870	1880	1870	1880
Foreign-born	14.4	3.2	4.0	*	trace	*	1.1	0.9
Native White	59.6	65.5	66.0	*	75.0	*	83.1	84.8
Native Black	26.0	31.3	30.0	*	25.0	*	15.8	14.3

*No data available

SOURCE: U.S. Department of Commerce, Bureau of the Census, Ninth Census, 1870: Population Manuscripts; Tenth Census, 1880: Population Manuscripts, Tennessee, Roane County; Compendium of the Ninth Census, 1870, 337; Compendium of the Tenth Census, 1880, 371.

The remaining minority were white United States citizens from Tennessee, Kentucky, and Ohio. Of the twenty-five natives of the British Isles living and working in Rockwood in 1870, twenty-one (84 percent) were working as coal miners for the Roane Iron Company.

This pattern also extended to other representative industrial occupations. Jobs at the coke ovens, which involved long days of heavy labor, working at high temperatures, were dominated by African Americans. No foreigners worked at the coke ovens, and only a small minority of native whites were employed there. Iron ore mining, considered to require less skill than coal mining because of the surface character of the deposits, was also limited to certain groups. Native whites were the predominant group found in the iron mines, with a significantly smaller number of blacks involved in that occupation. Again, no foreigners were employed in iron extraction.

Rockwood developed as a decidedly more ethnically diverse settlement than Roane County as a whole. In 1870 over 14 percent of Rockwood residents were foreign born, as opposed to about 1 percent for the county as a whole. In fact, 94 of the 148 foreign-born residents of the county lived in Rockwood at this time.[73] The Roane Iron Company made a concerted effort to attract skilled foreign labor during its early stages of operation. During the late 1860s and early 1870s General Wilder made several trips to England and Wales, from which he brought back skilled workers.[74] The town also had a significantly larger proportion of black residents than other settlements in the county in 1870 (table 4). This was also no happenstance. The company apparently preferred, and recruited, African American workers for unskilled positions. Chamberlain explained Roane Iron's labor practices:

> As far as unskilled labor is concerned, we always employed colored men. All the heavy work about the rolling mill was done by colored labor, and the same is true of the heavy work about the mines. . . . Around the furnaces, the great bulk of labor is colored labor, and it is almost entirely so about the blast furnaces. As far as our experience goes, we have found it to be a good, reliable character of labor. I think it is by far the best labor in the South—I mean native to the South.[75]

By 1880 the settlement of Rockwood had existed for twelve years, and some significant changes had occurred both regionally and locally. Principal among these was the completion of the Cincinnati-Southern Railway in 1879. The Cincinnati-Southern stretched from Cincinnati to Chattanooga, and its route cut through Roane County and directly past Rockwood. The Roane Iron Company had made strong efforts to convince the Cincinnati-Southern to construct this route, negotiating with the railroad since the early 1870s.[76] The successful completion of the rail line ended the isolation that had characterized Roane Iron's early operations in the Upper Tennessee River Valley. The company no longer had to operate according to wet and dry seasons and water levels on the Tennessee River. Building materials, supplies for the company store, and other items could be shipped in as readily as pig iron could be shipped out. The connection of Rockwood to the north-south rail line ended the community's initial pioneer phase and linked it to numerous potential customers and outside influences.

The work regime prevalent in the settlement changed little during 1870s. By 1880 the blast furnace operation itself was larger, with the addition of a second furnace in 1872. But the major changes over the course of the decade were the relative lack of foreigners in Rockwood, and a decrease in the number of workers employed in skilled blue-collar occupations in 1880 (compared to 1870). By 1880 the proportion of foreigners had decreased to slightly over 3 percent of Rockwood's population. In skilled blue-collar occupations, they had been replaced to a large extent by native whites (table 4). This was, more than likely, the result of the migration of the foreign-born skilled workers to other mining and manufacturing areas, and the substitution of native whites who had acquired needed mining skills. Once the iron production process had been perfected, there was probably less need for skilled iron workers, who could be replaced by lower-skill workers or eliminated altogether. The percentage of blacks living in Rockwood increased slightly over the decade, and they became

Table 5
Population of Upper Tennessee River Valley Towns, 1860, 1870, and 1880

Town	1860	1870	1880
Rockwood	–	649	1,011
Kingston	307	739	858
Loudon	*	*	832

*No data available

SOURCE: U.S. Department of Commerce, Bureau of the Census, Ninth Census, 1870: Population Manuscripts; Tenth Census, 1880: Population Manuscripts, Tennessee, Roane County; Compendium of the Ninth Census, 1870, 337; Compendium of the Tenth Census, 1880, 295; Compendium of the Eleventh Census, 1890, 380.

the dominant labor source in the Roane Iron furnaces (tables 3, 4). The other employment pattern evident in 1880 Rockwood was the entrenchment of natives from northern and midwestern states such as Indiana, Ohio, and New York in the few white-collar jobs available in the town.[77] These white-collar workers were, more than likely, close associates or relatives of principals in the Roane Iron Company, most of whom came from these states.

The social landscape of Rockwood through 1880 seems to have been characterized by microscale segregation. White and black residents were most often clustered in groups by race. The dominant pattern was one in which blacks and whites lived on different streets or different blocks on the same streets. There were, however, instances of black and white men residing in the same boardinghouses. In 1870 some clustering was evident among the foreign-born, but this pattern had diminished by 1880, with foreigners being almost totally intermixed with native whites. The 1880 census also shows the emergence of boardinghouses that housed workers involved in same-class or closely related occupations. For example, all residents might be skilled blue-collar workers or coal miners.[78]

During the 1870s the population of Rockwood grew with industrial production, and by 1880 the settlement was the largest in the Upper Tennessee River Valley (table 5). In twelve years Rockwood had grown into a larger urban place than Kingston or Loudon, settlements that had existed for more than half a century. The engine for this fast growth was industrial production and its labor requirements. Throughout the late 1860s and 1870s, the Roane Iron Company employed more than two-thirds of all working residents of Rockwood at jobs within its industrial complex.[79]

The Introduction of Industrial Capitalism

A plan for the growing town was not filed with Roane County until 1887, nineteen years after Roane Iron began operation. The plan shows the Roane Iron complex (including coal mines, coke ovens, and furnaces) at the far northwest extent of the settlement. This was where coal could be most easily and efficiently extracted from Walden's Ridge. The company-built Rockwood & Tennessee River Railroad spur line was built south of the production facility, connecting it to the Cincinnati Southern main line. The plan for the rest of the settlement, which stretched out onto a flat valley site to the south and east of the furnaces, incorporated a block pattern that had been incrementally created during the construction of early company housing (map 5). By waiting to formalize Rockwood's community plan until 1887, the company did not

MAP 5. The Roane Iron Company's Plan for the Village of Rockwood, 1887. By 1887 the Cincinnati-Southern rail line (visible on the lower part of the map) ran through the town, and the Rockwood and Tennessee River spur line paralleling Rockwood Avenue had been built by Roane Iron to transport iron from its production facility (top right). Source: Roane County Register of Deeds, Deed Book A-2, Page 233.

attempt to impose a predetermined plan on the landscape but developed the community in fits and starts of housing construction related to the production process. The 1887 plan was simply an articulation of the incremental, need-based urban pattern that the Roane Iron Company had created during its early period of operation.

Throughout the mid- to late nineteenth century, the Roane Iron Company used paternalism as a way to attract and retain a labor force at the Rockwood production facility. The company assumed the responsibility of providing housing for a majority of the workforce, especially in the early years. It also supported institutions that it felt were positive influences in the community and that the labor force might desire. Roane Iron built a schoolhouse in Rockwood early on, and provided $25 a month for the building's upkeep. Later, when a new school building was constructed, the company donated $750 toward the project. Soon after the furnaces opened, a church was built with company funds and was made available for nonsectarian services. A lot was also donated for a school for blacks in Rockwood, indicating both that African Americans had become a significant part of the town's population and that the company saw institutionalized segregation as a way of dealing with a multiracial workforce.[80]

On numerous occasions, Roane Iron donated lots in Rockwood to religious groups, so that they could build churches in the community. Social clubs such as the Masonic Lodge and the Independent Order of Odd Fellows were also supported by the company.[81]

The limits to Roane Iron's generosity were apparent in some of its other policies, however. Through the late 1880s, the company prevented outside commercial establishments from doing business in Rockwood, preserving the monopoly of the company store. Restrictive covenants against commercial activities in lease agreements were the major avenue through which this was accomplished. When a resident made a specific request to remove this restriction from his deed agreement in 1883, the motion was voted down handily by the board of directors, maintaining the monopoly.[82] Roane Iron also paid its employees in scrip[83] if they desired, a form of currency issued by the company through the company store. Once a worker's wages had been paid in scrip, they could not be converted back into U.S. currency and had to be redeemed at the company store for merchandise. The scrip system was a way for the company to siphon much of its payroll back into its coffers, while at the same time making a profit on the merchandise sold. Because the company store was the only commercial enterprise in Rockwood, it was possible for workers to be caught up in the scrip system, receiving little cash take-home pay. The company also balked at paying for certain amenities that it felt were unnecessary. For example, the board of directors voted against a motion by Hiram Chamberlain to build a reading room for employees at the furnaces.[84]

The activities of the Roane Iron Company in the Upper Tennessee River Valley in the period between the close of the Civil War and 1890 were representative of early industrial capitalist business methods. Although the company was incorporated from the outset, it was very closely held, and principal investors were involved in the management of production facilities. Until the late 1880s, the company depended on its small group of stockholders for expansion capital, operating with a closed ownership structure and limited capital availability. Roane Iron made groundbreaking attempts at technological innovation and vertical integration, but these efforts were plagued by problems with production processes, raw materials, and capital availability. When the company looked to an outside source for capital, it did not change its ownership structure to any degree, but gained access to large-scale loan capital through the well-connected Charles McGhee, a business associate of Hiram Chamberlain. This was a watershed event, as McGhee proved to be a very important "capital injector" for the Upper Tennessee River Valley, a man who brought not only money to the region but also innovative capitalist strategies. However, McGhee's influence didn't change Roane Iron's business structure, and it couldn't improve the inherently poor quality of the region's iron ore.

Roane Iron's development of Rockwood as a company community was influenced by its business goals and its capital situation. In its early years, the company had barely enough money to get its iron production facility up and running in isolated western Roane County. Housing for workers was considered a necessity, and was built with little emphasis on planning or amenities. Rockwood's development mirrored the needs of the iron production facility—when the size of the workforce increased, more housing was built by the company. Roane Iron's investment in the development of the community was relatively large—the company's original capitalization in 1867 was $100,000, yet over $52,000 had been spent on the housing construction by 1870. There is no question, however, that the company's primary profit strategy was iron production, not urban development. The company did what it felt had to be done to maintain a stable labor force at Rockwood. Thus, rather than become involved in community planning, Roane Iron used its influence to dictate aspects of life in Rockwood that directly influenced economics (housing rent, company store, prohibition of private vendors) or labor stability (provision of nearby housing). Roane Iron did not draft a plan for its community until nineteen years after its establishment. A plan wasn't needed. Because Roane Iron had neither the capital nor the inclination to rigidly plan the residential landscape of Rockwood, the social geography that emerged was largely a reflection of societal norms and the industrial division of labor. The result was a settlement in which there was microsegregation by class and race on the street and block level, even though the company played little or no role in encouraging more institutionalized segregation. Both the profit strategy and the development pattern would change in the Upper Tennessee River Valley in the near future, with the operation of new types of companies and the establishment of urban communities with new, distinct settlement patterns.

CHAPTER 3

The Advent of Corporate Capitalism:
Railroads, Land Companies, and Model Industrial Real Estate Ventures

> *The "new" investors typically operated on a much grander scale . . . [their] investments contributed in a major way to . . . the transformation of land into capital.*
> —Alan Banks, *"Class Formation in the Southeastern Kentucky Coalfields, 1890–1920,"* 1995

In the late 1880s, a new form of capitalism appeared in the Upper Tennessee River Valley—one based on increased access to capital and a functional separation between ownership and management of companies. *Corporate capitalism* was introduced to the Upper Tennessee River Valley through railroads, and later land companies used corporate strategies to undertake development programs that were larger in scale than the region had ever seen before.

Corporate Capitalism and Its Contexts

As the problems of capital availability converged with the intensely competitive conditions of the late nineteenth century, pressures began to develop that were too great to be withstood by old-style industrial business institutions. Capital-intensive producers began to reorganize legally into ownership structures that had large umbrella companies owning smaller subsidiaries. The business entity that emerged from this process—the corporation—was based upon limited-liability ownership by multiple individuals. Investment capital was generated by corporations as potential owners purchased corporate stock and, in turn, provided funds for vertical integration, facility retooling, or product development.[1] The emergence of a national market for industrial securities was a key development, for without it the spread of stock ownership would have been delayed, and the creation of large industrial mergers would have been much more difficult.[2]

As the corporate business form emerged, other organizational changes occurred within business enterprises. One of the most significant of these was the functional separation between owner-stockholders and managers within companies. Corporations developed management structures that were hierarchical in nature with stockholders and board directors at the top, and plant managers, superintendents, foremen, skilled, and semiskilled and unskilled workers following respectively at lower levels. To coordinate the flow of information through this hierarchical management structure, management practices and accounting procedures were routinized and standardized. Corporate headquarters and regional management planned production strategies and oversaw the movement of raw, semifinished, and finished materials to and from various resource extraction areas, production points, and markets on a weekly basis. Top-echelon company managers and directors assembled periodically to assess business performance and formulate future production and marketing policy. Through this corporate system information moved upward to top-level management, and policy flowed downward from the top through the hierarchy to individual production and work sites.[3]

Railroads were among the fastest-growing corporations in the late nineteenth century, and they strongly influenced regional development in Southern Appalachia. In 1870 the only major railroad line in the region was the East Tennessee, Virginia & Georgia Railroad, which connected Norfolk, Virginia, with Dalton, Georgia, via Knoxville, Tennessee. By 1900 several major railroads had built lines into Southern Appalachia, including the Cincinnati-Southern, connecting Cincinnati with Chattanooga; the Louisville & Nashville, extending into eastern Kentucky and eastern Tennessee; the Norfolk and Western, extending into western Virginia; and the Chesapeake and Ohio into southern West Virginia. Southern railroad growth between 1870 and 1900 was driven mostly by northern capital—in contrast to the relatively few regional antebellum railroads that had been financed by mostly local/regional capital.[4] In many instances, these railroads worked closely with major northern banking firms headquartered in major cities such as New York, Philadelphia, and Boston to access the capital needed to buy right-of-way and construct lines. As rail lines were extended into previously isolated areas, absentee capitalists (sometimes associated with the railroads and sometimes not) moved to acquire resource-rich land along routes in efforts to profit. This process was repeated again and again throughout Southern Appalachia in areas where resources such as coal, iron ore, and timber were identified.[5] Railroads, in addition to physically connecting previously remote areas of Southern Appalachia to the economic core of the country, also served as a conduit to the outside capital that drove land acquisition and resource exploitation.

As railroad building and land acquisition in Appalachia moved forward, some capitalists began to organize activities in more efficient ways. Specifically, the practice of concentrating landownership within land companies became widespread. Eller (1982) has documented the establishment and activities of land companies in the coal fields of southern West Virginia and southwestern Virginia during the period between 1870 and 1900. Cobb (1984), Gaventa (1980), and Benhart (1995) have also detailed the existence of land companies in Alabama, Kentucky and Tennessee, respectively, that were involved in the acquisition of large amounts of land for the purpose of mineral extraction, industrial activity, and city building.[6] The emergence of land companies in Southern Appalachia can be viewed as a move toward corporate capitalism, in that most of these companies were publicly owned and/or worked closely with northern banking firms in an effort to access large amounts of capital needed for their development activities. The key point here is the distinction between individual or small group acquisition of land and resources, which was limited by personal access to capital (characteristic of industrial capitalism), and corporate entities that could access larger amounts of money for investment and development because of their ownership structure. The advent of corporate capitalism played a significant role in the economic development of Southern Appalachia, through the activities of railroads, land companies, and vertically integrated industrial corporations.

The National Capital Market Situation in the Late 1880s

The development and maturation of the American capital market was one of the most important factors impacting the progress of industrial corporatism in the United States in the 1880s. Eastern capital markets had developed as a result of the demand for loan money by American railroads. The market for rail securities began during the railroad boom of the 1840s, when rail companies for the first time needed more capital for construction than could be obtained from farmers and merchants living along their rail lines. Those seeking funds for new lines in the late 1840s increasingly came to New York City, which had emerged as the major national financial center because of its low interest rates on borrowed capital.[7] During the same period, European investors also began to look for opportunities in the United States in lieu of those in politically unstable European countries. To meet the needs of American railroads seeking funds and Europeans seeking investment opportunities, a number of importing and exporting firms in New York began to specialize

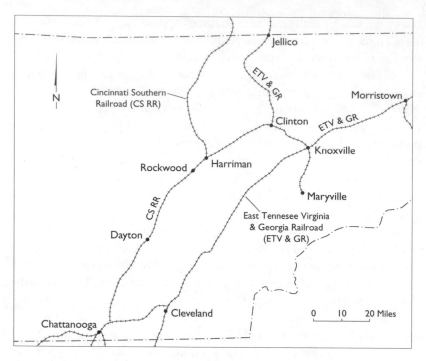

MAP 6. Rail System in the Upper Tennessee River Valley, 1889.

in handling railroad securities. Some of these firms eventually dealt almost entirely in railroad securities and became the nation's first specialized investment banking firms acting as agents for railroads, selling securities for a fee or on commission, acting as transfer agents in New York, and advising on financial matters. At the same time, these firms also became agents for larger European investors who were interested in purchasing American railroad stocks and bonds. This supply-and-demand cycle of railroad capital provided the impetus for the development of the New York City capital market (as well as for secondary markets in Boston and Philadelphia) by the mid-1850s.[8]

Responding to the needs of railroad financing, the New York financial district had, by the onset of the Civil War, become one of the largest and most sophisticated capital markets in the world. The volume of business generated on the New York Stock Exchange through the buying and selling of railroad securities brought about trading and speculation in its modern form. Whereas hundreds of shares had been traded weekly in the 1830s, hundreds of thousands of shares were traded in the 1850s. The modern call-loan market began in the 1850s, as New York banks began to lend speculators money on call in order to provide funds for the interest they were beginning to pay on their

The Advent of Corporate Capitalism

deposit accounts. Skillful railroad securities speculators such as Jay Gould made their first fortunes through the call-loan market and became nationally known figures.

The capital market spawned by railroad activity was thus fully developed and institutionalized by the late 1880s. The railroad industry had matured by this time, however, and its demand for capital relative to investment funds available had begun to diminish. Until this time, the market had been used almost exclusively by railroads and allied enterprises such as telegraph, express, and sleeping-car companies. These had been the only enterprises operating on a large enough scale to require significant amounts of outside capital. The relative decrease in the railroads' demand for capital, beginning in the late 1880s, opened the capital market to other potential users for the first time.[9]

The Regional Economic and Transportation Situation in the Late 1880s

By the late 1880s transportation in the Upper Tennessee River Valley had improved markedly from the early postwar period. In 1887 *Goodspeed's History of Tennessee* reported that Roane County had "transportation facilities [that] are the best of any county in East Tennessee."[10] This was mainly because rail lines had been constructed in the region in the late 1870s and 1880s. The Cincinnati-Southern Railway had been completed through western Roane County by 1880; and the East Tennessee, Virginia & Georgia Railroad (ETV&G) also expanded its network in the region during the 1880s.

The ETV&G initially acquired a locally owned, coal-extraction rail line (the Walden's Ridge Railroad) in the spring of 1887. It then added trackage to the line, connecting it to the Cincinnati-Southern Railway at Emory Gap and to the Knoxville & Ohio Railroad (already part of the ETV&G system) at Clinton, Tennessee. The major impetus for the ETV&G's rail development in the region was potential service to coal extraction areas, as its principals felt the Walden's Ridge line would have "excellent connections to the coal fields of the Cumberland Mountains, and that the coal tonnage would justify acquiring it, and that the entire region is rich in iron ore, coal, limestone, and timber."[11] The resulting network linked the Upper Tennessee River Valley to the national rail system, as well as to the two largest urban markets in East Tennessee—Chattanooga and Knoxville (map 6).

The 1880s were a period of economic expansion and increasing industrialization in the South. This was related to the upturn of the national economy in 1879 after the depressed conditions of the 1870s. The subsidence of the depression once again created a positive investment environment and allowed northern and European capitalists to pursue perceived investment opportunities in the South. The combination of available investment capital with increasing acceptance of industrialization by southern capitalists created an environment where New South hopes could become realities.

Evidence of the South's increasing reliance on the industrial sector was abundant in the 1880s. Southern cities were at the forefront of the industrial conversion. Several cities held large industrial expositions during the 1880s. Atlanta held the International Cotton Exposition in 1881 and the Piedmont Exposition in 1887; Louisville, Kentucky, hosted the Southern Exposition in 1885; and New Orleans sponsored thirty acres of exhibits at its Cotton Centennial Exposition of 1885. Each of these events touted the industrial development of the South (despite names evoking the prewar plantation economy), and each was geared toward attracting outside capital and immigration. Production statistics in important industrial sectors such as ironmaking also suggest that southern industrialization was on the rise. By the late 1880s, southern states were producing more pig iron than had the entire nation prior to the Civil War. The capital invested in blast furnaces was also increasing faster in the South as a whole than in any northern state during this period.[12]

The combination of an institutionalized national capital market, a favorable business environment in the South, and a vastly improved regional transportation system in the late 1880s created a situation that attracted investment. The Roane Iron Company had already demonstrated that pig iron could be made successfully in the region under primitive conditions. Vast timber and mineral resources were known to be present in the area, but prior to the 1880s these resources were relatively isolated from transportation systems and urban markets. In this context new groups of capitalists decided to undertake regional development in the Upper Tennessee River Valley in the late 1880s.

The Activities of Land Companies

The regional development that took place in the Upper Tennessee River Valley during the late 1880s and early 1890s came mostly through the activities of land companies. Railroads such the East Tennessee, Virginia & Georgia and the Cincinnati-Southern predated land companies in the Upper Tennessee River Valley and were instrumental in creating the infrastructure and the financial environment in which they could operate. Specifically, three land companies—the East Tennessee Land Company, the Cardiff Coal & Iron Company, and the Lenoir City Company—coordinated the industrial development, mineral extraction, and community building that took place during this period. These companies differed from the previous industrial entities that had operated in the region with respect to their organizational structure, their financial methods, and their development strategies. These enterprises took advantage of capital available in the securities market of the late 1880s, using it to fund their development programs in the Upper Tennessee River Valley. These programs diverged from those of earlier industrial capitalists, in that they were comprehensive in their scope and had city building at their core.

Each of the three land companies began operation in the Upper Tennessee River Valley during 1889 and 1890. The East Tennessee Land Company was the first of these, obtaining its charter from the state of Tennessee in April of 1889. The Cardiff Coal & Iron Company and the Lenoir City Company followed soon after, incorporating with the state in March and April of 1890 respectively.[13] An analysis of the activities of these companies suggests that they had similar methods of operation.

The East Tennessee Land Company

The East Tennessee Land Company (ETLC) was formed by a group of notable northern capitalists. Frederick Gates, a New York native who had moved to Chattanooga in the mid-1880s for health reasons was the driving force behind the formation of the company. Before his move to Chattanooga, Gates managed a large Diamond Match Company plant in Frankfort, New York. He also invested in real estate and helped route the West Shore Railroad connecting New York City and Buffalo through Frankfort. While in New York, Gates had been a member of the Prohibition Party and was the party's candidate for New York secretary of state in 1883.[14] He would found the East Tennessee Land Company on the basis of capitalist objectives (profit making) and Prohibition principles (no alcohol and clean living).

While in Chattanooga, Gates initiated a plan to combine temperance beliefs and business strategies in an industrial-urban development project in the Upper Tennessee River Valley. He sought out friends and associates to invest in the venture and, with them, created the East Tennessee Land Company. All of the company's initial principals were staunch Prohibitionists, and most were prominent politicians and/or businessmen. Perhaps the best known was General Clinton B. Fisk, former commissioner of the Freedman's Bureau for Kentucky and Tennessee, founder of Fisk University for freedmen in Nashville, and Prohibitionist candidate for president of the United States in 1888.[15] A native of New York, Fisk was appointed president of the East Tennessee Land Company because of his prominence in the Prohibition movement, and he was successful in attracting capital to the company.

Other inaugural officers and directors of the company included Dr. I. K. Funk and Adam W. Wagnalls, president and vice president, respectively, of the New York City publishing firm Funk & Wagnalls Company;[16] Ferdinand Schumacher of Akron, Ohio, a pioneer in the manufacture of oatmeal and president of the F. Schumacher Milling Company (predecessor of the American Cereal Company [1891], which later became the Quaker Oats Company [1901]);[17] John Hopewell Jr. and Ernest M. Goodall, both members of prominent New England textile families and principals in the Sanford (Maine) Mills blanket manufacturing company; Walter C. Harriman Jr., former United States congressman from New Hampshire; William H. Russell, former attorney for the Louisville, New Albany & Chicago Railway and senior member of the Chattanooga law firm of Russell, Daniels and Garvin;[18] and Alphonso A. Hopkins, former Prohibition party candidate for governor of New York [1882], and well-known author and biographer of Clinton B. Fisk [1888].[19] Thus, in addition to sharing temperance philosophies the East Tennessee Land Company's directors also shared strong ties to some of the most important institutions of American business, finance, and politics.

The company made it very clear that its development activities would be different from those of industrial capitalist firms. In a bound, illustrated prospectus targeted at potential investors, the company explained: "The East Tennessee Land Company will not expend its energies and its working capital in general mining or manufacture, nor in any miscellaneous fashion distributed over such broad territory. It is what its name indicates, primarily a Land Company, and having acquired magnificent heritage in lands, its one purpose is to turn these, by systematic development, to the best advantage possible."[20] Unlike industrial companies, which focused on resource extraction or processing, the ETLC wanted to profit essentially from real estate. Under a heading "Plans and Policy of the Company" in the prospectus, the following items were listed:

> To sell 250,000 acres of farming land, reserving all mineral rights.
> To do this by systematic colonization.
> To establish a manufacturing city, at a strategic valley point.
> To establish an upland town, as a health resort and an agricultural outlet.
> To sell 3,000 acres of land in town and city lots.
> To develop 250,000 acres of coal and iron deposits.
> To do this largely through subordinate companies, organized under supervision of the parent Company, in which this Company shall hold controlling interest wherever control is essential to insure best results.
> To secure from such interest in these companies, and from the royalties they will pay, a large and perpetual revenue.[21]

The role that the company envisioned for itself in the development process was as an overseeing body that would coordinate these wide-ranging activities.

The company needed a large amount of capital to pursue this strategy. It had a sophisticated financial structure for the time period and was organized from the outset to be publicly owned.[22] When the company was incorporated in April of 1889, the amount of its capital stock was specified at $3 million. More than half a million dollars of the stock was subscribed before the organization of the company, suggesting that this amount was probably bought by those who became its officers and directors. The ETLC planned to obtain the rest of its stock capitalization from outsiders and published its prospectus in 1890 to woo investors. Much of the document was devoted to convincing potential investors that the company's development project was a sound investment:

> Whoever has carefully read and fully comprehended the pages preceding, must perceive how small is a capitalization of $3,000,000 on such a basis as has been described, compared with the capital of every other company of this kind. The capital stock of this Company represents actual value, without inflation, but does not approximate the entire values of the properties on which it is based. It was the intention of the projectors and incorporators to shape this enterprise so that its stock should be as solid as that of a national bank.[23]

On the last page of the prospectus, potential stock purchasers were directed to inquire at the company's New York City headquarters, located in the Times Building.

The organizational structure and profit strategy employed by the East Tennessee Land Company indicate that it was introducing a new type of capitalism to the Upper Tennessee River Valley. The organizational structure implemented by the ETLC was compartmentalized, with different development activities being assigned to specific subsidiary companies. Casting itself in the role of parent company, the ETLC described its plan to use subsidiaries: "[The company] has organized, and will organize, other companies, with abundant capital drawn from its own individual membership and from investors outside, and to these subordinate companies it will transfer by lease the timber upon its lands, or the excess thereof beyond the need of settlers, and the minerals under them, devoting itself chiefly to surface development and improvement."[24]

The three subsidiary companies established in the first year by the East Tennessee Land Company were the East Tennessee Mining Company, the Harriman Coal and Iron Railroad, and the Harriman Manufacturing Company.

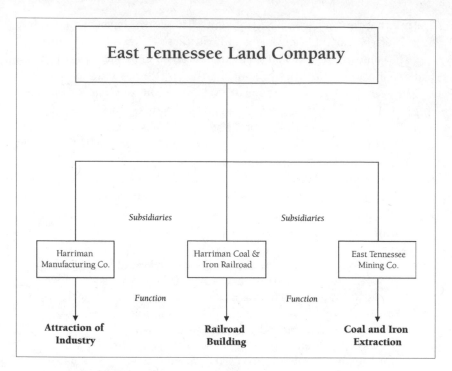

FIG. 4. Organizational Structure of the East Tennessee Land Company.

The East Tennessee Mining Company leased all the coal and iron properties owned by the ETLC and administered all coal and iron ore extraction operations on company lands. The Harriman Coal & Iron Railroad Company's function was to build rail lines over company lands, including a belt line around a proposed town site and branch lines into iron and coal extraction areas. The Harriman Manufacturing Company was to attract industry to the ETLC's landholdings by providing from one-third to one-half of the start-up capital for desired firms, in exchange for significant stock holdings in them (fig. 4).[25]

This profit strategy was advanced for the era and indicative of corporate capitalism. The acquisition of common and preferred stock in the ETLC's subsidiary companies, and in manufacturing concerns that received start-up capital from the Harriman Manufacturing Company, was a major profit tactic. This profit strategy was explained to potential investors:

> The Manufacturing Company will thus hold a large inter-
> est, as it does already, in many substantial factories at Harriman,
> and through proper officers will exercise careful supervision
> over these, making sure they are conducted to the best possible
> advantage, and that all means within the power of the Harriman

The Advent of Corporate Capitalism

MAP 7. Map Showing Harriman, Tennessee, with Adjoining Cities and Railroad Connections. Notice how the map symbol denoting Harriman is the same as those representing the locations of Chattanooga, Knoxville, and Nashville, which were much older cities in 1892. In addition, existing and proposed rail lines are shown running through Harriman in an effort to convince potential investors of the town's permanence as a community and its importance as an industrial center. Source: G. M. Connelly, *City Directory of Harriman, Tennessee* (Chattanooga: Times Printing Co, 1890)

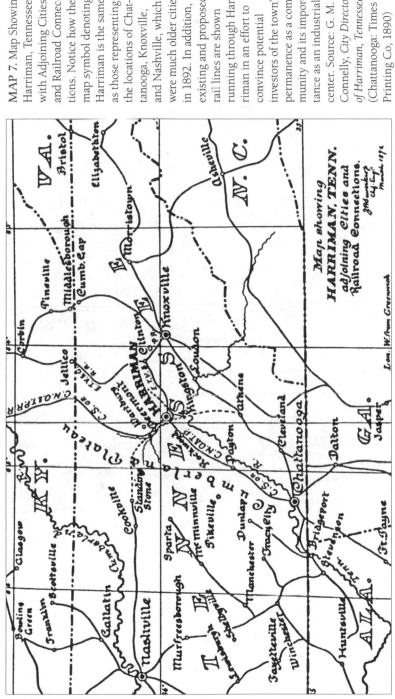

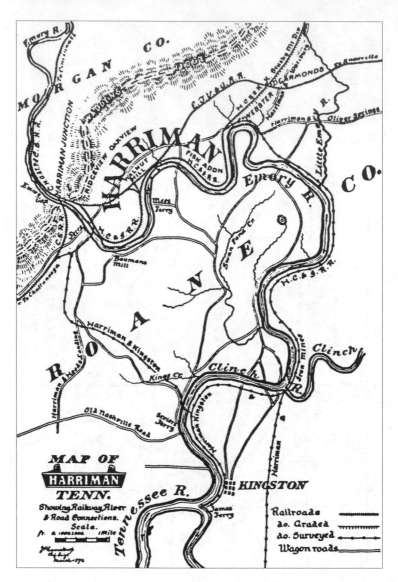

MAP 8. Map of Harriman Showing Railway, River, and Road Connections. This map shows Harriman stretching into two oxbows of the Emory River, when in fact only the area to the left (west) was ever developed by the East Tennessee Land Company. Note also the representations of existing, graded, and surveyed rail lines, the Clinch, Emory, and Tennessee Rivers, Walden's Ridge, and Emory Gap—the location where the Emory River carved a narrow pass through the ridge. The town of Kingston is shown at the bottom center (south), near the confluence of the Clinch and Tennessee Rivers. Source: G. M. Connelly, *City Directory of Harriman, Tennessee* (Chattanooga: Times Printing Co, 1890)

Manufacturing Company and the East Tennessee Land Company are used to promote their welfare and assure a wide market for their products.

This plan, it is believed, will carry to the utmost point yet attained, the spirit and method of co-operation among manufacturing establishments of different character, so that all shall work as one concern for their own interest, the interest of the town, and the consequent greater success of the parent company. . . . It follows that the stock to be held in each, by the Harriman Manufacturing Company, must be a profitable source of income to that Company, and must make its own stock return handsome dividends and increase handsomely in value. This is more certain because the stock which the Harriman Company will hold in many subordinate companies will be preferred stock, with six per cent dividend fairly assured upon it, by such preference from the start.[26]

The ETLC's organizational structure delegated many development responsibilities to subsidiaries but ultimately ensured that revenues would return to the parent company through common and preferred stock dividends.

The properties alluded to in the company's prospectus were obtained during the first months after its incorporation in 1889. By March of 1890, less than a year after its incorporation, the company had purchased 268,124 acres of land in the Upper Tennessee River Valley for $2,095,879.30.[27] Most land was purchased from locals for between $12 and $14 per acre, although the company paid as much as $92 an acre for what must have been considered prime property.[28] The ETLC got some of the money to purchase land from stock sales, but also some from the national bond market. In late 1889 or early 1890, the ETLC negotiated a $1 million bond issue with the Central Trust Company of New York,[29] one of the foremost financial institutions in the nation, having administered trust conversions for the cottonseed oil (1884) and sugar (1887) industries, as well as bond issues for several American railroad companies.[30] The fact that the ETLC was able to negotiate this bond issue is indicative of the important business connections that its principals must have had. Certainly these capital reserves were important in enabling the ETLC to acquire large tracts of land, allowing it to pursue its comprehensive development strategy.

The ETLC drew upon the logic of industrial capitalism—resource extraction and processing—as a rationale for the development of Harriman. The company expressed its belief in the relationship between the location of raw materials, industrial production, and urbanization:

The selling of city lots, where growth is rapid and where great industries congregate, is more productive of wealth than a gold mine. . . . Locate your town where railroads are, or are bound to be, and where minerals are abundant close at hand, and you may build as many as you please during the next decade without overdoing it. . . . For iron will be made where it can be made cheapest; it can be made cheapest where iron-plants have place in close proximity to the iron mines, and where coal supplies exist in the same neighborhood. To establish furnaces, coke ovens and iron-works, and to open coal beds at any given point, is to create a town. . . . Considerations like these determined the East Tennessee Land Company to establish the CITY OF HARRIMAN.[31]

The city of Harriman was to be the centerpiece of the ETLC's development strategy in the Upper Tennessee River Valley. If the ETLC felt that community building in association with industrialization was a logical progression, it also recognized that the endeavor could be lucrative: "While so large a proportion of the East Tennessee Land Company's territory can be sold for agricultural purposes, and at handsome profit . . . the Company expects to reap its chief gains, after those realized from coal and iron interests, from its work of town building."[32]

The location chosen by the ETLC for its industrial-temperance city was at Big Emory Gap, where the Emory River had eroded a narrow valley through Walden's Ridge. This site was approximately eighty miles northeast of Chattanooga via the Cincinnati-Southern Railway, and fifty miles west of Knoxville via the Walden's Ridge division of the East Tennessee, Virginia & Georgia Railroad (map 7).

The town was named Harriman in honor of Colonel Walter C. Harriman, a Union officer who had operated in the area during the Civil War and father of ETLC director Walter Harriman Jr. The original city site was on a large oxbow in the Emory River, with the Cincinnati Southern Railway directly to the west and the East Tennessee, Virginia & Georgia Railway to the north (map 8). A location chosen, the ETLC "staked out" a portion of the site on Christmas Day, 1889, and commissioned a plat for Harriman.[33] From this point forward, Harriman became the focus of the ETLC's development strategy in the Upper Tennessee River Valley.

The Cardiff Coal and Iron Company

The Cardiff Coal & Iron Company (CCIC) was likewise an enterprise conceived by northern capitalists. The company's origins were rooted in an exploratory expedition taken by W. P. Rice and some of his associates to the Upper Tennessee River Valley in the spring of 1889. Rice was a native of Maine who had been an executive with several financial institutions in Kansas City, Missouri, during the 1880s, and who had presided over the establishment of the new industrial city of Fort Payne, Alabama, in late 1888.[34] Apparently

Rice and his group were impressed with the area, for in the next six months they commissioned an agent to buy significant landholdings in the region. By March of 1890, the Cardiff Coal & Iron Company had been incorporated.

In large part, the group of investors that became principals in the Cardiff Coal & Iron Company were from Rice's native New England. The first president of the company was B. B. Smalley of Burlington, Vermont, president of the Ogdensburg & Lake Champlain Railroad, vice president of the Burlington Trust Company, and former secretary of the National Democratic Committee. Other officers and directors from the New England region included General Joshua L. Chamberlain, former four-term governor of Maine and president of Bowdoin College (Brunswick, Maine); Charles L. James, head of the Boston lumber firm James & Abbott, as well as partner in the finance banking firm of Cordley & Company; Samuel Pingree of Hartford, Vermont, former governor of Vermont and member of the state legislature, as well as chairman of the Vermont Board of Railroad Commissioners; John M. Whipple of Claremont, New Hampshire, a member of the New Hampshire legislature; Carlos Heard, a partner in the Biddeford, Maine, hardware firm of McKenney & Heard; and Henry C. Young, a junior partner in the Boston finance banking firm of Cordley & Company.[35] Some members of the inaugural board of directors were businessmen from East Tennessee, such as J. F. Tarwater, T. G. Montague, and Robert Pritchard. Each of these men was a regional business leader: Tarwater was head of the Rockwood iron-mining firm of Tarwater & Brown and a director of the Roane Iron Company; Montague was president of the First National Bank of Chattanooga; and Pritchard was the head of the Chattanooga law firm of Pritchard, Sizer, and Moore.[36] This combination of regional and national capitalists as administrators was used by the company as a selling point when the time came to cultivate additional investors.

From the outset, the Cardiff Coal & Iron Company's development program in the region focused on industrialization. The company's view of the worth of its landholdings in the Upper Tennessee River Valley was linked to the presence of industrial resources and the area's location relative to southern competitors and northern markets:

> The Allegheny Belt is full of coal and iron and limestone fluxes, and possesses other useful mineral resources in great abundance, with vast supplies of timber. It contains places where many manufactures [and the iron manufacture in particular, by reason of the richness of the ores and the facility of charcoal and coking coal] can be carried on to more advantage than anyplace else in the world. . . .
>
> With these preliminary considerations, [the Cardiff Coal and Iron Company] has selected a town site adjoining some of the

richest mineral deposits in the great Allegheny Belt, two hundred miles nearer than Birmingham to Northern and Western markets, with the advantage of the good-will and hearty cooperation of the resident and neighboring population, combined with the experience of successful managers of similar enterprises in the South, as the guarantee for its steady development into a flourishing centre of industry.[37]

Similar to the ETLC, the CCIC planned to administer most aspects of development on its land, including mineral extraction, the construction and management of some industrial facilities, and the development of a new city. That the company advertised its intention to use this approach is suggested in an early edition of the *Cardiff Herald,* the local newspaper:

> The Cardiff Coal & Iron Co., officered by men of national reputation, men whose good name is above reproach, has pledged itself to expend a vast amount in the development of our fair city.
>
> One million and two hundred thousand dollars in cash to be put into iron furnaces, coking ovens, rolling mills, planing mills, churches, store houses, water supplies, ice manufactories, etc., etc., ad infinitum.[38]

The CCIC's comprehensive development strategy required requisite capital, which the company obtained through two avenues. The first was a public ownership structure. When it was incorporated in March of 1890, the company declared its capitalization at $5 million, consisting of fifty thousand shares at a par value of $100 each. A prospectus, published to advertise CCIC stock to investors, emphasized the company's advantages over other similar enterprises. Under the heading "Personal and Financial Strength of the Company," the company suggested why it would succeed where others had failed:

> Unlike many of the corporations organized for Southern development, a number of the corporators of the Cardiff Iron and Coal Company consist of respected, wealthy and influential citizens of the neighborhood where the property is located, which is a local guarantee of the solidarity and success of the corporation, and of the friendship of the people and government of the State of Tennessee, that claims respectful attention. With them are associated representatives of capital and labor of other States, and men of approved experience in kindred enterprises; the whole making an aggregate of wise counsel, executive ability, and monetary strength such as has been seldom combined. Too many of the attempts at development in the South have been prosecuted by

promoters without sufficient resources to counterbalance the mistakes inevitable from the lack of experience and absence of local associations. From the present undertaking, every such source of weakness is eliminated.[39]

Thus, in its literature the CCIC invoked several factors to demonstrate to investors its ability to succeed in its endeavors—connections to regional business leaders, state institutional support, and access to development capital.

The second avenue through which the CCIC derived its initial "monetary strength" was from its association with the Boston banking firm of Cordley & Company. Two of the members of the company's board of directors—Charles James and Henry Young—were partners in the banking firm, and it is likely that capital for early land purchases came from it in association with the American Loan & Trust Company of Boston.[40] In fact, Cordley & Company was very much involved in land acquisition in the Upper Tennessee River Valley, sending an agent to the region several months before the incorporation of the CCIC.

Most of the property eventually acquired by the CCIC was actually purchased by Henry Young, the agent acting on behalf of Cordley & Company. Young went to Roane County early in 1890 and soon began surveying land and investigating titles in anticipation of purchasing several large tracts. According to a resident of Rockwood, who eventually purchased land from the CCIC:

> Young represented himself as being a member of the banking house of Cordley & Co., of Boston, Mass., and that his said firm, in whose behalf he claimed to be acting, as well as upon his own account, was possessed of large means and practically unlimited credit, and that there was associated with him and them in said scheme and enterprise a syndicate of gentlemen of unlimited means and national repute, who would give to said enterprise all requisite attention and afford to it all requisite capital to carry to a full consummation all the plans and schemes of industry, enterprise and development.[41]

By April of 1890, fifty thousand acres of land in the Upper Tennessee River Valley had been purchased by Young acting for Cordley & Company and the CCIC. During that same month, the CCIC assumed ownership of the land, issuing Young stock in exchange. Thus, the Cardiff Coal & Iron Company's initial landholdings in the region were accomplished almost entirely through the activities of northern financiers.

As with the East Tennessee Land Company, the focus of the CCIC's industrial complex was to be a planned urban settlement. The location selected for the city was on the Cincinnati-Southern line, five miles north of Rockwood and approximately the same distance southwest of the new town of Harriman (map 9).

The town was named Cardiff, with the expectation that the settlement would emulate the bustling coal-mining town of Cardiff, Wales. The city site encompassed two thousand acres between Walden's Ridge on the northwest and a range of lesser ridges on the southeast. The CCIC explained the proposed city's advantageous location in relation to transportation and urban markets:

> The company's possessions comprise lands not taken at haphazard, but carefully chosen for their natural wealth and adjoining them the town site (chosen with equal care) at the foot of Walden's Ridge, in the fertile Tennessee Valley, traversed north and south by the Cincinnati Southern Railroad (the main highway of travel and transportation between Cincinnati and Louisville, the great cities of the Ohio Valley, and Chattanooga and Birmingham, the great cities of the mineral belt), and so situated in relation to the mountain gaps eastward, and also to those westward . . . that it is sure to command the lateral lines of railroad communication which are multiplying in Northeastern Tennessee.[42]

The company also had definite ideas about how the internal structure of Cardiff should be arranged, and turned next to planning the urban landscape of the settlement.

The Lenoir City Company

The Lenoir City Company (LCC) was established by a partnership of Knoxville entrepreneurs and New York City financiers and businessmen. The early catalyst was E. J. Sanford, a prominent regional entrepreneur involved in a wide range of business undertakings in Knoxville and East Tennessee. In early 1890 Sanford was at the apex of his business career: he was president of the Knoxville drug firm of Sanford, Chamberlain & Albers, as well as the Mechanics National Bank of Knoxville; vice president of the East Tennessee National Bank; and on the board of directors of the Knoxville Woolen Mills, the Knoxville Iron Company, the Coal Creek Mining & Manufacturing Company, and the East Tennessee, Virginia & Georgia Railroad (ETV&G).[43] Sanford's ability to initiate a regional development initiative in the Upper Tennessee River Valley was directly related to his relationship with another successful East Tennessee native—Charles McClung McGhee. McGhee, a native of Knoxville, had been involved in railroad development in the South since before the Civil War. In 1886 he had moved from Knoxville to New York City

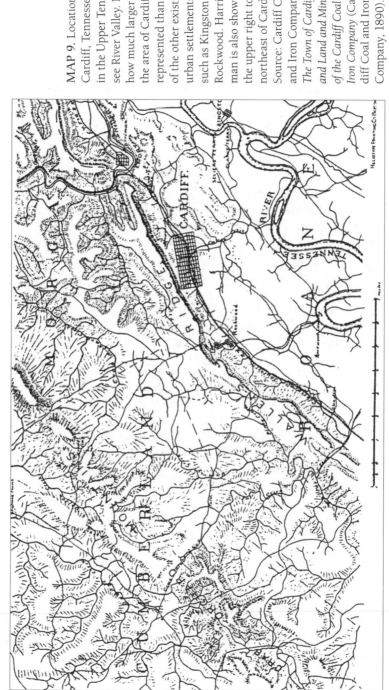

MAP 9. Location of Cardiff, Tennessee, in the Upper Tennessee River Valley. Note how much larger the area of Cardiff is represented than any of the other existing urban settlements such as Kingston and Rockwood. Harriman is also shown at the upper right to the northeast of Cardiff. Source: Cardiff Coal and Iron Company, *The Town of Cardiff, and Land and Mines of the Cardiff Coal and Iron Company* (Cardiff Coal and Iron Company, 1890).

in order to fulfill his administrative duties with the East Tennessee, Virginia & Georgia Railway. By 1889 he had become a vice president of the ETV&G. Although he had left East Tennessee, McGhee maintained a continuing interest in the economic development of the region and remained an investor in several companies operating there (the Roane Iron Company, for example). Sanford and McGhee had become close friends and business associates when they were Knoxville residents, and they continued their business dealings after McGhee's departure. The two frequently corresponded during the late 1880s, with McGhee inquiring about investment opportunities in East Tennessee and Sanford providing regional business news.[44] The Lenoir City development came to fruition largely through this relationship.

In June of 1887 Sanford first suggested to McGhee that an urban-industrial development in East Tennessee would be a sound investment. McGhee rejected the idea at the time but expressed to Sanford what his role would be if it were ever undertaken:

> I fully agree with you in the views that you entertain with reference to the City . . . and would like very much to see the enterprise undertaken and carried through. But I do not feel willing that our Syndicate should embark in the enterprise. We have as you say made a success and I do not feel like embarking in anything that will take the profits that we have already made. A capital of one million dollars would be required to ensure the success of a city and while I would be willing to put in $50,000 as my part of the venture, yet the temper and spirit here is not now favorable to the giving of the other $950,000. I think if I would father the scheme and undertake to do so I could secure the needed amount of money but if I did so I would have to assume the management of it to some extent and would have to be become morally responsible to my friends who I would induce to go into it, this I feel unwilling to do.[45]

McGhee's response to Sanford's inquiry is very telling in that he describes a scenario under which he could access the capital to fund the city-building project. This was surely the reason why Sanford brought his idea to McGhee in the first place—he knew that McGhee had the right connections in New York to make his idea happen. Without McGhee's leadership in obtaining outside financing, Sanford abandoned the idea for the immediate future. Less than two years later, however, the project was underway, and McGhee had enlisted his "syndicate" to fund and participate in the management of a company to administer development activities.

The syndicate to which McGhee belonged was made up in large part of New York financiers and businessmen whom he had gotten to know during his work with the East Tennessee, Virginia & Georgia Railway. These men were among the most powerful and respected businessmen of their era, and most had begun their careers working for railroads in some capacity. Probably the best known at this time was Samuel Thomas, president of the East Tennessee, Virginia & Georgia Railway.[46] Also part of the syndicate with McGhee, Sanford, and Thomas were Calvin S. Brice, vice president of the East Tennessee, Virginia & Georgia Railroad, as well as president of the Lake Erie & Western Railroad;[47] Oliver H. Payne, a principal in the innovative Standard Oil Company in association with John D. Rockefeller;[48] and John G. Moore and Elverton R. Chapman, partners in the New York brokerage firm of Moore & Schley.[49] McGhee and Sanford also included some of their Knoxville relatives and business associates in the enterprise. These were E. T. Sanford, J. M. Thornburgh, Calvin M. McClung, A. J. Albers, William P. Chamberlain, and T. H. Heald. Sanford and Thornburgh were prominent Knoxville law partners, while McClung, Albers, Chamberlain, and Heald were principals in some of the city's largest businesses (C. M. McClung & Co., wholesale hardware; Sanford, Chamberlain & Albers, wholesale and retail drugs; Knoxville Iron Company; and Black Diamond Coal Co., respectively).[50]

Like the East Tennessee Land Company and the Cardiff Coal and Iron Company, the Lenoir City Company was planned from the outset to be a publicly owned enterprise. Upon its incorporation with the state in April of 1890, the company declared $800,000 worth of stock, in the form of eight thousand shares worth $100 each. The LCC planned to issue $400,000 of this to the public at par value. It added a new twist, however, to the sale of stock to the public. Each buyer received not only stock certificates, but also a lot, or lots, in a city development worth the value of the stock subscription.[51] To cultivate potential investors, the company assured them of the stability of the planned development and the advantages of its stock sale strategy:

> Lenoir City is not a "boom town"; it is not the effort of speculators to build upon some old, worn-out fields, a mushroom city that cannot withstand future financial storms, and by taking advantage of popular excitement to sell out the lots to outsiders at unreal and fancy prices, and then silently retire from the field, leaving the investors and so to speak, to "hold the bag," the poorer from their investment in everything except experience. . . .
>
> Having started out with this determination, they realize the fact, pointed out by reason, that the way to permanently utilize the unexcelled natural advantages of Lenoir City, is to offer this property to the public in such a manner that INVESTMENTS SHALL BE PROFITABLE TO THE INVESTORS, AND THAT EVERY INVESTOR SHALL BECOME DIRECTLY INTERESTED WITH THEM IN THE ENTERPRISE, and a zealous and co-operating agent in the upbuilding of the City.[52]

Half of the proceeds of public stock sales were to be used to "pay for the original purchase of the property and debt contracted in the formation of the Company."[53] This indicates that bonds were floated to fund the early activities of the company, although no primary evidence has been found to support this.

The focus of the Lenoir City Company's developmental strategy was the development of a city, to be "one of the healthiest, most attractive and prosperous manufacturing and commercial cities in the entire South."[54] The company based its expectations of industrial development largely on the proximity of its landholdings to the mineral resources of the Upper Tennessee River Valley. In its prospectus, the LCC quoted ironmaking experts of the period, I. Lowthian Bell and Abram S. Hewitt, who stated that the Tennessee Valley was an ideal locale for iron production.[55] It emphasized that industrial facilities locating in Lenoir City would have access to the region's vast coal deposits. In fact, the same syndicate that was involved in the LCC had a controlling interest in the Coal Creek Mining & Manufacturing Company (CCMMC), an enterprise principally involved in coal extraction. The Coal Creek Mining & Manufacturing Company at this time owned ninety thousand acres of coal lands in Anderson County, Tennessee, and the Lenoir City Company planned to use the coal from this property to promote industry in its Lenoir City urban development.[56] The company was also cognizant of the site's transportation situation, noting: "Lenoir City will be the meeting point of two great trunk lines, where the two streams of immigration and capital flowing southward—from the Eastern and Middle States, by the East Tennessee, Virginia & Georgia Railway; and from the valleys of the Ohio and Upper Mississippi rivers, by the Cincinnati-Southern Railroad—will unite and build up a great industrial center."[57] This combination of the availability of industrial resources and rail accessibility served as the LCC's major selling point in convincing investors of the future success of its proposed development.

The property that was purchased by the LCC for its development was part of the Lenoir Estate, which had been ceded to General William Lenoir by the state of North Carolina for service in the Revolutionary War.[58] The proposed town site consisted of a 2,700-acre tract located on the north shore of the Tennessee River, near its confluence with the Little Tennessee River. The site was located on the main line of the East Tennessee, Virginia & Georgia Railway, approximately twenty-three miles southwest of Knoxville and eighty-five miles northeast of Chattanooga (map 10). Soon after the purchase of the property, the LCC commissioned a detailed plat of the proposed urban area. The development of Lenoir City became the primary focus of the LCC's activities, as it attempted to oversee the growth of a "commercial and industrial center of the first importance."[59]

MAP 10. Lenoir City in the "Valley of East Tennessee." On this map, Lenoir City (left center) is represented with a map symbol much larger than those for the existing cities of Bristol (upper right/northeast of Lenoir City), Chattanooga (bottom left/southwest), or Knoxville (center/northeast). Other regional towns are not shown. Notice the dark, primary line symbols used for railroads on the map—the Lenoir City Company suggested to its potential investors that rail connectivity would be one of the major advantages of the town. Source: Lenoir City Company, Prospectus of the Lenoir City Company (Lenoir City Company, 1890).

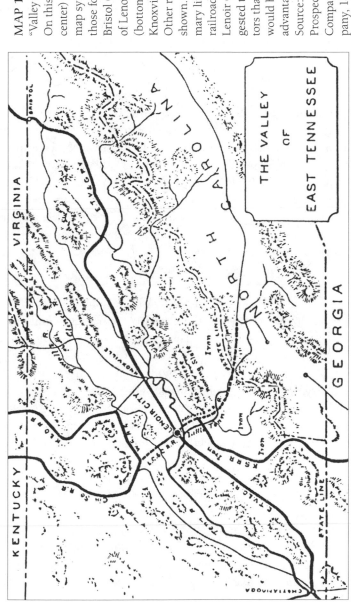

Late-Nineteenth-Century Reform Movements and Urban Development

The land companies operating in the Upper Tennessee River Valley were using a new corporate capital-based profit strategy, and they had a new approach for the planning and marketing of city developments as well. Land companies proposed developing new types of industrial cities—cities that would be better in many ways than the unhealthy, unplanned manufacturing districts of existing urban centers. Their plans for new cities in the Upper Tennessee River Valley drew on reform movements that had grown out of the much-publicized negative effects of industrial and urban growth that were also a product of corporatism.

The scale of capitalist enterprise increased significantly as corporate capitalism emerged in the late nineteenth century. The centralization of capital in the corporate structure created situations that had not previously existed. Because corporations developed innovative ways of increasing their access to capital (such as open ownership structures), they had larger amounts of money to pursue economic development than did their industrial capitalist predecessors. Industrial capitalists hoped to increase efficiency and profit margins by gathering labor and machinery in one place and closely monitoring the production process. But with their access to capital limited by personal wealth, secondary activities like community building were usually unplanned and undertaken on a cost-minimization basis. In contrast, some corporate entities—such as the ones that operated in the Upper Tennessee River Valley during the late 1880s and early 1890s—used accumulated capital to initiate development projects in which the planning, selling, and building of cities were to be primary components. These corporations used specific planning and marketing strategies to attempt to profit from community development itself.

As the scale of industrial production increased during the nineteenth century, larger factory labor forces were needed by manufacturers. In many American urban areas, large boardinghouses or tenements were constructed by landowners or even workers themselves. Often this demand for worker housing that was convenient to factories led to overcrowding and unsanitary living conditions.[60]

It was conditions such as these in American cities that spawned the urban reform movements of the late nineteenth century. Reformers—mostly middle and upper-class urbanites—believed that the squalid conditions created in cities by rapid industrialization were dangerous and unhealthy, and they had definite ideas about what needed to be done to improve urban environments. In particular, reformers believed that sanitation infrastructure and aspects of rural settings such as open space, trees, and parks could positively influence the mental and physical health of city dwellers.[61] Reform ideas were gradually embraced by the masses as the nineteenth century progressed, leading to popular organized sanitary reform and urban parks movements.[62]

Urban reform generally resulted in the commitment of governmental resources to the construction of infrastructural facilities. Professional civil engineers and architects were retained to design sewer and water systems, as well as public parks for major American metropolitan areas such as New York City, Boston, Philadelphia, and Chicago.[63] Later, in the 1880s and 1890s, urban reformers began to recognize the interconnected nature of urban problems—that infrastructure must be approached as a group of interconnected systems. The comprehensive planning movement began to address a wide range of urban issues through the planning, construction, and maintenance of many infrastructural facilities.[64]

Urban and sanitary reform movements also influenced industrialists of the period. Some began to believe that uplifting urban environments could improve not only workers' lives, but also their productivity at the plant. As a result, some industrialists chose to create *model company towns*. Larger investments were made to create a pleasant environment for workers by making available running water, appropriate drainage, and adequate light and ventilation. Worker housing was part of an ordered and usually professionally designed company-owned settlement. Despite their differences, model company towns still included the basic staples of all company towns: production areas, infrastructural facilities, and commercial functions.[65]

Paternalistic industrialists believed that good housing in concert with educational, cultural, and civic awareness would make workers into better individuals, citizens, and even Christians. Housing was seen by factory owners and urban reformers as an opportunity for workers and their families to experience a morally uplifting lifestyle that included religious observance and educational attainment. Thus, the development of model company towns seemed both a socially and economically beneficial use of capital.

Model company town builders believed in their own modified version of environmentalism: that a good living environment made better people and better people made better workers.[66] Paternalism was not only a way to uplift workers, but a way to make them more efficient. Industrialists incorporated environmentalism into the model company towns that they developed because they believed that their manufacturing operations would be made more secure and profitable by doing so. Having been influenced by their pleasant surroundings, model company town residents would be more reliable workers because they could cope better with the strenuous nature of industrial life than their contemporaries who lived in cities or less hospitable company towns. They would also appreciate the benevolence of industrial employers who made it possible for them to live high-quality surroundings at low cost. Hopedale, Massachusetts (1875), and Pullman, Illinois (1884), developed by the Draper Company and the Pullman Palace Car Company, respectively, are well-known examples of model company towns developed during the latter nineteenth century.[67]

In the urban settlements of the Upper Tennessee River Valley, the influence of reform movements was not apparent until the late 1880s. Settlements established during the mercantile period (Kingston and Loudon) predated the movement and did not have large production facilities with the associated urban problems. The Roane Iron Company, which founded Rockwood, Tennessee, was focused more on iron production than on community building. It was only when labor requirements dictated it that the company provided minimal infrastructure to the town. The first evidence of reform influence in urban development in the region appears with the activities of land companies. Each of the land companies that operated in the Upper Tennessee River Valley planned its city in advance and incorporated reform concepts such as urban parks, public sewer and water facilities, graded streets, and public lighting. In contrast to previous business entities, the land companies had determined that including urban reform aspects in their cities was integral to their success.

Harriman, Cardiff, and Lenoir City: Model Industrial Real Estate Ventures

As the land companies operating in the Upper Tennessee River Valley made the development of planned urban-industrial communities central to their corporate agenda, they were faced with decisions about the form and function of these settlements. Company housing was not incorporated into any of the community plans. Instead, the companies used infrastructural improvements and professionally designed community plans as selling points, and attempted to make money on the sale of land to buyers. In addition to residential tracts, the land companies were especially interested in selling land to manufacturing enterprises, which they envisioned would be the major employers in the communities. Thus, rather than model company towns, Harriman, Cardiff, and Lenoir City can more accurately be described as *model industrial real estate ventures*.[68]

In planning and developing their model industrial communities, the land companies operating in the Upper Tennessee River Valley drew upon urban sanitary reform ideals. For example, with respect to city site choice, each of the companies emphasized the favorable living conditions in that particular community.[69] In describing the location of Harriman, the East Tennessee Land Company explained: "It is nearly 1,000 feet above sea level, and beyond the

yellow fever range. Its location is cool in summer, warm in winter, and healthful all of the time. There the days are never tropically hot, and the nights are
deliciously cool."[70] The Cardiff Coal and Iron Company used similar reform
references to describe Cardiff's situation: "The town site of Cardiff lies like an
undulating ocean at the foot of Walden's Ridge, and by it is protected from the
March winds—those active agents and confederates of pulmonary diseases.
It is an area within which malarial fevers and epidemic diseases have never
been known."[71] Similarly, the Lenoir City Company summarized the healthful
aspects of its city site:

> Lenoir City is situated in the Central South, 1000 feet above
> the sea-level, with a climate singularly equable and exhilarating,
> midway between the severity of the New England climate and the
> heat of the extreme South; lying north of epidemics, and south of
> blizzards. . . . All the conditions of a sanitarium are found here;
> elevation, pure air, healthful waters, and an atmosphere dry and
> bracing, acting as a tonic on debilitated persons. The elevated
> location of the City exempts it from the dangers of overflows and
> malarial diseases; its topography assures the advantages of perfect
> drainage.[72]

Obviously, the companies were convinced that potential investors needed to
be assured that their model industrial cities would not foster the unhealthy
environments found in earlier (unplanned) industrial cities. Each of the companies articulated reform ideals in the development and planning of their
urban industrial communities: urban infrastructure and services that were
thought to positively impact people's physical and mental health would be
provided. As the East Tennessee Land Company spelled out to potential
investors and buyers: "The fixed policy of this Company, in town-building, is
to establish all original town improvements—to lay the sewers, the sidewalks
and the paving, to put in the water-works, and the lighting system, and the
streetcar system—and then to operate all these, and secure the profit thereon,
through subordinate companies which it shall control, by retaining a majority
of stock in each."[73]

The Cardiff Coal & Iron Company reported through its media conduit,
the *Cardiff Herald*: "No where is greater care exercised in all matters relative
to the health of a place than in Cardiff. Every precaution is taken, the utmost
vigilance is observed in all sanitary matters. The sewerage system will be
perfect, and the work already done indicates the policy to be followed. Health
is of primary importance, and while nature has done her share for the place,
sanitary science will keep abreast of the constantly changing condition of
affairs here."[74]

Also:

> In establishing industrial towns, the advantages of a site from a business point of view too commonly decide the question of locality, while the inestimable value of health as a prime factor in the successful growth and development of all industrial centers is apparently lost sight of. No such mistake has been made in locating the town of Cardiff. It would be difficult to find anywhere in the South, or in fact, in the entire country, a site where the conditions necessary to the maintenance of a high standard of health prevail to a greater extent than they do here.[75]

In each company's promotional literature, the references were explicit: sanitary reform was to be a major selling point. The companies recognized sanitary infrastructure not only as promoting public health but as a sound business investment.

The land companies of the Upper Tennessee River Valley also incorporated moral reform measures in their planned cities. Like model company town builders before them, the land company capitalists felt that the work ethic and business success could be fostered by the promotion of temperance. The East Tennessee Land Company made a concerted effort to identify its development with the movement, dubbing Harriman "The City of Temperance" during its early advertising campaign. The ETLC explained in one of its publications:

> It is a well-known economic fact that sober labor, away from saloons, yields a positive percentage of gain to the capital employing it, over labor in a community where the liquor traffic is allowed. Statistics could here be cited were it necessary, to show that this is the fact, and that large manufacturing plants have actually yielded a much larger interest upon their capital in years when the liquor traffic around them was forbidden and abolished, than in years when the liquor traffic was permitted, but with the same financial conditions otherwise. By the policy of the East Tennessee Land Company the liquor traffic is prohibited in title deeds, and saloons can never be permitted, with their inevitable influences upon labor and its product.[76]

It is perhaps instructive to note that in the above passage the ETLC refers to both manufacturers and workers in abstract terms.

The Lenoir City Company echoed these sentiments, albeit less bluntly. In its prospectus, under the bold-letter heading "NO BAR ROOMS," the LCC justified its temperance policy:

The promotors of this Company, as a matter of business, and for the protection and general welfare of the people already living on this property, and of those who will soon make this City the home of their families, and to prevent disorders and lawlessness, have determined to put into each deed executed by the Company a clause forfeiting the title if liquor shall ever be manufactured or sold on the premises conveyed. All manufacturers know that it is the convenient dram shop which does the most to demoralize workmen and impair their usefulness.

This will be especially valuable to the Furnace plants and all other manufacturing enterprises that are now and soon will be established here.[77]

In this literature, the objective was to convince potential investors that social conditions would exist in Harriman and Lenoir City that would encourage stable industrial labor and efficient production. In turn, the cities and their residents would thrive.

Upper Tennessee River Valley land companies made property and home ownership defining elements of the urban communities they were developing. This was related to two goals that were part of the model company town ideologies. The first was intrinsic to the city development strategy employed in the establishment of model company cities such as Pullman, Illinois, and Hopedale, Massachusetts: cities should be considered first and foremost as business ventures. Land companies understood that their investment in land and improvements could be recovered most quickly through the sale of lots. The second was related to the longer-term profitability of the urban developments: the creation of a favorable labor environment for industrial production. In relation to this, the East Tennessee Land Company wrote: "No class of workingmen ever is so profitable to its employers as the class which can come and does come, by reason of its labor, into the ownership of its own homes, covets permanency of employment, strives after superiority, and seeks that mutual welfare which labor and capital should each assure to each. Already the number of homes owned at Harriman by the workingmen employed there surpasses, as is believed, that of any other town of like proportion."[78]

Obviously, the ETLC and the other land companies operating in the region were selling a specific vision of capital-labor relationship, which they believed industrialists were in the market to buy. Rather than selling resources or commodities, they were selling the concept of industrial capitalism and a new urban ideal as a package: the juxtaposition of resources, the transportation infrastructure, the capital-labor relationship, and the new healthful uplifting industrial American city.

The Geographic Manifestation of
Model Industrial Communities: The City Plans

Because land companies were marketing the development of their cities based on the growth of industry, they made every attempt to meet the needs of potential manufacturers. The companies, tapping into the increasingly accepted logic that particular types of urban environments could produce stable pools of labor and more efficient industrial production, spent a considerable amount of effort and capital in planning model industrial communities. But what social, infrastructural, and geographic characteristics did these capitalists market to sell their cities? The land companies had very explicit ideas about what kinds of urban places would sell as "industrial utopias" in the late 1880s.

The city plans created by the land companies had some components in common. One of these was a general grid pattern of streets and blocks, with service alleys bisecting most blocks. The grid pattern of subdivision was not distinctive and suggests the companies' concern with ease of subdivision and obtaining large numbers of lots to sell in their city sites. Each of the plans also set aside large tracts of land for industrial use adjacent to railroad lines. Undoubtedly this design feature was incorporated as an attraction to manufacturers considering location in the cities. Rail-side sites would make loading and unloading of raw materials and finished products easy and efficient and would contribute to the low-cost operation of any industrial facility.

The site that the East Tennessee Land Company chose for Harriman was a piece of land bounded by an oxbow of the Emory River. The grid subdivision pattern was altered somewhat to fit the hexagonal shape created by the river and a proposed rail belt line. Some more distinctive urban reform-related elements of the plan included a block set aside for public buildings that faced Roane, Walden, Trenton, and Morgan Streets, and the designation of an extensive public park (Block 36). Lots were not subdivided to uniform size throughout the city site. Residential lot sizes were significantly larger (50 x 190 feet compared to 25 x 127 1/2) in an area bounded by Clinton, Union, Clifty, and Walden Streets, that occupied a ridge looking down on the rest of the area (map 11).

The Cardiff Coal and Iron Company's plan for Cardiff incorporated the grid plan in most of the area north of Georgia Avenue (map 12). The Cincinnati-Southern rail line ran east to west through the city site, bifurcating it, and land was designated for a depot at a central location on the north side of the tracks. Large parts of blocks (numbers 38, 45, 52, 59, 66, 73, 80, 87) were left open for industrial facilities to the south of the rail line. Lot sizes were significantly larger to the south of Georgia Avenue, and in much of this

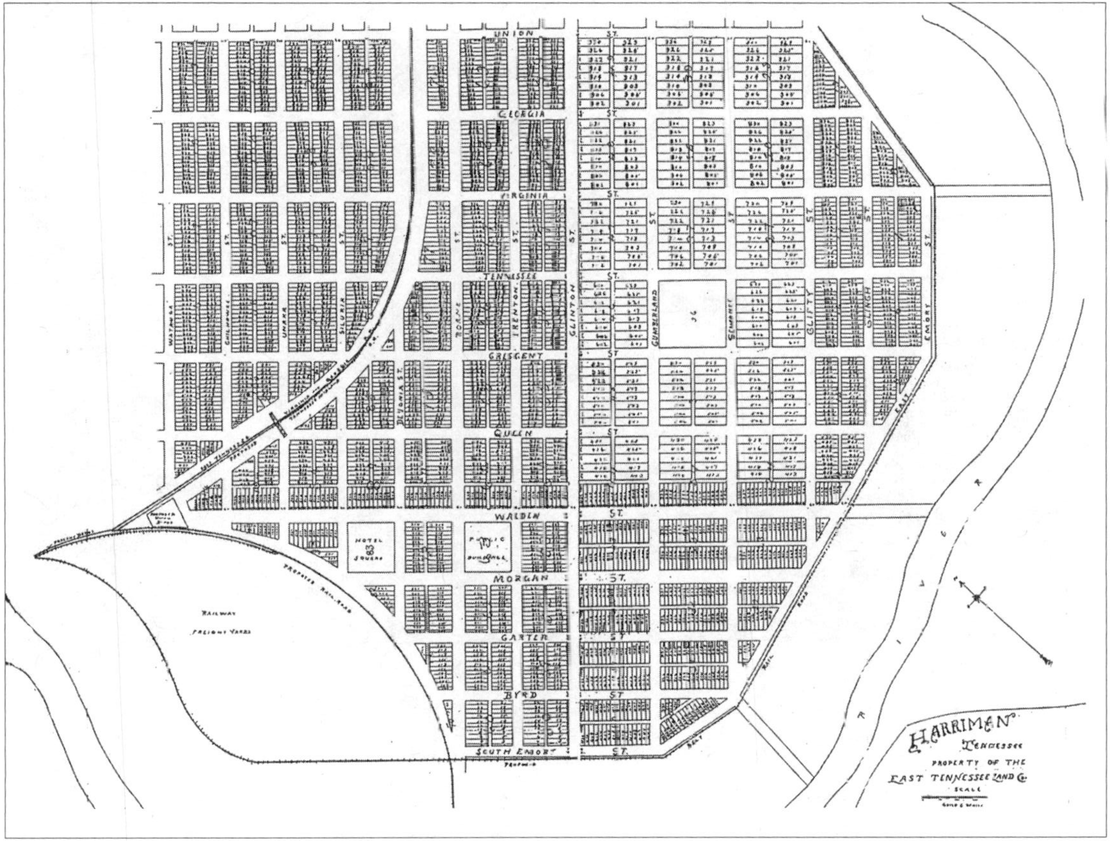

MAP 11. Harriman, Tennessee, Property of the East Tennessee Land Co.

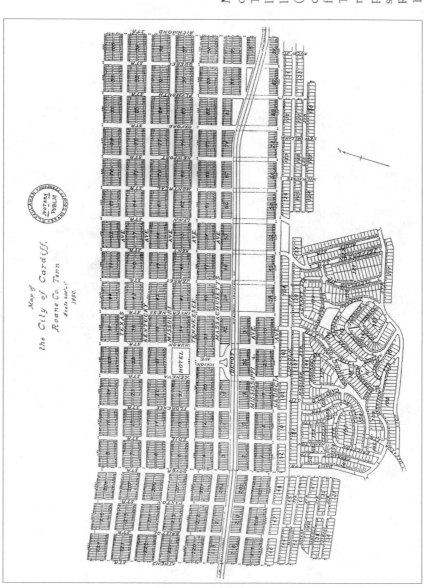

MAP 12. Map of the City of Cardiff, Roane County, Tennessee, 1890. Note the larger lot sizes and curvilinear streets in the lower (southern) portion of Cardiff, setting this area apart from the rest of the plan. The Cincinnati-Southern railroad line is also shown passing through the city site. Source: Roane County Register of Deeds, Cabinet 1, Slide 4

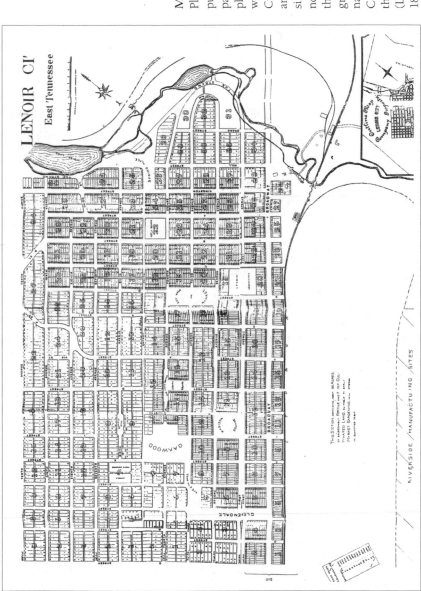

MAP 13. The Lenoir City Plan. Note the numerous public spaces that were part of the Lenoir City plan (for example, Oakwood, Madison Square, City Hall and Market, and Spring Place). Lot sizes were larger in the northwestern portion of the plan, although the grid pattern still predominated. Source: Lenoir City Company, Prospectus of the Lenoir City Company (Lenoir City Company, 1890).

area curvilinear streets and irregularly shaped lots were laid out. In contrast to the grid pattern, streets and lots in this part of Cardiff followed the natural topography. For example, Upper, Middle, and Lower Terrace Streets were designed (and named) specifically to correspond with the site's topographic variation. Obviously, the CCIC wanted this southern part of the city to have a distinct identity. The company succeeded in this, as the urban design of this residential area employed curvilinear streets, irregularly shaped lots, and other design features popularized by Frederick Law Olmsted during this period.[79] This area was also set apart by a change in street naming protocol, with streets named after various American statesmen, politicians, and commanders rather than states or cities (map 12).

There was considerable evidence of reform and English garden influences in the Lenoir City Company's plan for Lenoir City. Within the grid plan, public spaces such as Madison Square, Oakwood, the City Mall, the City Hall and Market, and The Piran Court Square interrupted the general pattern. The Strand was designed to run along Town Creek, with public space and large residential lots extending west. These reflected the urban reform emphasis on access to public open space for the maintenance of public health. The original Lenoir family reservation was preserved between blocks 19 and 20, and a market gardening area was designated to the south of the platted area between the East Tennessee, Virginia & Georgia rail line and the Tennessee River. As in the other plans, there was variability in lot sizes throughout the plat, with "standard" size lots found in the southern and eastern sections, and an area of larger lots in the northwestern part of the site. A block was also designated by the company for public schools and other public buildings (Block 7) (map 13).

In planning and selling their industrial cities, the land companies of the Upper Tennessee River Valley were marketing a specific geographic vision of what American industrial urban landscapes should be. They articulated the vision in high-quality promotional literature, hoping to appeal to industrialists and urban middle- and upper-class investors. In addition to urban reform, home ownership, and temperance, race and class segregation were also to be part of the new industrial city. These were also features that, apparently, land company capitalists perceived to be part of a profit strategy that would work in the Upper Tennessee River Valley in the late nineteenth century.

Capitalist Perception of Urban Space in the Planning of Model Industrial Cities: Land Company Literature

Some of the Upper Tennessee River Valley land companies published extensive literature describing their model industrial real estate ventures to potential investors. In these prospectuses and pamphlets, the companies often provided clear expressions of how urban space would be organized within their planned cities. The information in these publications provides insight into how land companies were marketing their ventures, and what they felt would sell to potential investors. Examination of this literature facilitates interpretation of the urban geography created by land company capitalists.

The East Tennessee Land Company made it clear in its literature that it envisioned different areas of Harriman for various classes of residents:

> Cumberland Street . . . traverses the crest of the high ridge which runs across the town, and upon this street are many residences of an excellent class. . . . At the eastern end of this street . . . stands the elegant home of Mr. Frederick Gates, in whose brain Harriman was conceived. . . . his home commands a splendid prospect of the city which he and his colleagues have established.
>
> Still another Cumberland Street home . . . is the residence of Mr. S. K. Paige, President of the Paige Manufacturing Company, which vies with that of Mr. Gates . . . in costliness and architectural design. From this, as from all residence sites in this part of town, a magnificent view of Emory Gap is had, with much of the town spread out below you upon the lower slopes.
>
> . . . Even the homes of the cheapest class, such as abound in the manufacturing district, upon Clifty, Sewanee, Carter, Emory, and other streets, are noteworthy for their neatness, and their general average as above homes of a similar class in other manufacturing places.[80]

The ridge area was to be an upper-class residential area, and lower elevation areas on the periphery of the site adjacent to manufacturing facilities were to be for the working classes. The spatial delineation was clear enough in the company's eyes that specific streets could be associated with particular socioeconomic groups. Although not articulated down to the street, the other companies demonstrated similar methods of spatially partitioning their urban landscapes. The LCC summarized its geographic vision for Lenoir City:

> By reference to the map of the Lenoir City site . . . it will be seen that the East Tennessee, Virginia & Georgia Railway traverses the central portion of the City from north-east to south-west, and that Town Creek flows through the central portion from north-west to south-east, at nearly right angles to the railroad, thus dividing the site into four quadrangular divisions.
>
> That portion which is north of the railroad and west of Town Creek will be the residence portion of the City, with several longitudinal and lateral streets near the railroad. The central and northern portions of this division consist of a succession of beautiful

hills and vales covered with magnificent groves, which are most suitable for residential purposes.

Upon that portion lying south of the railroad and west of Town Creek, on a river front at considerable distance from the City site, will be located the larger and heavier factories, such as blast furnaces, steel works, saw mills and lumber yards. Upon that portion lying south of the railroad and east of Town Creek, will be established woodworking plants, wagon spoke, handle and furniture factories, and canning establishments. On either side of Town Creek, cotton and woolen mills, and all kinds of textile factories will be located.

The northern portion of the remaining division, lying north of the railroad and east of Town Creek, will be laid off into lots, and sold to operatives and wage workers on the most liberal terms.[81]

Again, the LCC had specific, preconceived ideas about how urban land was to be used. The railroad and Town Creek served as the boundaries for quadrants where the company had defined desired land uses: (1) northwest—middle class and affluent residential, (2) northeast—industrial worker housing (not platted), (3) southwest—heavy manufacturing (blast furnaces, lumber yards), (4) southeast—lighter manufacturing (woodworking plants, woolen mills, textile factories). These types of descriptions tell us that land companies had translated their development strategies into plans with particular spatial characteristics. How were these plans implemented, and how well did they sell?

Capitalist Strategies to Geographic Realities: The Selling of Urban Land

One of the major tests of the model industrial real estate venture as a profit strategy was the inaugural land sale. The East Tennessee Land Company and the Cardiff Coal & Iron Company advertised their sales both regionally and nationally. In the case of Harriman, initial sales were accomplished through a company-administered auction. The East Tennessee Land Company touted its land sale in newspapers in New York City, New Jersey, Pennsylvania, Ohio, and throughout New England during January and February of 1890. From the company's offices at No. 96 Broadway in New York's financial district, letters and leaflets were sent to prospective buyers and investors (fig. 5).[82] The ETLC's sale ran from February 26 to February 28, 1890, and attracted from three to four thousand prospective buyers from all over the eastern United States.

During the three-day period, 574 lots were sold for a total of $604,703.[83] Although the sale was conducted under an open auction format, the company

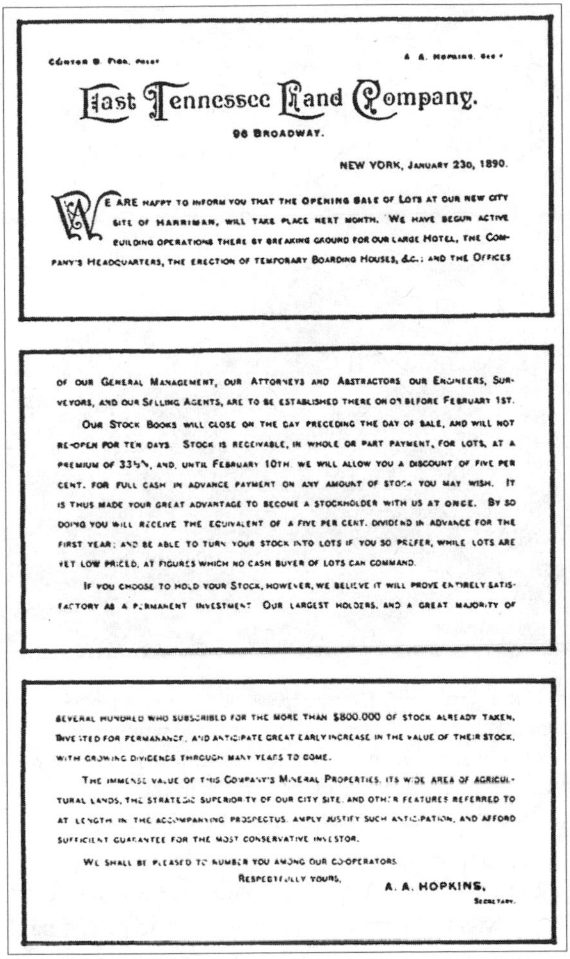

East Tennessee Land Company.

96 BROADWAY.

NEW YORK, JANUARY 23D, 1890.

WE ARE HAPPY TO INFORM YOU THAT THE OPENING SALE OF LOTS AT OUR NEW CITY SITE OF HARRIMAN, WILL TAKE PLACE NEXT MONTH. WE HAVE BEGUN ACTIVE BUILDING OPERATIONS THERE BY BREAKING GROUND FOR OUR LARGE HOTEL, THE COMPANY'S HEADQUARTERS, THE ERECTION OF TEMPORARY BOARDING HOUSES, &C.; AND THE OFFICES OF OUR GENERAL MANAGEMENT, OUR ATTORNEYS AND ABSTRACTORS OUR ENGINEERS, SURVEYORS, AND OUR SELLING AGENTS, ARE TO BE ESTABLISHED THERE ON OR BEFORE FEBRUARY 1ST.

OUR STOCK BOOKS WILL CLOSE ON THE DAY PRECEDING THE DAY OF SALE, AND WILL NOT RE-OPEN FOR TEN DAYS. STOCK IS RECEIVABLE, IN WHOLE OR PART PAYMENT, FOR LOTS, AT A PREMIUM OF 33⅓%, AND, UNTIL FEBRUARY 10TH, WE WILL ALLOW YOU A DISCOUNT OF FIVE PER CENT. FOR FULL CASH IN ADVANCE PAYMENT ON ANY AMOUNT OF STOCK YOU MAY WISH. IT IS THUS MADE YOUR GREAT ADVANTAGE TO BECOME A STOCKHOLDER WITH US AT ONCE. BY SO DOING YOU WILL RECEIVE THE EQUIVALENT OF A FIVE PER CENT. DIVIDEND IN ADVANCE FOR THE FIRST YEAR; AND BE ABLE TO TURN YOUR STOCK INTO LOTS IF YOU SO PREFER, WHILE LOTS ARE YET LOW PRICED, AT FIGURES WHICH NO CASH BUYER OF LOTS CAN COMMAND.

IF YOU CHOOSE TO HOLD YOUR STOCK, HOWEVER, WE BELIEVE IT WILL PROVE ENTIRELY SATISFACTORY AS A PERMANENT INVESTMENT. OUR LARGEST HOLDERS, AND A GREAT MAJORITY OF SEVERAL HUNDRED WHO SUBSCRIBED FOR THE MORE THAN $800,000 OF STOCK ALREADY TAKEN, INVESTED FOR PERMANANCE, AND ANTICIPATE GREAT EARLY INCREASE IN THE VALUE OF THEIR STOCK, WITH GROWING DIVIDENDS THROUGH MANY YEARS TO COME.

THE IMMENSE VALUE OF THIS COMPANY'S MINERAL PROPERTIES, ITS WIDE AREA OF AGRICULTURAL LANDS, THE STRATEGIC SUPERIORITY OF OUR CITY SITE, AND OTHER FEATURES REFERRED TO AT LENGTH IN THE ACCOMPANYING PROSPECTUS, AMPLY JUSTIFY SUCH ANTICIPATION, AND AFFORD SUFFICIENT GUARANTEE FOR THE MOST CONSERVATIVE INVESTOR.

WE SHALL BE PLEASED TO NUMBER YOU AMONG OUR CO-OPERATORS.

RESPECTFULLY YOURS,

A. A. HOPKINS,

SECRETARY.

FIG. 5. Advertising Leaflet for the East Tennessee Land Company and Harriman, Tennessee; New York, January 23, 1890. This leaflet accompanied the East Tennessee Land Company's prospectus and was designed to encourage investors to buy stock in the company, land at the Harriman city site, or both. Source: Walter T. Pulliam, *Harriman: Town That Temperance Built.* (Maryville, TN: Brazos Press, 1978).

had already established de facto land use patterns and land values through its city plan. According to an account of the sale:

> Just such a land sale was probably never seen before in this country, under such conditions, and its like may never be witnessed again. Faith in the Company's character, and confidence in the location of the town, had created enthusiasm of a remarkable degree. . . . It would have run the aggregate sales to a round million dollars, had not the Company sought in unusual ways to discount the speculative spirit, and hold men down to reasonable business bidding.[84]

FIG. 6. The Great Land Sale at Harriman, February 26, 1890. Potential buyers descend on the Harriman city site on February 26, 1890. Note the large white tent where, presumably, the land auction was held, and the areas cleared by the East Tennessee Land Company in advance of the lot sale. Walden's Ridge is in the background. Source: Roane County Heritage Commission Photograph Collection, Kingston, TN.

What the ETLC determined to be "reasonable business bidding" was based on its preconception of how space was to be used in Harriman. The prices paid for lots during the land sale seem to correspond with the company's vision of how the settlement should be spatially arranged. Prices paid for city lots varied greatly. In general, lot price variation corresponded to the land uses that the company had envisioned (map 14).

Lots that sold for less than $500 were principally located on the periphery of the original platted area, to the south of Carter Street and the east of Clifty Street, the area intended for "homes of the cheapest class" encompassing Clifty, Carter, and Emory streets.[85] The other area where lots sold for under $500 was not shown on the original plat, but it lay to the west of the East Tennessee, Virginia & Georgia Railway line. Lots purchased for above $2,000 were located in the ridge area on Cumberland and Walden Streets, or along Roane Street to the west. In its literature the ETLC had described the ridge area, and Cumberland Street in particular, as an upper-class residential area. Roane Street had been envisioned as the main commercial boulevard in the city, the company

The Advent of Corporate Capitalism

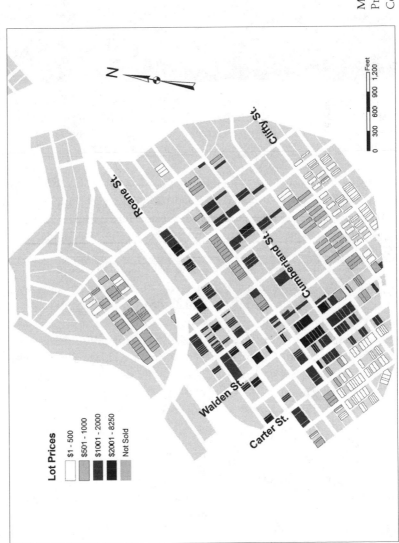

MAP 14. Inaugural Land Sale Lot Prices, Harriman. Source: Roane County Register of Deeds Records.

FIG. 7. The Cardiff Land Sale, April 22, 1890. Note the Pullman railcars used to bring potential land buyers to the Cardiff site, and the wooden planks needed to protect those who made the trip from the spring mud in East Tennessee. Source: Roane County Heritage Commission Photograph Collection, Kingston, TN.

promising that it would "in due time [be] the central thoroughfare of Harriman . . . [which] will approximate three miles in length."[86] The ETLC's strategy had been successful—large numbers of investors had purchased lots, producing satisfactory monetary returns—and its plan for the city would the basis for future development.

The Cardiff Coal and Iron Company also attempted to influence land use in its city through its land sale methods. The company assigned values to lots before any buyers bid on them or offered a price. Land in Cardiff was sold at an auction similar to that held by the East Tennessee Land Company. In addition to national newspaper advertisements, the CCIC commissioned at least one agent to travel to major cities of the United States and Canada soliciting buyers and investors in advance of the land sale.[87] The Cardiff sale began on April 22, 1890, and continued for three days. A total of thirty-five Pullman railcars, bringing an estimated four thousand prospective buyers from the New England states, New York, Cincinnati, Louisville, Atlanta, and several other cities arrived in Cardiff for the sale (fig. 7).

By the end of the auction, the CCIC had sold over a million dollars worth of lots, for prices ranging from $500 to $7,000.[88] The method of sale was described by the CCIC: "A definite price has been fixed upon each offered lot, which will be the maximum price for the Company to receive therefore. The lots will be put up at auction and sold to the highest bidder for whatever price

The Advent of Corporate Capitalism

they bring, whether it amounts to more or less than the maximum price, but all premiums (of $50 or any multiple thereof bid on lots) above the maximum price will be returned to the successful bidder in the stock of the Company, full paid and non-accessible."[89] This method of selling lots served to preserve the valuation of land and, by extension, land use in Cardiff, as set out initially by the company. For instance, lots that the company envisioned for prime commercial sites or high-class residential areas were assigned high(er) prices, and those for lower-class worker housing low(er) prices. If the bidding on a particular lot took the selling price over the prescribed amount, the buyer was issued CCIC stock for the monetary difference.

The Lenoir City Company treated urban land in essentially the same way, although it did not conduct a public auction. The company assigned values to lots in advance and placed those values on a map of the city site that was distributed with each company prospectus (see map 13). Lots were not sold outright but were included as a "bonus" when a purchase of Lenoir City Company stock was made. The company described this process, which it dubbed the "Mutual Plan":

> A large tract of land belonging to the Company, lying in the center of the locality where the City is to be built has been already laid off in streets and lots, and an accurate map has been made of the entire property showing in detail these streets and lots. These lots have been estimated in value, the valuations being as nearly uniform as possible, after making allowances for the different locations and sizes of the various lots and the uses to which they can be put. . . .
>
> These lots . . . are to be disposed of by the Company in connection with the $400,000 of stock, in the following manner: THIS $400,000 WORTH OF STOCK WILL BE SOLD TO THE PUBLIC AT PAR. EVERY PURCHASER OF THIS STOCK WILL, HOWEVER, RECEIVE NOT ONLY PAID-UP STOCK TO THE AMOUNT OF HIS SUBSCRIPTION BUT ALSO A LOT (OR LOTS) WHOSE ESTIMATED VALUE IS EQUAL TO THE AMOUNT OF HIS SUBSCRIPTION.[90]

Again, land use and value within the city site were determined by the LCC through its city plan and maintained through the land sale process. The company's plan was a geographic manifestation of the period "ideal" of the industrial city, and even with this slightly different approach in land sales, the LCC had a stake in maintaining its urban vision on the former Lenoir Estate.

What kinds of urban places were created in the Upper Tennessee River Valley by these land companies? Some idea of the urban and social geography found in land company urban settlements is possible by looking at several sources of historical data.

The Development of a Model Industrial Real Estate Venture—Harriman, Tennessee

An especially large amount of information regarding the East Tennessee Land Company and the town of Harriman, Tennessee—company literature, Sanborn fire insurance maps,[91] a city directory, and the town's newspaper (the *Harriman Advance*)—has been preserved by various institutions and researchers over the past century. This information allows a glimpse of the urban and social geographic patterns that were created through the model industrial real estate venture development strategy in Harriman, Tennessee. It is conceivable that urban geographic patterns identified in Harriman could be representative of those in other model industrial real estate ventures developed by land companies in the Upper Tennessee River Valley and Southern Appalachia.

For all of the planning that went into the early development of Harriman, the East Tennessee Land Company added two additional residential areas only three months after the inaugural land sale. The two additions were laid out approximately one mile northeast of the original city site, separated from it by the East Tennessee, Virginia & Georgia line and a tract of unplatted, undeveloped land. The company explained the need for these additions and its rationale in developing them:

> In May, 1890, an addition was platted one mile east for the special accommodation of workingmen who could not afford such prices as had been for a time established by the auction sale, and one hundred neat houses were built and occupied that year. It is known as Walnut Hills Addition, and forms a thriving suburb of the city proper, of which it is a corporate part. It has a school and a church, and number over 600 population. Oak View Addition joins it, nearer the ridge, where colored residents have grouped themselves, with their own churches and schools.[92]

It is highly unlikely that African American residents "grouped themselves" in Oak View Addition. A more plausible explanation is that the ETLC set up an additional real estate development for low-skill industrial laborers when it became absolutely necessary. The capitalists behind the ETLC were not stupid, nor did they forget that low(er)-class whites and blacks would be part of Harriman's industrial workforce. After all, seven years before, Hiram Chamberlain had testified before the U.S. Senate that African Americans were a major part of the iron industry workforce at Rockwood. The ETLC was simply more concerned with selling real estate than with manufacturing goods, and the company realized that the investors they were trying to court might be scared away by the prospect of living near "undesirable" social and ethnic groups. Thus, the company put off dealing with the messy issues of race and class until industrial development made it unavoidable.

With this in mind, two important ideas were expressed in the ETLC's description of the Walnut Hills and Oak View Additions. First, the new residential areas were "additions," subordinate and apart from Harriman. They were separated from the original city site by a quarter-mile buffer and they had their own institutions such as schools and churches. Second, these new areas were developed for defined groups of people. Walnut Hills was a residential area for the lower-paid, blue-collar, white working class (workingmen), while Oak View was the section where any African Americans working in the city would "group themselves." This initial omission of working-class residential areas from the plan gives an indication of the ETLC's priorities: it was more concerned with making money from the sale of urban land than it was in *actually* creating the labor conditions needed for industrial production.

Construction of the city began in the months before the land sale and intensified in the months after it. Initially, temporary shacks were built to house workers and businesses in the settlement. This "Shacktown" area was gradually abandoned as permanent structures were constructed. The ETLC graded the entire city site, and carved streets and blocks out of the previously undeveloped landscape.

FIG. 8. "Shacktown," Harriman, 1890. The first buildings constructed in Harriman, Tennessee. If you look closely, you can see that some businesses have signs hanging from the temporary structures. Source: Roane County Heritage Commission Photograph Collection, Kingston, TN.

FIG. 9. Development of the Harriman City Site, 1890. From this vantage point on a ridge to the south of Harriman, streets, alleys, and the outlines of blocks laid out by the East Tennessee Land Company are visible in 1890. The area on top of the hill that has not been cleared is the block 36 on the previous Harriman plan map, set aside for a public park. Source: Roane County Heritage Commission Photograph Collection, Kingston, TN.

In its first two years of operation, the company spent over $50,000 in street improvements; established municipal electric power and water infrastructure; funded the construction of a public school building at a cost of more than $6,000; constructed an exposition building to be used for public meetings; began construction of a public sewer system; and completed construction of an imposing company headquarters building.[93] The East Tennessee Land Company headquarters building was designed to be a symbol of the permanence and future prosperity that Harriman would attain. According to the company, it was "a substantial brick and stone structure, erected upon a square reserved for public buildings. . . . The four Norman towers of the office building give it a peculiar appearance of grace and strength combined. It is pronounced the finest building of any kind in Roane County, and the finest private office building in the State (figs. 9–11)."[94]

By 1892 the ETLC reported that nine industrial enterprises had located in Harriman as a result of the activities of the Harriman Manufacturing Company. The largest of these was the Lookout Rolling Mills, which had previously operated in Chattanooga, and employed 250 to 300 workers (fig. 12). Other production facilities included a furniture factory, a machine works, a brick works, an agricultural implement factory, a tack factory, and a tool works. Several of these had previously been in operation in other locations such as Knoxville; Chattanooga; Lancaster, Ohio; and Auburn, New York. The stock held by the Har-

FIG. 10. East Tennessee Land Company Headquarters, Harriman, date unknown. In an 1892 publication, the East Tennessee Land Company pronounced its building as the "finest private office building in the state," with "four Norman towers . . . [providing] . . . it a peculiar appearance of grace and strength combined." The company reported that it cost $26,000 to construct the building, which was completed in August of 1891. Source: Roane County Heritage Commission Photograph Collection, Kingston, TN.

riman Manufacturing Company in these industries in 1892 was $268,000.[95] After two years of implementing its development strategy, the ETLC seems to have been successful in building an industrial base in Harriman.

The Urban/Social Geography of Harriman, Tennessee

In 1892 the first and only Harriman city directory was printed. Its publisher, G. M. Connelly, proclaimed: "The upbuilding of a great city will undoubtedly be the result of the united labors of the community which so liberally supported the publication of volume 1 of the Harriman City Directory. No town of double the population has ever exhibited such enterprise. The book is as complete in its arrangement as all large directories." The East Tennessee Land Company at this time must have hoped that the city directory would serve as evidence of Harriman's urban legitimacy. Over one hundred years later, the Harriman City Directory of 1892 serves another unanticipated purpose. It provides data with which to reconstruct the social landscape created by the East Tennessee Land Company in Harriman.

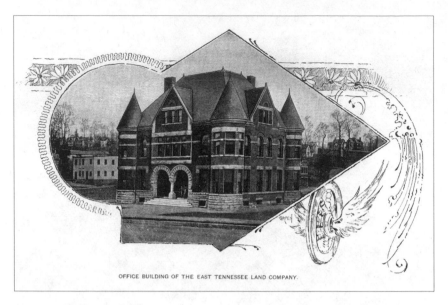

OFFICE BUILDING OF THE EAST TENNESSEE LAND COMPANY.

FIG. 11. Office Building of the East Tennessee Land Company. The company's depiction of its headquarters in the publication *Two Years of Harriman, Tennessee* published in 1892. Source: East Tennessee Land Company, *Two Years of Harriman, Tennessee* (New York: The South Publishing Co., 1892).

FIG. 12. Lookout Rolling Mills, Harriman, 1891. Source: Roane County Heritage Commission Photograph Collection, Kingston, TN.

In 1892 Mr. Connelly reported in the Harriman City Directory that the town had grown from one family in January of 1890 to a population of 3,762. The directory reported the name, address, occupation, and race of each head-of-household in the city in 1892. By using plat maps and Sanborn insurance maps to determine the location of each head-of-household's address, this information offers some insights into the social geography of Harriman at this point in time. One way of assessing the urban geography of Harriman is to use the ETLC's own literature as a way of studying geographic patterns. In addition, various descriptive spatial statistical methods can be used to characterize, for example, observed versus expected occurrences of particular residential groups in defined areas.

In examining the ETLC's literature and its development methods, there are two fairly obvious ways to spatially delineate the town of Harriman. One is simply to distinguish between the area recorded in the company's original plan for the town, and those areas on the "other side of the tracks" to the northwest of the town (described as additions) (map 15). Examination of company literature

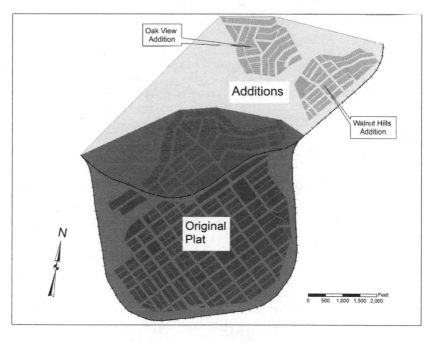

MAP 15. Map of Original Harriman Plat and Additions. The shaded area was part of the original plan filed for the City of Harriman. The lighter area was developed more than a year later by the company as "additions." Source: Author.

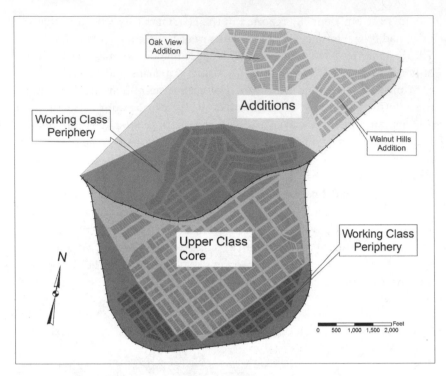

MAP 16. Map of Urban Geography Defined by the East Tennessee Land Company in Harriman. The areas delineated on this map were described in the East Tennessee Land Company's prospectus and in subsequent promotional publications. Source: Author.

also reveals the delineation of three distinct social geographic areas: (1) a middle- and upper-class residential core area, bounded by Carter Street on the south and Clifty Street on the east; (2) a blue-collar, working-class residential area stretching around the lower-elevation periphery of the original plat; and (3) the Walnut Hills and Oak View "addition" residential areas to the northwest of the ETV&G railroad tracks (map 16).

The spatial distribution of African Americans among 1892 Harriman residents leaves little doubt that the ETLC had created a racially segregated settlement by design. Data from the city directory reveal a geographic pattern of virtually complete residential segregation of blacks (map 17). Almost all African Americans living in the Harriman area in 1892 were located west of the railroad tracks in the Oak View Addition.[96] In fact, there was only one instance of African Americans living to the east of the tracks in the original city site, where a boardinghouse for single men was located. It appears that African Americans, although crucial to the industrial labor force, were not to

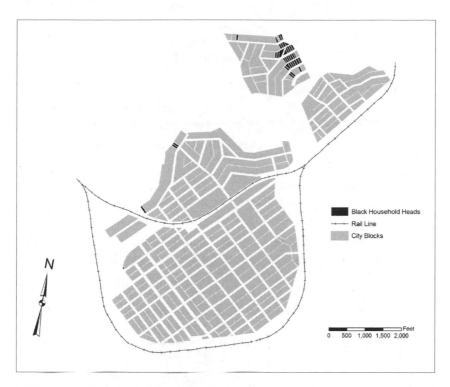

MAP 17. Residential Distribution of African Americans in Harriman, 1892. Note that almost all African Americans lived north and west of the railroad tracks, a significant distance from the central part of Harriman. Source: G. M. Connelly, *City Directory of Harriman, Tennessee* (Chattanooga: Times Printing Co, 1890); Sanborn Map Company, Sanborn Fire Insurance Maps, Harriman, TN, 1895.

reside in Harriman or benefit from its amenities. They were, apparently, not part of the ETLC's vision of the profitable planned model industrial city.

Characterization of spatial patterns in Harriman based on socioeconomic class distinctions is somewhat more difficult. One mechanism for grouping Harriman residents into socioeconomic classes is to use a classification system developed by Olivier Zunz for his study of late-nineteenth- and early-twentieth-century Detroit[97] (table 6). One issue in using this classification method in conjunction with city directory data is that only the head of a household can be classified, therefore not taking into account the total income of multiple earners within households or income from boarders.[98] Recognizing this significant limitation, some general statements can be made about the social geography of 1892 Harriman.

The distribution of heads-of-household of some occupational class groups were significantly different from what would be expected under an assumption

Table 6
Occupational Classification
Adapted From Zunz (1982)

High White-Collar Occupations
  architect, dentist, large business owner, lawyer, merchant, physician

Low White-Collar Occupations
  bookkeeper, civil engineer, clerk, contractor, insurance agent, salesman, schoolteacher

Skilled Blue-Collar Occupations
  blacksmith, cabinetmaker, carpenter, iron molder, iron puddler, plumber, printer, railway engineer

Semiskilled and Unskilled Blue-Collar Occupations
  domestic, janitor, laborer (various), messenger, peddler, policeman, porter, waiter, watchman

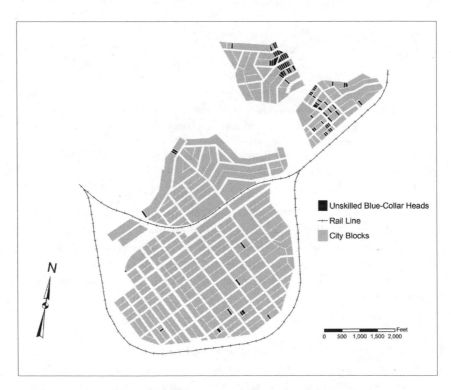

MAP 18. Residential Distribution of Unskilled Blue-Collar Heads-of-Households in Harriman, 1892. Note the clustering of unskilled worker residences in Walnut Hills and Oak View Additions and in the low-elevation periphery of Harriman. Sources: G. M. Connelly, *City Directory of Harriman, Tennessee* (Chattanooga: Times Printing Co, 1890); Sanborn Map Company, Sanborn Fire Insurance Maps, Harriman, TN, 1895.

of geographic randomness. Two patterns were very obvious in examining the geographic distribution of Harriman heads-of-household. One was the relative lack of unskilled blue-collar heads-of-household in the original city plan. A much larger than expected number of unskilled blue-collar heads lived northwest of the tracks in Oak View Addition.[99] Conversely, high white-collar heads were concentrated in the central core area of the original city plat. In 1892 Harriman, no high-level white-collar heads lived northwest of the tracks. The class group that was represented at close to expected frequencies in all parts of Harriman was skilled blue-collar heads-of-household. Their residences were found both in the original plan (mostly in the periphery) and in Walnut Hills and Oak View Additions north of the tracks. The same was generally true of low-level white-collar heads in the original plan, although they were significantly underrepresented in areas north and west of the ETV&G tracks (maps 18–20).

Even with the limitations of the data, some aspects of the urban social geography of Harriman in 1892 are apparent. One is the almost complete segregation of the races that was encouraged through the ETIC's development

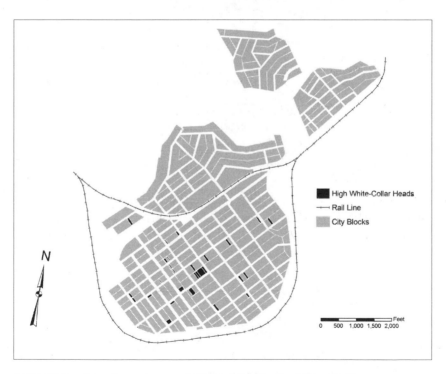

MAP 19. Residential Distribution of White-Collar Heads-of-Households in Harriman, TN, 1892. Most high white-collar heads-of-households lived in the central area of Harriman in 1892. None lived north or west of the railroad tracks. Data sources: G. M. Connelly, *City Directory of Harriman, Tennessee* (Chattanooga: Times Printing Co, 1890); Sanborn Map Company, Sanborn Fire Insurance Maps, Harriman, TN, 1895.

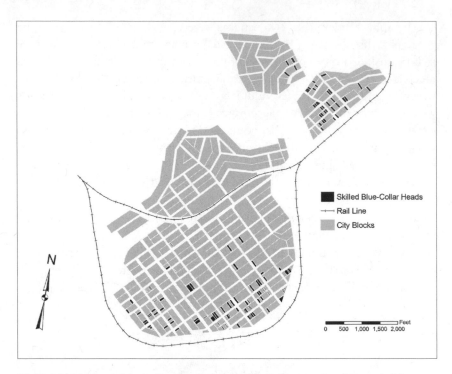

MAP 20. Residential Distribution of Skilled Blue-Collar Heads-of-Households in Harriman, 1892. Skilled Blue-Collar heads-of-households had the least clustered distribution of all of the occupation class groups, although they were less evident in the central part of Harriman. Source: G. M. Connelly, *City Directory of Harriman, Tennessee* (Chattanooga: Times Printing Co, 1890); Sanborn Map Company, Sanborn Fire Insurance Maps, Harriman, TN, 1895.

plan. The company almost certainly knew that African Americans would be working in Harriman's factories (when those factories began operation), yet the company had no intention of recognizing this while it was marketing the proposed city as a real estate venture. The idea that African Americans had chosen to "group themselves" in Oak View Addition is ludicrous. In fact, the ETLC must have determined at some point that a residence area for blacks was needed, and conveyed to them where it would be (although no primary evidence exists to confirm this). This spatial pattern imitated the segregation in northern cities with respect to foreigners and free blacks drawn by industrial employment opportunities.[100] Thus, the East Tennessee Land Company in Harriman created a racially segregated urban settlement in the Upper Tennessee River Valley years before a Jim Crow law was ever passed in the state of Tennessee.[101]

In relation to the residential patterns of socioeconomic classes (as defined by Zunz), there seems to be some correlation between the East Tennessee Land Company's literal descriptions of Harriman's urban geography and reality in 1892. Evidence of this can be found in the very different residential patterns of unskilled blue-collar workers and white-collar heads-of-household. This pattern in itself was not significantly different from that of many other towns and cities in the United States during this period. What is notable, however, is that it appears that the ETLC planned Harriman to be this way in an effort to maximize its profits. Ironically, the social and ethnic groups that would make up the majority of the anticipated industrial workforce—African Americans and uneducated, unskilled Whites—were left out of the plan until it became absolutely necessary to include them. This, more than anything, indicates that the ETLC was selling a real estate venture—the idea of industrialization—rather than focusing on production itself.

Soon the ETLC and the other land companies were not able to continue operating on the large scale with which they had begun their activities in the late 1880s. Their comprehensive development schemes were interrupted by adverse economic circumstances in the early 1890s. The national business environment took a nosedive, and development plans were put on hold, modified, or abandoned completely. The United States was entering a depression.

CHAPTER 4

The Postboom Period

*The boom comprises only a part of the story — a
tale that continues to ripple outward.*
—Brian Black, *Petrolia*, 2000

The Financial Panic of 1893

The economic downturn that affected the entire country during the early to
mid-1890s impacted the land companies in the Upper Tennessee River Valley.
The Panic of 1893, during which the New York Stock Exchange endured several severe drops, initiated a depression that lasted more than three years, one
of the most severe economic depressions in American history.

The decade of the 1890s opened with the nation approaching the end
of a business-cycle expansion. Foreign trade had been favorable since the
mid-1880s, and European capitalists had invested large amounts of capital in
railroads, cattle ranching, and other American enterprises. Employment was
increasing, output was growing, and general economic conditions were positive in the United States.[1]

The generally positive conditions that existed in the country through
1892 belied significant harbingers of economic downturn. There was a significant recession in England in 1890, marked by the failure of the large and
prestigious Baring Brothers investment banking house, a pioneer merchant
banking firm founded in 1763, which had long served as an intermediary
between British investors and American entrepreneurs.[2] By November of
1890, the Baring House had overextended itself in Argentine speculation.
Argentina's economy collapsed, leaving Baring Brothers with a large amount

of its resources locked up in now-worthless land and securities. Although the Bank of England bailed Baring Brothers out, the near-failure of England's foremost banking house shocked European investors. This caused a run on gold by English investors, many of whom liquidated their stock holdings in American companies.[3] The result was a net loss of $68 million in gold exported from the United States in 1890.[4]

Another destabilizing factor for the American economy by 1890 was the struggle for bimetalism. Congress had passed a measure in 1873 that discontinued the further minting of the standard silver dollar.[5] The United States had also returned to a policy of specie payments in 1879, following passage of the Resumption Act by Congress in 1875.[6] The result of these two bills was a contraction of the currency supply in the United States.

By the early 1890s, the silver movement and Europe's general economic downturn threatened the maintenance of the de facto gold standard in the United States. The amount of silver to be purchased under the Sherman Act was too large to be readily absorbed by the United States Treasury, as notes issued for silver were more often than not redeemed for gold at a later date. Through this process, $156 million in Treasury Notes was added to the national money supply between 1890 and 1893, leading to a significant loss of gold from the national reserve over this period. At the same time, skittish European investors were withdrawing their capital from American companies at a heightened pace as their confidence in the American economy and the dollar waned. In 1893 alone, the United States suffered a net loss of $87 million in exported gold.[7]

The dwindling supply of gold caused by the Sherman Silver Act and foreign withdrawal of capital from the United States had dire consequences. In 1893, for the first time since the de facto institution of the gold standard (1873), national gold reserves dropped below the $100 million that had long been regarded as the minimum safe treasury reserve. The breaking of the $100 million reserve barrier began speculation that the gold reserve was in jeopardy, causing trepidation among investors who regarded maintenance of the gold standard as paramount. As this speculation continued, the net result was a general loss of confidence in the soundness of the dollar.[8]

During the early months of 1893 investors rushed to dispose of stocks, bonds, and other securities, causing a sharp downward trend in stock prices on the New York Stock Exchange. Loss of confidence in the monetary system also produced runs on banks, especially in the South and West. In turn, these banks called on larger eastern financial institutions for the return of their reserves. Such demands strained the capital resources of these foremost financial institutions, creating a situation in which loans became almost impossible to obtain and the hoarding of gold and currency was common.[9]

Large-scale business failure characterized the economic downturn in the United States in 1893. Two of the foremost examples were the Philadelphia & Reading Railroad, which went into receivership in February 1893, and the National Cordage Company, which followed in May. These corporations were among the most respected in the United States, and their failures did not bode well for the national economy. In fact, more than fifteen thousand commercial failures involving liabilities of $346.8 million occurred during 1893. In addition, more than six hundred banking institutions and seventy-four railroad corporations failed during the same year. The Panic of 1893 was followed by three years of economic depression during which business failures were accompanied by falling agricultural prices, high unemployment levels, and declining industrial production. It wasn't until the latter part of 1896 that the depression began to break, as silver proponents were defeated and a shift in the balance of foreign trade stemmed the outflow of gold from the national reserve.[10]

Nationwide Depression and the Land Companies

The economic depression had profound effects on companies operating in the Upper Tennessee River Valley. In fact, the only large industry-related company there to remain in its pre-depression form by 1896 was the Roane Iron Company. The mid-1890s held varying degrees of failure and reorganization for the others, ending the large-scale infusion of capital into the region that had characterized the late 1880s and early 1890s.

The first casualty of the depression in the Upper Tennessee River Valley was the Cardiff Coal & Iron Company. The Cardiff Company, begun with lofty aspirations, soon found that the economic conditions of the early 1890s had left the company in an impossible situation. Following its land sale in April of 1890, the CCIC advertised that it had sold over a million dollars' worth of property at its city site. However, this amount was never collected. Buyers were required to pay only one-third of the total purchase price at the auction, with the other two-thirds due after six months and one year, respectively. As economic conditions worsened during the year following the sale, a significant number of property buyers defaulted on their installments. At the same time, the CCIC's creditors were demanding payment on the large loans that the company had taken out to purchase land. During its early period of activity in 1889 and early 1890, conditions were favorable, and the company assumed that these conditions would continue. By mid-1891 it was obvious, however, that investors were retaining their capital in times of increasing uncertainty. This left the CCIC with bills to pay and no money to pay them with. Its plan of paying off its debts with the proceeds of continued land sales was no longer viable. The company was sued by land buyers and creditors during 1891. The former sued for improvements and infrastructure not provided to the city site as promised, the latter for loan payments not made on time. The CCIC went into receivership in June of 1891.

Events impacting the national capital market doomed Cardiff. The CCIC had begun just early enough to appear to be a profitable venture, but too late to develop a solid financial base before the economic downturn. Most of the company's advertised plans were stopped by the receivership. This created more suits by investors and land purchasers who felt that the company had not made good on its pledge to "build" the town and provide it with certain infrastructure (a blast furnace, graded and paved streets, water and sewer systems, a hotel). Charles Haley's description of events was representative of the opinions held by Cardiff investors:

> Of the large amount of money agreed to be expended . . . only a small amount was spent, just enough to fool the bidders at the public sale in April, and to cajole the buyers into paying the six month notes maturing in September and October following. Then the whole work was abandoned. The hotel which had been partially constructed was left uncovered and exposed to the elements, the streets washed into gullies, the trenches for the furnace filled up and caved in, the cottages were deserted, the people moved off, and the whole fraud and sham has been blown up and dissipated.[11]

Although Haley was apparently biased about the initial intentions of the Cardiff company, his description of the situation in the town in 1892 was accurate. Most of the infrastructure that the CCIC was supposed to have built was not completed before the company's financial troubles in mid-1891. This led to the abandonment of several projects and the completion of few.

Events associated with the Panic of 1893 proved to be the end of the CCIC and the city of Cardiff. The company had survived its two years in receivership mainly on the strength of proceeds from the sale of coal mined on its lands to iron production facilities in East Tennessee. The effects of the Panic caused many of these facilities to decrease production or shut down completely, creating a corresponding reduction in demand for coal. This was devastating to the CCIC, since income from land and stock sales had been almost nonexistent since mid-1891. The company declared bankruptcy and discontinued operations in the Upper Tennessee River Valley in 1893. A Chattanooga publication described Cardiff in 1895: "The collapse came, and today the town does not contain twenty people. The only signs of it that can be seen are a few deserted stores, rain-washed streets, overgrown with grass and weeds and the electric light poles which ornament the vacant fields."[12] By late 1893, the capitalist blueprint drafted for Cardiff by the CCIC could not be followed, as previously available capital markets had disappeared. The planned city did not last long enough to rate even a mention in the federal census of 1900.

The East Tennessee Land Company and the city of Harriman were also adversely impacted by the economic conditions of the early 1890s. The ETLC and its planned city had benefited from an earlier start in the region (April 1889), and because of this had been able to complete several projects associated with the development of Harriman by 1893 (the ETLC Building, several business buildings along Roane Street, the Belt Line Railway, and street grading on the city site). Between 1890 and 1892, the company was fairly successful in obtaining capital through its land sale (held in early 1890) and the sale of stock. But a decision made in mid-1890 to raise additional capital for development by obtaining one million dollars worth of first mortgage bonds through the Central Trust Company of New York was one that the ETLC would regret in the years to come, however. The company used this money to finance improvements for the city of Harriman and to subsidize the establishment of its satellite companies and new industries and businesses. Unfortunately for the ETLC, neither the subsidiary companies or the new industries and businesses earned sufficient profits in the ensuing years to pay even the interest on this large mortgage. By late 1892 the ETLC found it very difficult to meet payments on the loan. In September of 1892 a program called the Million Dollar Plan was initiated to recapitalize the company through the issuance of first-lien and second-lien preferred stock. The goal of the plan was to sell stock, use the proceeds to pay off the Central Trust bonds, and return the company to a sound financial situation. The ETLC declared the plan an overwhelming success in January of 1893, when it informed the public that it had received subscriptions for the entire one-million-dollar amount. The account of this announcement in the local newspaper indicates the amount of importance attributed to the plan:

> The Directors have satisfied themselves that the subscriptions to the new stock are bonified [sic] and can be relied upon. They are further satisfied that the One Million of Dollars which these will yield will meet the entire bonded and floating indebtedness on the Company, and relieve its immense properties from incumberance. . . . the success of the Million Plan is immediate, the effects of it will be increasingly shown, and the final results should tell wonderfully for the benefit of Harriman and all concerned in its future.[13]

The events of 1893, however, dampened enthusiasm regarding the Million Dollar Plan. Although the stock offered by the ETLC had technically been fully subscribed, the subscribers had not paid the money to the company by mid-1893. This is when the most extreme drop in the stock market took place, and when financial institutions were under the most demand for capital. The Central Trust Company demanded payment from the ETLC and, when it was not forthcoming, filed suit in federal court. This resulted in the company's filing for bankruptcy in November of 1893. Receivers over the next four years sold off the ETLC's assets in an effort to recoup any money that could be paid to creditors. Thus the Panic of 1893 also caused the demise of the ETLC as a corporate entity.

The city of Harriman was able to survive, however, thanks to its strong start and the determination of its Prohibitionist founders and population. Although many industries shut down during the Panic, the major railroads and some smaller companies continued to operate throughout the depression. During this difficult time, residents who remained in Harriman established other institutions that generated economic activity in the town. Prominent among these was the founding of the American Temperance University in 1894, which was housed in the former ETLC building. In the ensuing years, as many as 250 students attended the university, to learn in an environment free from "smoking, gambling, theft, lying, profanity, obscenity and drunkeness."[14]

Lenoir City was the latest of the land company developments to be initiated and, because of this, did not find itself in as dire a debt situation as its predecessors. The Lenoir City Company was not incorporated until April of 1890, and its stock and land sale was not held until September of that year. This later start proved important because the LCC was able to anticipate impending economic conditions to some extent and to avoid larger-scale speculative spending and debt accumulation. By June of 1892, however, the company was experiencing problems paying on debt it had accrued earlier. Sales of property had been much slower than expected, and the board of directors attributed this to "the unusual and stringent conditions of the money market."[15] Charles J. McClung, a prominent Knoxville businessman, came to the company's aid in this situation and personally paid the debt, effectively removing the lien from its property.[16] The situation did not improve in the next six months, however. Company records indicate that by November of 1892, the LCC had sold only 144 of the 3,448 lots platted in Lenoir City.[17]

Lenoir City ultimately survived the depression of the 1890s because of the work and dedication of E. J. Sanford and Charles McGhee. Sanford was the originator of the Lenoir City project and took responsibility for overseeing many of the early activities of the company. He, more than anyone, worked to make the development successful in an uncertain economic environment. His dedication to the project was reflected in a letter to his friend McGhee in 1891: "I have not yet lost faith in Lenoir, and I feel it will all work out yet, although as I stated before I have had more disappointments in it than in than any other business attempt in my life."[18] Besides his financial influence, McGhee spent considerable time attempting to attract industry to Lenoir City. His biggest success, and probably the savior of the development during the 1890s, was the Lenoir Car Company. McGhee convinced J. H. Bass, an experienced railcar producer from Fort Wayne, Indiana, to locate a new facility in Lenoir City. He then went to the board of the Lenoir City Company and made a motion that a fifty-acre tract of land adjacent to the East Tennessee, Virginia & Georgia mainline be given to the Car Company.[19] The Lenoir Car Company immediately became a major employer in the town and remained so for the next thirty years.

Each of the land companies ceased large-scale operation after the economic downturn of 1893. The late 1880s and early 1890s had been a watershed for investment because of the evolution of the national capital market, which allowed land companies access to development capital needed to buy land and initiate their development projects. In the years following the Panic of 1893, the American economy was unstable at best, and financial institutions and investors were reluctant to become involved in any type of speculative venture. In addition, by the mid- to late 1890s it had become apparent that the region was not going to become a major iron and steel production center. The main problem lay in the high phosphorus content of local iron ore deposits. High-quality steel simply could not be made. Meanwhile, other industrial entities had successfully mass-produced steel in Pittsburgh and Johnstown, Pennsylvania, in Chicago, and in Birmingham. By the mid-1890s, the financial and industrial situation had changed, bringing an end to the land company investment era in the Upper Tennessee River Valley.

The Aftermath: The Regional Economy and Settlement Pattern of the Upper Tennessee River Valley, 1895–1920

The settlement patterns that had emerged from the agricultural economy in the Upper Tennessee River Valley prior to 1860 were altered by industrial capital investment during the study period. In 1880, twelve years after the Roane Iron Company began operation, Rockwood was the most populated urban settlement in the region. Twenty years later, in 1900, Rockwood had been supplanted by Harriman as the largest city, and both were more than triple the size of the river towns of Loudon and Kingston. Through the first two decades of the twentieth century, Lenoir City, Rockwood, and Harriman emerged as the largest urban settlements in the region, each with populations of between 3,000 and 3,700 in 1910, and between 4,000 and 4,700 in 1920 (table 7).

Perhaps more significant is the longer-term reorientation of the regional settlement pattern. In 1860 (prior to the advent of industrial capitalism), the proportion of the Roane County population that was urban was approximately

Table 7
Population of Upper Tennessee River Valley Towns, 1860–1920

Town	1860	1870	1880	1890	1900	1910	1920
Cardiff	*	*	*	430	*	*	*
Harriman	*	*	*	716	3442	3061	4019
Lenoir City	*	*	*	**	**	3392	4210
Loudon	**	**	832	942	875	**	**
Kingston	307	739	858	**	548	824	516
Rockwood	*	649	1011	2305	2899	3660	4652

*Community was not recognized by the Bureau of the Census in the census year.
**Data was not reported on the community by the Bureau of the Census for the census year.

Source: U.S. Department of Commerce, Bureau of the Census, Ninth Census, 1870: Population Manuscripts; Tenth Census, 1880: Population Manuscripts, Tennessee, Roane County; Compendium of the Ninth Census, 1870; Compendium of the Tenth Census, 1880; Compendium of the Eleventh Census, 1890; Compendium of the Twelfth Census, 1900; Compendium of the Fourteenth Census, 1920.

11 percent and fluctuated only slightly (13.4 percent in 1870, 12.3 percent in 1880) during the ensuing twenty years. Between 1880 and 1890, however, the percentage of urban population in the county more than doubled to 25.1 percent and continued to increase through the 1920 census (35.2 percent). When the numbers from both counties comprising the Upper Tennessee River Valley (Roane and Loudon) are combined, a similar trend emerges, although Loudon County had a lower proportion of urban population throughout the study period than did Roane (table 8). This suggests that although the period of intense influence by industrial and corporate capitalists was relatively short, it significantly altered the preexisting settlement pattern.

The period between 1870 and 1893 also seems to have had a significant long-term impact on the regional economy. In 1870 the value of farm products in the study area was more than two and a half times that of manufactured products. This situation persisted through 1880, although the ratio of the value of agricultural products to manufactured products decreased. In 1890 the situation changed as the value of manufactured products exceeded the value of agricultural products for the first time. This was mostly the result of investment and production by the Roane Iron Company, as the land companies were just beginning to operate when the census was conducted. By 1900 a major economic shift was evident, as the value of manufactured products exceeded $2.4 million, more than double the value of agricultural products. From 1870 to 1900, industrial employment increased more than fivefold, from 160 workers to 911 in the study region (tables 9 and 10).

Table 8
Percent Urban Population—Loudon and Roane Counties and the Upper Tennessee River Valley, 1870–1920

	1870	1880	1890	1900	1910	1920
Loudon	*	9.1%	10.2%	*	24.9%	25.9%
Roane	13.4%	12.3%	25.1%	27.9%	29.4%	35.2%
Upper Tenn River Valley	**	10.7%	17.7%	**	27.2%	30.6%

*Data was not reported on the county by the Bureau of the Census for the census year.
**Not able to be determined as data was not reported on one of the counties for the census year.

Source: U.S. Department of Commerce, Bureau of the Census, Ninth Census, 1870: Population Manuscripts; Compendium of the Eleventh Census, 1890; Compendium of the Fourteenth Census, 1920.

An examination of census data indicates that the Upper Tennessee River Valley economy had made a significant shift toward industrial production by 1920.[20] In 1920 the value of manufactured goods produced in the region was $18,512,122—an increase in the value of industrial production of more than seven-and-one-half times since 1900 (table 10). A trend begun in 1890 of increasing imbalance in favor of industry continued, as the proportion went from more than two-to-one industry to agriculture in 1900 to more than five-to-one in 1920. A look at the region from a statewide perspective offers further evidence of regional economic reorientation. In 1920 Loudon County ranked fifth among Tennessee counties in the cost of industrial input materials and sixth in the value of industrial commodities (out of ninety-six counties). Roane County had slightly lower rankings of ninth and eighth, respectively in 1920. This level of productivity was much higher than might be expected based on the region's population, as Loudon County had a population rank of 57 (16,275) and Roane County a rank of 27 (24,624) in the state in 1920. With respect to industrial wage earners, Loudon and Roane Counties ranked fifth and sixth in Tennessee, respectively, in 1920. Loudon County was second in the state in proportion of county population employed in industry at 11.4 percent (to Hamilton County, the political unit where the city of Chattanooga is located), and the average combined proportion employed in industry for both Roane and Loudon counties in 1920 (9.5 percent) exceeded that in Tennessee's two most populous counties: Shelby (Memphis) and Davidson (Nashville).

But what kind of industrial production was taking place in the Upper Tennessee River Valley after 1895? The answer to this question illustrates

Table 9
Value of Agricultural Production,
Upper Tennessee River Valley, 1870–1920

	1870	1880	1890	1900	1910	1920
Loudon Co.	*	$368,420	$348,900	$514,591	*	$1,657,998
Roane Co.	$619,768	$512,937	$341,490	$678,831	*	$1,968,994
Total	$619,768	$881,357	$650,390	$1,193,422	*	$3,626,992

*Data not available.

SOURCE: U.S. Department of Commerce, Bureau of the Census, Ninth Census, 1870: Agriculture, Tennessee; Tenth Census, 1880: Agriculture, Tennessee; Eleventh Census, 1890: Agriculture, Tennessee; Twelfth Census, 1900: Agriculture, Tennessee; Fourteenth Census, 1920: Agriculture, Tennessee.

both the lasting influence of the industrial and corporate stages of capitalism, and the impact of changing capitalist contexts. Examples of the lasting impact of the industrial and corporate stages in the Upper Tennessee River Valley include the Lenoir Car Works and the Roane Iron Company. In Loudon County, one of the major industrial producers after 1895 was the Lenoir Car Works. Charles McGhee had used his influence and connections as a director of the East Tennessee, Virginia & Georgia Railroad to facilitate the location of the Lenoir Car Works in Lenoir City. He had successfully convinced J. H. Bass of Fort Wayne, Indiana, to locate a new freight car production plant in the town. Although no evidence exists, it is likely that McGhee promised Bass that his company would receive preference for East Tennessee, Virginia & Georgia freight car contracts if a production facility were located in Lenoir City. McGhee had delivered contracts for orders before to preferred suppliers, as he had secured iron and steel rail contracts for the Roane Iron Company. John White, referring to the practice as the "home-purchase rule," points out that it was typical for railroads to purchase rolling stock from railcar builders located on their lines, as they could avoid paying shipping costs.[21] So the location of the Lenoir Car Works in Lenoir City was a direct result of the corporate capitalist stage and, in particular, the influence of Charles McGhee.

The Roane Iron Company—a product of the early industrial capitalist stage—remained in business the longest of any of the Upper Tennessee River Valley companies examined in this story. Hiram Chamberlain, and later Charles McGhee, spent much time and effort working to make the company a success. The Roane Iron Company's focus on production, and its adaptation to its role as a regional producer of pig iron after the Panic period allowed it to remain viable. The company managed to produce pig iron at Rockwood

Table 10
Industrial Production - Upper Tennessee River Valley, 1870-1920

County	1870			1880		
	Capital Invested	Value of Products	Number Employed	Capital Invested	Value of Products	Number Employed
Loudon	*	*	*	$157,100	$254,730	83
Roane	$162,750	$235,321	160	$774,250	$327,082	455
TOTAL	$162,750	$235,321	160	$931,350	$531,812	538

County	1890			1900		
	Capital Invested	Value of Products	Number Employed	Capital Invested	Value of Products	Number Employed
Loudon	$77,089	$99,199	118	$873,936	$921,489	311
Roane	$671,370	$669,212	388	$1,449,838	$1,511,721	600
TOTAL	$748,479	$768,411	506	$2,323,774	$2,433,240	911

County	1910			1920		
	Capital Invested	Value of Products	Number Employed	Capital Invested	Value of Products	Number Employed
Loudon	*	*	*	*	$10,294,713	1,862
Roane	*	*	*	*	$8,217,409	1,843
TOTAL	*	*	*	*	$18,512,122	3,705

*Data not available.

Source: U.S. Department of Commerce, Bureau of the Census, Ninth Census, 1870: Manufactures, Tennessee; Tenth Census, 1880: Manufactures, Tennessee; Eleventh Census, 1890: Manufactures, Tennessee; Twelfth Census, 1900: Manufactures, Tennessee; Fourteenth Census, 1920: Manufactures, Tennessee.

continuously through the depression of the mid-1890s, although production slowdowns took place. Even after the depression had ended, however, Rockwood did not become a major regional production center for iron or steel. The reason for this was articulated by Hiram Chamberlain in an October 1887 letter to Charles McGhee, when he stated "I think it better that we have some foreign iron very low in phosphorus in our mixture."[22] Chamberlain, after two decades of experience making iron and steel in the Upper Tennessee River Valley, realized that the high-phosphorus iron ore in the Rockwood area did not make a high-quality steel product. This was a significant problem for

Roane Iron in the ensuing decades because it prevented the company from making cost-competitive steel products. Although the company experimented with using outside iron ore, each of these attempts was abandoned because of prohibitive cost. Because it could not produce for the emerging market for steel products, the Roane Iron Company remained a small regional producer, and Rockwood a small industrial town in the Upper Tennessee River Valley. The potential that Hiram Chamberlain and James Wilder dreamed of when they began their endeavor was instead realized at a place farther down the Tennessee Valley—Birmingham, Alabama.[23]

The Roane Iron Company continued operations until 1929. The company experienced a period of prosperity during World War I, when iron products were needed for the war effort. This demand disappeared after the war, however, and problems emerged for the company. Freight rates on the transport of its pig iron to the Northeast rose rapidly, decreasing competitiveness. The southern iron market was dominated by Birmingham, which was able to produce higher-quality steel at lower cost. Also, Roane Iron endured several mine disasters during the mid-1920s, which resulted in lost lives and worker compensation payments of more than $200,000 (over one-fifth of the total capitalization of the company). These circumstances, in concert with plunging iron prices in 1929, caused the company to suspend operations in January of 1930.[24]

In contrast to the Lenoir Car Works and the Roane Iron Company, the industrial base that emerged in the Upper Tennessee River Valley after 1895 was a product of the changing capitalist context of the region. In Harriman, the Panic of 1893 had severely restricted access to development capital, and it had become obvious that iron and steel were not going to be the economic future of the town. In 1900 the largest industrial employer in Harriman was the Harriman Rolling Mills (with three hundred workers), a branch of the Knoxville Iron Company. Other industrial companies employed fewer workers and produced fairly ubiquitous goods for a regional market. What would eventually form the longer-term industrial foundation for the Upper Tennessee River Valley had its inception in Rockwood in 1905. The Rockwood Hosiery Mill was established by local businessman J. F. Tarwater, bringing low-skill, low-wage, labor-intensive industry to the Upper Tennessee River Valley. Seven years later in 1912, the Harriman Hosiery Mills was established by J. F.'s son Tom Tarwater. Under the heading GIRLS WANTED, the Harriman Hosiery Mill advertised in the November 12, 1912, issue of the *Harriman Record* (the town newspaper) for "girls 14 years of age and over . . . [for] Steady work, pleasant employment, and good pay."[25]

Evidence exists that even in Lenoir City, where the Lenoir Car Works employed significant numbers of skilled blue-collar workers after 1890, the industrial base was evolving by 1910. Although the Lenoir Car Works was indisputably important in Lenoir City's development and is usually high-lighted in various historical accounts, census manuscript data show that less than twenty years after its establishment the car works was not the town's largest employer. By 1910 the Lenoir Knitting Mill employed 81 more workers than the Lenoir Car Works (454 Lenoir City residents were employed in the knitting mill, and 363 in the car works).[26] A vast majority of the knitting-mill workforce was made up of women and children. Eleven-year-old twins Dewey and Pisyck, two of seven children, worked in the knitting mill in May of 1910. So did thirteen-year-old Hester, a female knitting-mill laborer who had stopped attending school. The youngest documented worker in the mill was seven-year-old Lee, who although still attending school had not yet learned to read and write.[27] By 1910 the vision of the model industrial city in the Upper Tennessee River Valley appears to have all but vanished, replaced by a more realistic assessment by capitalists as to which strategies would yield profits. In Southern Appalachia, a region where wage rates were among the lowest in the United States, labor didn't come any cheaper than school-age children and unmarried young women. Rather than heavy industry, which required access to bulky, high-value raw materials and a certain amount of skilled labor, the economic base of the region between 1900 and 1920 became much less unique. It was beginning to look much like that of other parts of the American South, where activities like hosiery and apparel production had few geographic constraints, other than access to pools of low-cost labor.

CONCLUSION

What Does the Story of the Upper Tennessee River Valley Tell Us about Capitalism and Regional Development in Appalachia?

I suggested at the outset of this story that much of it would be about failure. On the surface, many of the capitalist strategies pursued in the Upper Tennessee River Valley during the period between 1865 and 1900 did appear to end in failure. None of the business entities that operated in the Upper Tennessee River Valley—the Roane Iron Company, the East Tennessee Land Company, the Cardiff Coal & Iron Company, or the Lenoir City Company—became national, or even regional, business leaders. Capitalist goals were often set and then not met, especially in such areas as steel production, urban development, and the sale of real estate.

There are two ways to view these capitalist "failures." One is to gloss over them with a shallow explanation as to why things didn't "work," and move on to study capitalists in places where much more development occurred and more money was made. This is the typical treatment of less-than successful capitalist strategies, and the reason why regions like the Upper Tennessee River Valley have remained on the periphery in the study of capitalism and its impact. But another approach is to look closely at the contexts and circumstances within which capitalists made their decisions and took their risks. Upon doing this, the difference between achieving "success" and facing "failure" seem very small, and very much subject to chance.

Let's take a closer look at capitalist success and failure in Appalachia. Eller believes that the persistent poverty within subregions of Appalachia "has not resulted from the lack of modernization. Rather it has come from the particular kind of modernization that unfolded in the years from 1880 to 1930."[1] From Eller's perspective, capitalist failure could have been a saving grace for the people of Appalachia, if it meant that their lives would be less affected by industrial and corporate capitalism. But in the Upper Tennessee River Valley, an Appalachian subregion where capitalists' aspirations to bring about modernization never came to fruition, even failed capitalist ventures brought about permanent changes.

In the introduction to this book, I suggested that the story of regional development in the Upper Tennessee River Valley could contribute to the literature of the impact of capitalism in Southern Appalachia during the years between 1865 and 1900. The Upper Tennessee River Valley was identified as representative of many subregions of Appalachia, with respect to physical geography, agricultural regimes, settlement patterns, and historical circumstances. But what has the story of this region really told us about the evolution of capitalism and regional development in Southern Appalachia? The literature discussed in the introduction can be used as a framework to evaluate what happened in the Upper Tennessee River Valley.

Stages of Capitalism and Their Implications for Regional Economic Development

Upon examination, the three stages of capitalism seem easy to identify in the development of the Upper Tennessee River Valley. Before the Civil War, *mercantile capitalism* was dominant in the region, and strongly influenced development patterns. The towns of Kingston and Loudon became small urban places because their locations allowed merchants to effectively perform their marketing function within the region. Early on, locational imperatives for markets were almost completely based on access to river and road transportation routes. The town of Kingston was established in 1799 at a location that met these criteria. Kingston remained the major urban settlement in the region for the next fifty years. In 1852 the regional transportation picture changed when the East Tennessee & Georgia (ET&G) Railroad constructed its line from Dalton, Georgia, to Loudon (Blair's Ferry), Tennessee. For a short period Loudon became a uniquely advantageous location for farmers and merchants, as it linked the Upper Tennessee River Valley to larger markets via a new mode of transportation—the railroad. But Loudon's location became less advantageous two years later (in 1854) when the ET&G built a bridge across the Tennessee River and extended its line northeast to Knoxville. Nonetheless, prior to the Civil War, the development pattern in the Upper Tennessee River Valley was a product of a mixed regional mercantile economy that was agriculture-based.

The Roane Iron Company (RIC) initiated the onset of industrial capitalism there in 1867. It was the first significant manufacturing entity to begin operation in the region. A close look at its operation methods and structure reveal that it was indeed a true *industrial capitalist* entity.

Throughout its entire period of operation (1868–1929), Roane Iron continued as a proprietary-competitive business entity that was owned and managed by the same people. The primary exemplar of this was Hiram Chamberlain, who was intimately involved with the operations of the company and sat on its board of directors for over forty years. Additionally, the Roane Iron Company suffered a problem common to many early industrial entities—a shortfall of capital to support its operations. Symptomatic of this were RIC's largely unsuccessful efforts to vertically integrate, both backward into the control of land and resources and forward into product-finishing processes and marketing and distribution. The company frequently struggled to gain access to capital to pursue expansion, innovation, and upgrades. Only when Charles McGhee used his influence to allow the RIC access to New York capital markets did this situation change. Even then, the closed ownership structure of the business remained the same.

Railroads and land companies brought corporate capitalism to the Upper Tennessee River Valley beginning in the 1880s. There, as in many parts of Southern Appalachia, railroads were very important in bringing about the transition from industrial to corporate capitalism. One of the most obvious reasons for this was increased access to transportation for vast new areas as rail lines were constructed. Once an area had been penetrated by rail lines, many other profit-making activities became feasible (mining, timbering, rough processing, manufacturing). For example, once the Upper Tennessee River Valley was connected by the East Tennessee, Virginia & Georgia and the Cincinnati-Southern Railroads to destinations north and south in the Great Valley and the Midwest, the region became much more attractive to investors.

But there were other, perhaps even more important, reasons why railroads brought changes in the way that capitalism was practiced. Railroads introduced outside business innovators to Southern Appalachia. These innovators had been exposed to advanced techniques of accumulating capital that had been devised to fund the expansion and construction needs of railroads. Stover has documented the transition that occurred in the ownership and administration of southern railroads, stating, "Prior to and during the war years southerners, using chiefly local finances, owned, controlled and managed the great bulk of southern railroads . . . in 1900, northern men and money exerted a considerable financial influence and control over a much enlarged southern railway network."[2] As northern capitalists gained control of southern railroads and incorporated them into integrated rail networks, they brought more sophisticated organizational and financial business methods to Appalachia.

Why are these ideas so important to understanding regional development patterns in the Upper Tennessee River Valley and Southern Appalachia? The answer lies in the fact that the methods that outside railroad capitalists brought with them to Southern Appalachia constituted a *spatial diffusion of capitalist strategies*. The capitalists who began to assert themselves in Southern Appalachia through the development of railroads were veterans at operating within corporate public ownership structures and knew how the capital markets of New York, Boston, and Philadelphia worked. They also had personal ties to trust companies and investment banking firms from previous business dealings—connections needed to successfully obtain funds through the issuance of stocks and securities.

As these capital accumulation strategies spread throughout Southern Appalachia, and as railroad expansion continued, a relative decrease in demand for capital by railroads occurred during the mid-1880s that created opportunities for other types of business entities to employ capital markets. At the same time, capitalists and investors began to search for other ways to use the infrastructure that railroad expansion had provided. They sought other innovative avenues to make profits. This is when *land companies* appeared in Southern Appalachia as new strategies to accumulate capital.

In the Upper Tennessee River Valley, land companies began their operations in late 1880s. The East Tennessee Land Company, Cardiff Coal & Iron Company, and Lenoir City Company each exhibited corporate capitalist characteristics that were directly related to the influence of railroads. In fact, each of the companies had at least one director who was also on the board of directors of a railroad. From railroads, the land companies borrowed both business structure and capital accumulation methods. Each of the three land companies operating in the Upper Tennessee River Valley employed a parent company/subsidiary model of business structure. The land companies themselves were the parent companies, and they established subsidiaries to perform specific development functions. The East Tennessee Land Company, for example, told its potential investors that it would "organize, other companies . . . and to these subordinate companies . . . transfer by lease the timber . . . and the minerals under them . . . devoting itself chiefly to surface development."[3] In addition, the three land companies demonstrated another characteristic often associated with corporate capitalism—a functional separation between ownership and management. Unlike the Roane Iron Company, where the same people were involved in ownership and production management activities, the land companies were very clear about their intention to keep corporate ownership activities separate from commodity production management. The company best articulated this approach in its literature: "The East Tennessee Land Company will not expend its energies and its working capital in general mining or manufacture. . . . its one purpose is to turn these, by systematic development, to the best advantage possible."[4]

The land companies used limited-liability public ownership structures and access to industrial securities markets to accumulate large amounts of capital to undertake development activities in the Upper Tennessee River Valley. Each company worked with investment banking firms to offer securities for public sale. The Cardiff Coal and Iron Company obtained some of its development capital through bonds issued by the Boston investment banking firm of Cordley & Company (in fact, two of the firm's partners were on the CCIC's board of directors). The East Tennessee Land Company worked with the Central Trust Company of New York to obtain a $1 million bond issue in 1889, which provided the money needed to buy large tracts of land in the Upper Tennessee River Valley. The Lenoir City Company, similar to the Cardiff Coal and Iron Company, had two partners of the New York investment banking firm of Moore & Schley on its board of directors, and it obtained development capital from the firm. Thus, public ownership structure and access to investment banking capital were crucial to allowing land companies to proceed with their development strategies in the region.

The Role of Institutions and Individuals in Regional Development

The story of the Upper Tennessee River Valley suggests that the institutional environment for the onset of industrial capitalism was in place in Tennessee. When New South conservatives came to power in the state in 1869, they changed many radical policies, but they continued those that encouraged industrialization. Examples include funding by the state legislature for a State Board of Immigration (1867) and a State Industrial Association (1869). By 1870 the state of Tennessee had instituted policies that strongly supported industrialization.

The Role of Land Speculators

In the literature on industrial development in Southern Appalachia between 1880 and 1920, researchers such as Gaventa, Eller, Lewis, and Banks have suggested that control of land by "absentee" capitalists led to the exploitation of resources and people. In the Upper Tennessee River Valley, land speculators were active from the mid-1860s onward, with spikes in activity coming during the mid- to late 1860s and the late 1880s. The earliest speculators—the former Union officers John Wilder and Hiram Chamberlain—were outsiders who had become acquainted with the region during the Civil War. In September of 1865 Wilder and Chamberlain purchased approximately 728 acres of land from several owners for $3,641.56 ($5 an acre).[5] Little more than two years later, the Roane Iron Company paid $10,000 to purchase 1,000 acres from a local landowner ($10 an acre). These purchases tell us two things: (1) Roane Iron was an early industrial capitalist entity focused on iron production and had neither the capital nor desire to purchase large amounts of land; (2)

Roane Iron did not seem to be unfairly exploiting local landowners based on the prices that it paid for land. There is no question that Roane Iron brought about changes in the local economy and, to some extent, in the work and subsistence regimes of people living in the region. It does not seem, though, that it was among the firms documented by Gaventa and Eller that exploited and misled Appalachian freeholders into "trading a mountain for a hog rifle." In fact, the prices that Roane Iron paid for land were at their lowest 66 percent, and at their highest more than 200 percent, greater than the highest prices paid ($3 an acre) by companies some years later in Bell County, Kentucky.[6]

In the 1880s land speculators in the Upper Tennessee River Valley worked in conjunction with land companies. Initially, individual speculators negotiated with landowners, acquiring land that was eventually transferred to the companies. The East Tennessee Land Company, for example, had an agent named W. C. Shaw, who was buying land in the area as early as 1887. He seems to have been authorized to pay around $13 an acre for land based on the purchase prices of various tracts.[7] Comparison of these prices to the Bureau of the Census's estimation of the value of agricultural land in the Upper Tennessee River Valley of $9.45 per acre (average for Loudon and Roane Counties) in 1900 shows that the company was paying more than the estimated market value for its land acquisitions.[8] Henry and Joseph Young were brothers originally from Boston who were "land agents" for the Cardiff Coal and Iron Company. The Youngs purchased land outright, but they also bought numerous options to purchase land from local owners.

The Role of Land Companies

Land acquisition patterns in the Upper Tennessee River Valley support previous findings that the advent of industrial and corporate capitalism brought increasing external control of land to Appalachia. The Roane Iron Company acquired slightly more than 1,800 acres of iron and coal land in the late 1860s. It did not have the need or the capital to acquire more, limiting its regional impact in this respect. The land companies, on the other hand, purchased tracts of land large enough to transfer complete control to outside interests. The ETLC alone purchased over 200,000 acres of land with funds it had acquired from the New York capital market. In 1890 the Cardiff Coal and Iron Company claimed to have "absolutely good and indefensible title" to over 50,000 acres. In its prospectus, the Lenoir City Company told potential investors that it "owned or controlled" 80,000.[9] Banks has asserted that land companies brought about qualitatively different forms of investment when they began operation within Appalachia, in that corporate entities (as opposed to individuals) were able to monopolize land and resources.[10] In the two-year period between 1888 and 1890, ownership of huge amounts of land in the Upper Tennessee River Valley was transferred from local individual landowners to corporate entities controlled by capitalists from outside the region. The land acquired by land companies was incorporated into comprehensive development plans, with resource extraction, industrial production, and city development as major components.

The land companies of the Upper Tennessee River Valley, even in their short period of existence, fundamentally changed both how land was used and the means by which local people made a living. Even after the land companies had been dismantled in the aftermath of the Panic of 1893, land for the most part did not return to local owners, nor did the regional economy go back to being dominated by mixed agriculture. Evidence of this is found in the census statistics covering the study period. Through 1880, the value of agricultural products in the Upper Tennessee River Valley continued to exceed the value of industrial products, even though the Roane Iron Company had been in operation for over ten years. In 1890, for the first time, the value of industrial production exceeded that of agricultural production in the region. With the economic downturn of 1893, it might be expected that agriculture would become relatively more important in the region in terms of value by 1900, but that was not the case. In fact, the trend of increasing disparity between the value of agricultural and industrial production in the region continued through 1920. In addition, the settlement pattern in the region from 1880 to 1920 continued to become more concentrated in urban settlements—primarily a result of industrial production. These data support assertions by Eller, Gaventa, Banks, and others that the activities of industrial and corporate capitalist entities had a dominant and lasting economic and social impact on Southern Appalachia, regardless of the fortunes of individual business entities.

The land companies documented in this book were not isolated instances of a seldom-used capitalist strategy. Rather, they were prevalent ways of doing business in Southern Appalachia during the late 1880s and early 1890s, and they were key agents in coordinating regional development patterns. In fact, numerous researchers have separately documented the activities of land companies in northern Alabama, southeastern Kentucky, southern West Virginia, southwestern Virginia, as well as East Tennessee.[11] I view land companies as intermediate corporate business forms that were characterized by (1) public ownership structure, (2) access to capital markets, and (3) comprehensive regional development schemes based on control of land. It was through the activities of such companies that urban settlements such as Birmingham, Bessemer, Fort Payne, Gadsden, and Sheffield in Alabama; Middlesborough in Kentucky; Marlinton in West Virginia; and Elizabethton, Harrogate, Harriman, and Lenoir City in Tennessee and probably many more were developed. The documentation of the land company form as an identifiable capitalist strategy is useful, as it allows for the recognition of a systematic development regime within Appalachia during the late nineteenth and early twentieth centuries. The land company development model was considered advantageous by capitalists because capital could be accumulated easily, there was no individual liability, and development activities could be pursued on a large scale.

The Role of Individual Capitalists

In his study of northeastern Pennsylvania, Burton Folsom found that the "quality of entrepreneurship" displayed by "venturesome economic leaders" had a strong impact on levels of "urban-economic development" within the

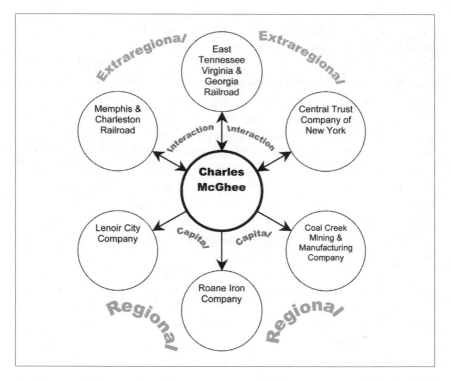

FIG. 13. Charles McClung McGhee, the Business Connections of a "Capital Injector." This diagram illustrates Charles McGhee's role as a capital injector. At the top, McGhee's connections with extraregional business organizations are shown, with two-way transactions showing both McGhee and the corporations benefiting from the relationship. At the bottom, McGhee's role as capital injector for the Upper Tennessee River Valley is shown, as he brokered the movement of capital and development from extraregional business organizations to regional ones. One could argue that these arrows could also be bidirectional; however, in the context of this study they point only in the direction of Upper Tennessee River Valley business organizations.

region.[12] Likewise, the impact of individual entrepreneurs on regional development patterns in the Upper Tennessee River Valley between 1865 and 1900 appears to have been very important. The most outstanding example of this was Charles McClung McGhee. Based on an analysis of a myriad of information sources, it is clear that the development pattern in the Upper Tennessee River Valley would have been significantly different were it not for the activities of this East Tennessee–born businessman.

Charles McGhee was without a doubt the most important and influential capitalist in the region during the late nineteenth century. He had the perfect combination of regional and extraregional contacts, business experience with railroads and investment banking firms, a personal embrace of industrial capitalist ideology, and a genuine desire to bring economic progress to his native region. I propose that McGhee was a unique entrepreneur who served as a *capital injector* in the Upper Tennessee River Valley. By this, I mean that McGhee was a capitalist who played a unique role in bringing about capital investment—by using his connections and influence to inject capital from the economic heart of the American economy (New York City) into the Upper Tennessee River Valley.

There were many examples of Charles McGhee's strong influence on regional development patterns. The earliest of these was his involvement in the merger of the East Tennessee, Virginia & Georgia Railroad. McGhee was instrumental in bringing about the merger, as he and a group of business associates formed a partnership to purchase large amounts of stock in 1866 in both the East Tennessee & Georgia and the East Tennessee & Virginia Railroads (they were separate entities prior to the Civil War). With large stock voting blocs in both companies, McGhee's partnership was largely responsible for merging the two rail companies into the East Tennessee, Virginia & Georgia Railroad (ETV&G) in 1868, creating a rail corridor under centralized management that stretched through the Upper Tennessee River Valley from Bristol, Virginia, to Dalton, Georgia.[13] McGhee served on the board of directors of the ETV&G for the next twenty-five years.

McGhee's involvement with the Roane Iron Company (RIC) is another example of his influence on the region. He became a member of the Roane Iron Company's board of directors in the spring of 1882 and served through 1889. During this period, he served as a crucial conduit to the capital that Roane Iron needed to expand into steel production. In 1886 McGhee handled Roane Iron's negotiations with the Central Trust Company of New York, securing $125,000 for the construction of a Bessemer steel production facility at Chattanooga. Later, when the Roane Iron Company had begun production of steel at Chattanooga in 1887, McGhee used his position on the boards of the ETV&G and Memphis & Charleston Railroads to make sure that they each ordered large lots of steel rails from Roane Iron. The Roane Iron Company could not take advantage of the opportunity that McGhee had provided it, however, as the poor quality of its steel rails caused both railroads to discontinue orders.

A third instance of McGhee's impact on the economy and settlement pattern of the Upper Tennessee River Valley was his role in the development of Lenoir City. Again, he served as a capital injector by assisting his friend E. J. Sanford, a Knoxville businessman, in obtaining the money needed to fund a real estate venture. In this case, McGhee promoted the Lenoir City development project to his business "syndicate," capitalists who had worked together on the board of directors of the ETV&G Railroad and other profit-making ventures such as the Coal Creek Mining & Manufacturing Company. The result was the establishment of the Lenoir City Company, a land company with an advertised capitalization of $800,000. Without McGhee's help, Sanford's idea would have been no more than a dream, as the capital to undertake such a project simply did not exist in East Tennessee at this time.

Hiram Chamberlain was another individual who arguably had significant unique influence on regional development within the Upper Tennessee River Valley. I describe Chamberlain as a *pioneer industrial innovator,* in that he was able to integrate changing technological imperatives and local natural resources to produce marketable industrial commodities. Although a northerner by birth, Chamberlain became an "adopted son" of East Tennessee, never leaving after his tour of duty during the Civil War. Chamberlain invested a large part of his life (over forty-five years) trying to make iron and steel in the Upper Tennessee River Valley. In the progression of the iron industry and industrial capitalism in the Upper Tennessee River Valley, Chamberlain was the entrepreneurial common denominator, experimenting with production processes and adapting techniques to make it possible for successful production to occur. Among his accomplishments were the first successes in the South in producing pig iron from coke fuel, and producing steel by any process. Because of his success in pioneering iron production at the isolated Rockwood site, and his long-term personal involvement in industrial production in the Upper Tennessee River Valley, it is hard to overestimate the regional impact of Hiram Chamberlain as an entrepreneur.

Other individuals also played important roles in the regional development of the Upper Tennessee River Valley. Men such as E. J. Sanford (Knoxville), J. F. Tarwater (Chattanooga), Calvin McClung (Knoxville), A. J. Albers (Knoxville), and T. G. Montague (Chattanooga) were regional business leaders who cooperated with outside capitalists in regional development projects. Eller suggests that the "receptive attitude" of such business leaders toward industrial development "eased the way for the penetration of southern regions by northern capital."[14] This is confirmed by events in the Upper Tennessee River Valley. Charles McGhee not only had a receptive attitude toward industrial capitalism, he personally orchestrated business dealings in his efforts to bring northern capital to the region (and beyond). In addition, two of the land companies—the Cardiff Coal & Iron Company and the Lenoir City Company—used the participation of regional business leaders as selling points in their promotional literature. There is little doubt that a core group of regional business leaders in East Tennessee had embraced the ideology of industrial development and actively worked in conjunction with outside capitalists to bring it about.

As in the Upper Tennessee River Valley, so too in many subregions of Southern Appalachia specific individual capitalists—*capital injectors* and *pioneer industrial innovators*—were crucial in bringing about the advent of industrial and corporate capitalism. These entrepreneurs did not transcend the contexts (geographic, financial, technological) within which they found themselves; rather, they were able to interpret them and adopt what Schumpeter refers to as "creative responses." In the Upper Tennessee River Valley, Charles McGhee and Hiram Chamberlain played these roles, and can be closely linked to the inception and progress of capitalism there. Capitalism evolved in a similar way in other Southern Appalachian subregions—it was not an invasion of faceless outsiders but a cooperative effort between key local business leaders and outside capitalists to bring about certain types of economic development within regional economies.

The Role of Business Entities in Creating Urban Settlements

Urban Development during the Industrial Capitalist Stage

The Roane Iron Company's approach in community development was typical of early industrial capitalist entities. The company chose to locate its production facility as near as possible to the resources needed for production (coal, iron ore, lime). This was done in an effort to produce iron as efficiently as possible, as transporting these bulky resources any distance would require infrastructure and be prohibitively expensive. When Roane Iron began its activities in western Roane County in 1867, the site was not connected to any road or river transportation route, and no settlement existed there. The primary business objective of the company was to meet the resource requirements of iron production—providing for the day-to-day needs of workers was a secondary concern. The unplanned, incremental development of Rockwood, Tennessee, is evidence of this.

The town of Rockwood exhibited several characteristics of "classic" company towns. One was company ownership of land and housing. The Roane Iron Company viewed housing for workers as necessary for production, and treated it as such. An inventory in May of 1870 showed that the company had spent over fifty thousand dollars in less than three years constructing housing for workers.[15] The RIC maintained ownership of the housing in Rockwood and rented it to workers employed at the blast furnace and mines. Very few if any workers owned their own homes in Rockwood during Roane Iron's first twenty years of operation. Although the company initially was compelled to build housing to maintain its labor force, in the longer term rent payments served as an additional source of revenue.

Other indicators of the Roane Iron Company's objectives in developing Rockwood had to do with how workers were paid, where they obtained essentials for daily survival, and the chronology of the town-planning process. Roane Iron workers were paid in both regular currency and scrip. The use of scrip to pay workers was a common strategy used by industrial employers to ensure that worker paychecks ended up back in company coffers. Workers who needed money could draw scrip payments anytime (as opposed to currency payments, which occurred on a weekly or monthly schedule); however, the scrip was accepted at full value only by the issuing company. In Rockwood, one of the first things that the Roane Iron Company did beyond iron production was to establish a company store in 1868. The company used clauses in rental agreements to forbid the sale of dry goods by individuals, creating a company monopoly on the sale of consumer goods in the town. Finally, the company did not develop or file a plan for the town of Rockwood until 1887, almost twenty years after the company began operation. This indicates that community development was indeed a secondary concern for Roane Iron, one that was driven by industrial labor needs rather than any other profit strategy.

Urban/Regional Development during the Emerging Corporate Capitalist Stage

The land companies that began operation in the Upper Tennessee River Valley during the late 1880s had business objectives quite different from those of industrial capitalist entities such as the Roane Iron Company. Their profit strategy was not to accumulate capital by processing raw materials into higher-value goods, but instead to make money from the sale of land and stock dividends from successful business ventures operated by others.

The urban communities created by land companies were not by-products of industrial production—they were the primary focus of development activities. In fact, the plans and features of these future cities were carefully designed to appeal to industrialists and investors. I have coined a term for these develop-ments—*model industrial real estate ventures.*

Model industrial real estate ventures in the Upper Tennessee River Val-ley shared the following characteristics: (1) large tracts of land were acquired by land companies; (2) they were predicated on the *potential* for industrial production; (3) development strategies were comprehensive in scope; (4) planned cities were a major focus; (5) sanitary and moral reform ideologies were emphasized. Each of the land companies in the Upper Tennessee River Valley purchased large amounts of land as a precursor to development. The companies were able to accomplish this because they were able to obtain large loans through New York and Boston capital markets.

By controlling thousands of acres of real estate, land companies were able to lay out multifaceted development strategies for potential investors. The logic of these strategies was based on widely accepted imperatives of indus-trial capitalism. Each land company published a handsome prospectus that clearly explained the industrial capitalist logic of why its development would succeed. A passage from the prospectus of the Cardiff Coal & Iron Company is typical: "The Allegheny Belt is full of coal and iron and limestone fluxes, and possesses other useful mineral resources in great abundance. . . . With these preliminary considerations, [the Cardiff Coal and Iron Company] has selected a town site adjoining some of the richest mineral deposits . . . two hundred miles nearer than Birmingham to Northern and Western markets." The circumstances had to be right for investors to believe that profit through industrialization was possible. Note the conditions that land companies felt the potential investor needed to be made aware of: (1) proximity to specific raw materials, (2) an advantageous location for manufacturing, and (3) rela-tive location to markets. In the late 1880s industrial capitalism was in full swing in the United States, and few questioned that these conditions could lead to profit.

The comprehensive nature of land company development strategies con-trasted with the production-focused approach of earlier industrial capitalist entities. The companies did not plan to extract resources directly or to manu-facture them into finished products. Their focus was on obtaining owner-ship of land, and profiting from *all types of capital accumulation activities that occurred on it.* The ETLC expressed this approach in its prospectus: "The East Tennessee Land Company will not expend its energies and its working capital in general mining or manufacture, nor in any miscellaneous fashion distrib-uted over such broad territory. It is what its name indicates, primarily a Land Company, and having acquired magnificent heritage in lands, its one purpose is to turn these, by systematic development, to the best advantage possible."[16] The one activity that each Upper Tennessee River Valley land company did commit to was city development. In fact, land companies spent an inordinate amount of time and effort describing the types of urban communities that they were planning to build.

City building was at the core of the model industrial real estate venture as a profit strategy. Land companies were compelled to convince investors that profitable industrial production would occur on their lands, but they also recognized that cities were the result of industrialization. The ETLC prospectus pointed out to potential investors: "To establish furnaces, coke ovens and iron-works, and to open coal beds at any given point, is to create a town." But the land company capitalists evidently believed that marketing just *any* industrial city wasn't going to sell.

Model industrial real estate ventures in the Upper Tennessee River Valley were variations of the model company town idea espoused by paternalistic industrialists of the period. In 1884 the Pullman Palace Car Company of Chicago, Illinois, established the town of Pullman, Illinois, as a place where employees would be "elevated and refined" by the living environment. In Hopedale, Massachusetts, the Draper Company hired professional architects and planners to create model neighborhoods for workers to live in. Model company towns were built by industrialists who believed that uplifting living environments made better people, and better people made better workers.[17] Model industrial real estate ventures, by contrast, were about creating the social and physical conditions for the optimal industrial city—in effect making money by laying the foundations for place-creation.

Thus, in developing the model industrial real estate venture as a capitalist strategy in the Upper Tennessee River Valley, capitalists co-opted reform ideologies of the period for profit. In marketing their cities, land companies made a concerted effort to tap into the ideology that the quality of the social and physical environment could positively affect the lives of workers and, by extension, the productivity of labor. Land company literature assumed that the reader understood and agreed that certain physical and social conditions would lead to better lives for workers and a higher profit margin for manufacturers. By preplanning their cities, the land companies were able to include and advertise characteristics that they obviously felt were crucial to the success of their real estate ventures—urban, sanitary, and moral reform aspects.

An examination of the promotional literature published by land companies in the Upper Tennessee River Valley reveals what Boyer refers to as "the two faces of urban moral reform in the 1890s."[18] One of the faces, or strategies, of reform was the coercive approach, in which measures were aimed at individuals in order to uproot vice and impose a higher standard of civic virtue. The goal was to undertake social control measures that would preclude the urban problems that had become commonplace in other American cities. Boyer describes the temperance movement as "the quintessential coercive reform," in that the saloon was viewed as a major bastion of urban vice.[19] Passages from the company literature of the East Tennessee Land Company and the Lenoir City Company, respectively, make very clear the point that land company capitalists were trying to make:

> It is a well-known economic fact that sober labor, away from saloons, yields a positive percentage of gain to the capital employing it.[20]

> The promoters of this Company . . . have determined to put into each deed executed by the Company a clause forfeiting the title if liquor shall ever be manufactured or sold. . . . All manufacturers know that it is the convenient dram shop which does the most to demoralize workmen and impair their usefulness.[21]

Although land companies did not plan on producing industrial commodities themselves, the success of their ventures hinged on convincing industrialists as well as investors that desirable social conditions for efficient production— such as a sober workforce—would exist.

The second face of urban reform evidenced in the model industrial real estate ventures of the Upper Tennessee River Valley involved the physical design of land company cities. The cities were to be built in such a way as to "elevate the moral tone" of their populations. The aim of what Schultz has called "moral environmentalism"[22] was not to destroy urban vice through rhetoric or legal repression, but to do so "by creating the kind of city where objectionable patterns of behavior, finding no nurture, would gradually wither away."[23] This normally involved the provision of parks, playgrounds, and facilities for concerts, lectures, and art exhibits. In many instances, the ideals of sanitary reform were included as components of these favorable urban environments, with connections being drawn between cleanliness, health, and the character of city dwellers.[24] Again, the companies were very explicit in describing how the physical environment of their cities would be different from, and superior to, unplanned urban-industrial settlements:

> The fixed policy of this Company, in town-building, is to establish all original town improvements . . . and then to operate all these, and secure the profit thereon.[25]

> No where is greater care exercised in all matters relative to the health of a place than in Cardiff. . . . Health is of primary importance, and while nature has done her share for the place, sanitary

science will keep abreast of the constantly changing condition of affairs here.[26]

All the conditions of a sanitarium are found here. . . . The elevated location of the City exempts it from the dangers of overflows and malarial diseases; its topography assures the advantages of perfect drainage.[27]

The land company development strategies brought new urban spatial patterns to the Upper Tennessee River Valley. With the money and inclination to create planned cities, the companies had the opportunity to shape the urban landscape to fit their vision of the ideal industrial city. The plans themselves reveal capitalist interpretations of the ideologies and value systems of the time. What do they tell us?

The city plans drafted by the land companies of the Upper Tennessee River Valley were geographic articulations of human value systems. Schultz has suggested that cities are "the results of cultural decisions about the most appropriate physical uses of land and the residential distribution of people."[28] If we view the urban developments undertaken by Upper Tennessee River Valley land companies in this way, we can draw some conclusions about the geographic implications of model industrial real estate ventures as capitalist development strategies. One way to view these conclusions is in terms of their urban planning and urban geographic contexts.

With respect to urban planning, the city development strategies employed by land companies in the Upper Tennessee River Valley seem significant. Examination reveals that land company plans were actually precursors of the City Beautiful movement in the United States. This is not to suggest that City Beautiful was in any way directly related to urban development in the Upper Tennessee River Valley—rather that the same forces that came together to define the movement were at work in the development strategies of the land companies. Major aspects that have been identified with City Beautiful include the aesthetic beauty of urban surroundings (including urban parks and other public spaces), sanitary conditions that would prevent the spread of disease, and modern infrastructure such as transit systems and street lights.[29] All of these elements were present in the city plans of Harriman, Cardiff, and Lenoir City more than three years prior to the Chicago World's Fair of 1893 (the Columbian Exposition), widely considered the event that ushered in the City Beautiful movement in the United States. Land companies used the popularity of these ideas to sell their developments as model industrial cities—places where urban dwellers could live the ideal existence and where industrial capitalism would be particularly successful. The development strategy employed by land companies in the Upper Tennessee River Valley suggests that capitalists had perceived the societal embrace of these various reform ideas by the late 1880s and used them as core elements of the model industrial real estate venture strategy.

As for the urban geography of land company towns, these capitalists planned for their cities to be segregated by class and race. Land companies clearly articulated in promotional literature the social geography they wanted in their cities. They wanted potential land buyers and investors to know how urban space would be organized. The cities developed as part of model industrial real estate ventures were not going to be haphazard, congested, or "disorganized." They were going to be places that fostered physical health and moral and social order. One of the geographic manifestations of this was race and socioeconomic segregation as a means of socially ordering the city. Land companies seemingly had no problem describing the social ordering of space in their cities, in some cases identifying particular streets with specific groups of people. Land company capitalists must have felt that the middle- and upper-class market they were trying to appeal to was much more concerned with the health and order of the city than with any negative effects from geographically separating socioeconomic groups.

In 1892 Harriman's African Americans experienced almost total residential segregation. It seems that the East Tennessee Land Company adopted what by the 1880s had become the common method of dealing with the "Negro question" in the South. By the mid-1880s, residential segregation of blacks had become the norm in southern cities. Prior to the Civil War, when fewer blacks lived in cities and most of those who did were slaves, residential intermixing of blacks and whites was common. But after the war, Reconstruction officials and New South business leaders were confronted with the reality of large numbers of African Americans migrating to cities and coming into contact with whites. The solution that these postbellum leaders usually settled on to keep the peace and to promote economic and social stability in southern cities was separation of the races. Through a combination of local and state laws, and coercion and intimidation by whites and the actions of blacks themselves to protect their own safety, blacks largely settled in separate residential areas around cities in the South. They were encouraged to develop their own institutions—separate from whites—such as schools, hospitals, and churches.[30] Many New South industrialists were strong proponents of what came to be known as "biracialism," as they believed it was a system that would limit social conflict in the city, improve the overall quality of life for whites and blacks, and maintain pools of low-wage labor (chiefly blacks) for efficient industrial production.[31] The East Tennessee Land Company must have embraced these "solutions," for even as it planned Harriman and published its promotional literature, African Americans were not mentioned. When African Americans did come to Harriman to work in newly established factories, almost all of them lived in Oak View Addition on the "other" side of the East Tennessee, Virginia & Georgia Railroad tracks and some distance north of the original town site. There is no documentation explaining exactly how this residential pattern came about, but certainly the company was involved in determining where Oak View Addition was located, and in informing African Americans that they would be living there.

The land companies of the Upper Tennessee River Valley did not originate race segregation in the American South or in Southern Appalachia. Indeed, some might argue that they created better residential conditions for African Americans in Harriman than existed in many other southern cities.[32] The land companies used segregation as they had other ideologies, as a way to increase the salability of their model industrial real estate ventures. Racial segregation was another (albeit less advertised) aspect of their model industrial communities—like temperance, open public spaces, and home ownership—another means to foster efficient industrial production and maximize profits.

Evidence from Harriman suggests that land companies were more straightforward when it came to socioeconomic stratification of urban space. Although difficult to document from the available data, geographic separation of socioeconomic/occupation groups apparently was part of the East Tennessee Land Company's plan for Harriman.[33] An examination of the company's promotional literature and the residential location of heads-of-household in 1892 indicates that the company planned and developed a socioeconomically segmented urban settlement in Harriman. The social geography—for example, the residential distribution of unskilled blue-collar heads-of-household and high-level white-collar heads shows that these groups had very different geographic patterns of residence. What's more, the residential distributions that can be documented correspond closely to the company's promotional literature, which highlighted the "social identity" of different parts of the town. In this respect, it seems that the East Tennessee Land Company took the separation of socioeconomic groups within cities to a new level in Southern Appalachia so as to convince investors that Harriman would be a socially "ordered" urban place.

Despite the previous discussion detailing capitalist strategies, and counter to the arguments of Banks, Gaventa and others, it does not appear that land companies in the Upper Tennessee River Valley were driven solely by the profit motive. We see examples of entrepreneurs in the region who went against all logic to see urban settlements built. For example, E. J. Sanford and Charles McGhee remained committed to Lenoir City through the downturn of the 1890s, even when it became obvious that the venture was probably going to lose money. Temperance advocates in Harriman remained committed to the town long after the boom was over, making attempts to attract other types of economic development after everyone knew that steel was no longer viable. These capitalists obviously believed in the ideas they were selling, and they personally invested themselves in the projects even when it made no sense financially. Granted, the Cardiff Coal & Iron Company did not demonstrate such loyalty, pulling out of its commitments when financial times got tough.

Land companies have often been overlooked in discussions of capitalism and regional development in Southern Appalachia, mainly because their period of operation was usually very short. I believe, however, that their activities were significant in that they reveal a progression in capitalist development strategies within Southern Appalachia. Capitalist implementation of model industrial real estate ventures required particular preconditions. The most important of these was capital availability. When the national economy was on an upswing and railroads had vacated the capital markets of New York and Boston in the mid-1880s, land companies with the right capitalists involved could access amounts of capital that previously had been available to very few business entities. With hundreds of thousands or millions of dollars at their disposal, land companies purchased land in the Upper Tennessee River Valley on a scale not seen before. Large amounts of land quickly came under external control. This relatively short time period was a watershed, for the economy of the Upper Tennessee River Valley never returned to its previous structure—it remained oriented toward industry after decades under a mixed-agriculture economy. Agriculture did not disappear, it just became relatively less important than it had been. Through 1920, increasing numbers of regional workers became part of an industrial labor force employed in labor-intensive, low-skill production. The same process was repeated in other subregions of Appalachia.

Capitalism as a Constant in Regional Development

The story of the Upper Tennessee River Valley demonstrates the value of capitalism as a framework for understanding regional development patterns. Through an analysis of capitalist decision-making contexts (technological, geographic, financial) and the roles of individual capitalists, I have attempted to develop a clear picture of regional development patterns in the Upper Tennessee River Valley and, by extension, other Appalachian subregions between 1865 and 1900. Crucial to "seeing" this picture is an understanding of the progression of industrial and corporate capitalism in the United States during this period.

In the Upper Tennessee River Valley, just as throughout Appalachia, post–Civil War entrepreneurs who had embraced the tenets of industrial capitalism were attempting to formulate effective profit strategies. They weren't robots, but human beings trying to align their ideologies and value systems with the land, resources, and technologies at their disposal. These early regional industrial capitalists saw a certain set of possibilities and created business entities such as the Roane Iron Company and urban places like Rockwood, Tennessee. Then, as capitalism evolved and spread in the United States, entrepreneurs perceived new possibilities and profit opportunities that increased their ability to influence development patterns. They also discovered that as industrialization progressed, what people had learned about its requirements and impacts had created a demand for a new type of urban community: the model industrial city.

What does the story of the Upper Tennessee River Valley tell us about capitalism and regional development in Appalachia and the United States? It tells us many specific things about the region and the time period, and about why some places became important urban centers and others didn't. In addition, it reinforces something we already knew—that capitalism is very adaptable and capitalists are often creative in their responses to varying contexts. The story of regional development in the Upper Tennessee River Valley, unlike the focus of this book, does not end in 1893 (or 1900). After 1893, the decision-making contexts for capitalists changed significantly: capital markets were gone, and the region's iron ore had proven to be too impure to make steel. To many capitalists, the Upper Tennessee River Valley ceased to be an attractive region for investment. For others who decided to stay, a new profit strategy seemed in order—low-wage manufacturing. This strategy had been adopted in many parts of the American South where the most advantageous feature of the local economy consisted of resident populations who for various reasons had ceased or reduced their farming and were willing and able to work for low wages.

If you travel to the Upper Tennessee River Valley in the early twenty-first century, it is difficult to imagine a time when capitalists saw unique profit opportunities in its physical and human geography. Harriman and Lenoir City, with populations of 6,744 and 6,819 in the year 2000 respectively, are still the largest urban places in Roane and Loudon Counties, Tennessee. No new urban settlements have been established in the valley since 1890. Little economic development has occurred in the region, as its location has not proven to be particularly advantageous for any capitalist activity in the recent past or present. A trip down the streets of Harriman, Lenoir City, or Rockwood is like a trip back in time—many of the structures depicted in land company literature of 1890 still stand, looking much as they did when they were first built. Even the trees seem not to have been disturbed. They are much bigger now, but it is almost always possible to determine which ones in the present were newly planted in 1890. This is how capitalism has always worked—places become advantageous and then disadvantageous based on the knowledge and perceptions of people who make decisions about how land and resources are used. Ironically, what attracts people to this region now (albeit in small numbers) are the same aspects of the landscape that capitalists of more than a century ago believed were necessary for profit-making. Features like open public spaces, certain types of architecture, and streetscapes that allow for pedestrians as well as cars—are increasingly rare on the contemporary landscape. I find them interesting not only as urban environments but as capitalist strategies.

Roane Iron Co's. Furnaces, Rockwood, Tenn.

FIG. 14. Entrance to the Roane Iron Company's Iron Production Facility, date unknown. Note the building at the entrance to the production site—it is all that remains of the Roane Iron facility.

FIG. 15. Entrance to the Roane Iron Furnace Site, Rockwood, Summer 2005. Note the presence of the same utilitarian, Italianate building in this 2005 picture, and the left foreground of the previous picture. Photo by Jacque S. Benhart.

FIG. 16. Modified Company Housing, Rockwood, Summer 2005. Rows of company-style houses still line streets near the former Roane Iron site in Rockwood. Photo by Jacque S. Benhart.

FIG. 17. Rockwood Avenue, Rockwood, TN, Summer 2005. Rockwood Avenue continues to be the main street in town as it was in the late 1880s. As you look up the street, it leads directly to what was the entrance of the Roane Iron Company production facility. Note Walden's Ridge in the background. Photo by John Benhart Jr.

FIG. 18. Cardiff Baptist Church, Roane County, Summer 2005. Although the town of Cardiff was never really built, its existence is still recognized on the landscape of the Upper Tennessee River Valley in the names of local institutions such as the Cardiff Baptist Church near Rockwood, Tennessee. Photo by Jacque S. Benhart.

FIG. 19. Harriman: Utopia of Temperance Historical Marker, Summer 2005. Harriman's unique origins are explained on this historical marker located directly in front of the former East Tennessee Land Company building along Roane Street in the downtown area. Photo by Jacque S. Benhart.

FIG. 20. Former East Tennessee Land Company Building, Harriman, Summer 2005. Presently, this building houses the Harriman Heritage Museum, the city administrative offices, and the Harriman city council chambers. Photo by Jacque S. Benhart.

FIG. 21. Roane Street, Harriman, TN, Looking South, 1892. Note the substantial buildings that had been completed along Harriman's main thoroughfare by 1892 in an effort to convince investors of the town's permanence. Source: Roane County Heritage Commission Photograph Collection, Kingston, TN.

FIG. 22. Roane Street, Harriman, TN, Looking South, Summer 2005. If you look closely, you can see the same corner tower topped with a mansard roof, and Italianate cornices on buildings along the right (west) side of Roane Street as in the picture from 1892. Photo by Jacque S. Benhart.

FIG. 23. Home of Frederick Gates, Cumberland and Crescent Streets, Harriman, 1891. The Gates home was located in the highest elevation part of Harriman envisioned by the East Tennessee Land Company for "residences of an excellent class." Source: Roane County Heritage Commission Photograph Collection, Kingston, TN

FIG. 24. Frederick Gates Home, Summer 2005. The home looks much as it did in 1890, with the major difference being the size of the trees, some of which were seedlings in the earlier photo. Photo by Jacque S. Benhart.

FIG. 25. Intersection of Cumberland and Crescent Streets, Harriman, Summer 2005. This part of Harriman, designated as an upper-class neighborhood by the East Tennessee Land Company in 1890, is now a National Historic Register District called Cornstalk Heights. Note the Gates house in the background. Photo by Jacque S. Benhart.

FIG. 26. Fisk-Killeffer Park, Harriman, Summer 2005. This park was set aside in the original Harriman plan as open space, reflecting the town's origins during the urban reform movement of the nineteenth century. Photo by Jacque S. Benhart.

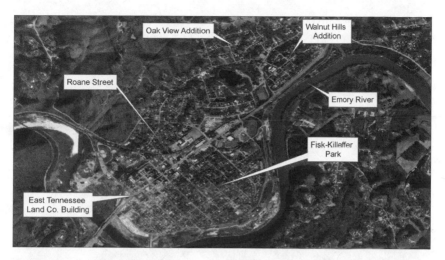

FIG. 27. Digital Orthophoto Quarter Quadrangle of Harriman, Flown March 16, 1997. This orthophotograph of the Harriman area from 1997 shows the location of some important human and physical geographic landmarks. Note that the urban geography is very similar to what it was in 1892—significant aspects of the East Tennessee Land Company's development plan for the town remain visible on the landscape more than a century after Harriman's establishment. Source: United States Geological Survey, edited by author.

FIG. 28. Harriman, Summer 2005. This is what part of the area along the banks of the Emory River looked like in the summer of 2005. The East Tennessee Land Company planned this area to be the industrial district of the town, with access to river and rail transportation. Photo by Jacque S. Benhart.

The name of the Walnut Hills Addition is still on the landscape in the early twenty-first century, as evidenced by these church and school signs on the outskirts of Harriman.

FIG. 29. Walnut Hill Baptist Church, Harriman, Summer 2005. Photo by Jacque S. Benhart.

FIG. 30. Walnut Hill Elementary School, Harriman, Summer 2005. Photo by Jacque S. Benhart.

FIG. 31. Working-Class Housing, Walnut Hills Area, on the Outskirts of Harriman, Summer 2005. This modified double-shotgun type of housing is still prevalent in residential areas that were developed by the East Tennessee Land Company as Walnut Hills Addition. Contrast this to the stately homes found in Cornstalk Heights. Photo by Jacque S. Benhart.

FIG. 32. The Lenoir City Museum Building, Depot Street, Lenoir City, Summer 2005. This building, which was built to be the headquarters of the Lenoir City Company in 1890, now houses the Lenoir City Museum. Photo by Jacque S. Benhart.

FIG. 33. Lenoir City Junction, Lenoir City, Summer 2005. The railroad, so important to the Lenoir City Company's original plans for the city, still runs through the town. Photo by Jacque S. Benhart.

Will the geographers and historians of the future be intrigued by the capitalism of our own early twenty-first century? Will the sameness of strip malls, "big box" retailers, and fast-food restaurants be as interesting as model industrial real estate ventures and towns? Will these capitalist landscapes exist as remnants on the landscape in another century, or will they disappear, replaced by other disposable temporary containers for capital transactions?

The capitalism of today doesn't require the specific geographic preconditions of nineteenth-century industrialization—its strategies can work almost anywhere. Just as in the late nineteenth century, people make decisions based on changing circumstances and new technologies. Now the geographic orientation of the U.S. economy is shaped more by the availability of amenities (climate, cultural opportunities, or specialized services) and access to transportation than by proximity to iron or coal. The constant remains the pursuit of profit by capitalists, who, like those of the Upper Tennessee River Valley more than a century ago, still endeavor to gain from new and ever-changing business strategies.

NOTES

Introduction

1. The drainage pattern within these watersheds (particularly the Tennessee River) has changed drastically since the focus period of this book (1865–1920), with the establishment and activities of the Tennessee Valley Authority (TVA) in recent decades.

2. It is not my intention to establish whether subsistence and barter or capitalist exchange of agricultural commodities was more dominant in the preindustrial economy in the Upper Tennessee River Valley. There has been some debate among "social" and "market" historians about the basis of preindustrial regional economies within Appalachia. See Dwight Billings, Mary Beth Pudup, and Altina Waller, "Taking Exception with Exceptionalism: The Emergence and Transformation of Historical Studies in Appalachia," in Mary Beth Pudup, ed., *Appalachia in the Making: The Mountain South in the Nineteenth Century* (Chapel Hill: University of North Carolina Press), 1995, 10–14. The preindustrial period in the Upper Tennessee River Valley is not a primary focus of this book, rather it provides a context for the onset of the ensuing stages of capitalism within the region.

3. Morrow Chamberlain, *A Brief History of the Pig Iron Industry in East Tennessee* (Chattanooga: Author, 1942), 6; James F. Doster, "The Chattanooga Rolling Mill: An Industrial By-Product of the Civil War," *East Tennessee Historical Society's Publications* 36, 1964, 51–52.

4. Roane Iron Company, Board of Directors Minutes, numerous dates.

5. *Prospectus of the East Tennessee Land Company* (New York: The South Publishing Company, 1890), 26.

6. Chattanooga *Tradesman* 32 (1895): 116.

7. James C. Cobb, *Industrialization and Southern Society, 1877–1984* (Lexington: University Press of Kentucky), 14–16.

8. This is not to suggest that there is broad agreement among researchers on all aspects of capitalism as an economic system, but simply that many researchers accept the general characteristics of these categories as a framework for academic investigation.

9. David Harvey, *Social Justice and the City* (London: Edward Arnold, 1973).

10. David Harvey, *The Urbanization of Capital: Studies in the History and Theory of Capitalist Urbanization* (Baltimore: Johns Hopkins University Press, 1985), 37–40.

11. Harry Braverman, *Labor Monopoly and Capital: The Degradation of Work in the Twentieth Century* (New York: Monthly Review Press, 1974).

12. Olivier Zunz, *Making America Corporate: 1870–1920* (Chicago: University of Chicago Press, 1990).

13. Ronald D. Eller, *Miners, Millhands and Mountaineers: Industrialization of the Appalachian South, 1880–1930* (Knoxville: University of Tennessee Press, 1982), 4–22.

14. Paul Salstrom, *Appalachia's Path to Dependency: Rethinking a Region's Economic History, 1730–1940* (Lexington: University Press of Kentucky, 1994), 23–25.

15. Cobb, *Industrialization and Southern Society,* 14–16.

16. W. B. Hesseltine, "Tennessee's Invitation to Carpetbaggers," *East Tennessee Historical Society's Publications* 4 (1932).

17. David R. Goldfield, *Cottonfields and Skyscrapers: Southern City and Region, 1607–1980* (Baton Rouge: Louisiana State University Press, 1982), 118–22; Cobb, *Industrialization and Southern Society,* 10–17.

18. Braverman, *Labor Monopoly and Capital,* 63–67.

19. Crandall A. Shifflett, *Coal Towns: Life, Work, and Culture in Company Towns of Southern Appalachia, 1880–1960* (Knoxville: University of Tennessee Press, 1991), 33–38; Margaret M. Mulrooney, A Legacy of Coal: The Coal Company Towns of Southwestern Pennsylvania (Washington: National Park Service, 1989), 9–19; Geoffrey L. Buckley, *Extracting Appalachia: Images of the Consolidation Coal Company, 1910–1945* (Athens: Ohio University Press, 2004), 39–43.

20. Sam Bass Warner Jr., *The Urban Wilderness: A History of the American City* (New York: Harper and Row, 1972); Robert Ernst, "Immigrants and Tenements in New York City, 1825–1863," in R. A. Mohl and N. Betten, eds., *Urban America in Historical Perspective* (New York: Weybright and Talley, 1970), 113–26.

21. Thomas Bender, *Toward an Urban Vision: Ideas and Institutions in Nineteenth-Century America* (Lexington: University Press of Kentucky, 1975); Paul Boyer, *Urban Masses and Moral Order in America, 1820–1920* (Cambridge: Harvard University Press, 1978).

22. Jon A. Peterson, *The Birth of City Planning in the United States* (Baltimore: Johns Hopkins University Press, 2003), 29–54.

23. Burton Folsom Jr. *Urban Capitalists* (Baltimore: Johns Hopkins University Press, 1981), 145.

24. Joseph A. Schumpeter, "The Creative Response in Economic History" *Journal of Economic History* 7 (November 1947), 149–59, as quoted in Burton Folsom Jr. *Urban Capitalists,* 7–8.

25. See Bender, *Toward an Urban Vision;* Boyer, *Urban Masses and Moral Order;* Peterson, *The Birth of City Planning.*

26. Stanley K. Schultz, *Constructing Urban Culture: American Cities and City Planning, 1800–1920* (Philadelphia: Temple University Press, 1989), xiii–xiv.

Chapter 1

1. Roy S. Dickens Jr., "The Origins and Development of the Cherokee Culture," in D. King, ed., *The Cherokee Indian Nation: A Troubled History* (Knoxville: University of Tennessee Press, 1979), 3–28.

2. Gilbert E. Govan and James W. Livingood, *The Chattanooga Country 1540–1951: From Tomahawks to TVA* (New York: E. P. Dutton, 1952), 23–24.

3. Thomas M. N. Lewis and Madeline Kneberg, *Tribes That Slumber: Indians of the Tennessee Region* (Knoxville: University of Tennessee Press, 1960), 156–59; Dickens, *Cherokee Culture*, 9–13; and Govan and Livingood, *The Chattanooga Country*, 23–25.

4. The Treaty of Holston was signed by William Blount, governor of United States territory south of the Ohio River, on June 2, 1791, but the treaty was not proclaimed until February of 1792.

5. Albert C. Holt, *The Economic and Social Beginnings of Tennessee* (Nashville: George Peabody College, 1923), 35–38; and Weston A. Goodspeed, ed., *Goodspeed's General History of Tennessee* (Nashville: Goodspeed Publishing Company, 1887), 93–103.

6. John Haywood, *The Civil and Political History of the State of Tennessee from its Earliest Settlement up to the Year 1796* (reprinted from 1823 edition, Knoxville: Tenase Co., 1969), 41–45; P. M. Hamer, *Fort Loudoun on the Little Tennessee River* (Raleigh, NC: Edwards & Broughton Printing Co., 1925).

7. Groups of Cherokee by this time had become disenchanted with settlers and the American government for constant encroachment on their traditional lands.

8. Mary U. Rothrock, ed., *The French Broad–Holston Country: A History of Knox County, Tennessee* (Knoxville: East Tennessee Historical Society, 1946), 26–27.

9. Stanley J. Folmsbee, Robert E. Corlew, and Enoch L. Mitchell, eds., *History of Tennessee, Volume 1* (New York: Lewis Historical Publishing Co., 1960), 194–202; Eugene M. Pickel, "A History of Roane County, Tennessee to 1860" (master's thesis, University of Tennessee, Knoxville, 1971), 25–27.

10. United States Eighth Census, *Volume 2: Agriculture* (Government Printing Office, 1865), 215.

11. Goodspeed, *History of Tennessee*, 229–32.

12. Roane County encompassed in 1860 the entire study area, and therefore its census statistics are applicable. Loudon County, in which Loudon and eventually Lenoir City were located, was formed in 1870 out of parts of Roane, Monroe, and Blount Counties.

13. United States Eighth Census, *Agriculture*, 136.

14. Pickel, "History of Roane County," 55–60.

15. Jack Shelley, Helen Galloway, Amy Wolfe, and Madge Sneed, "Towns—Old and New," in Jere Hall and Jack B. Shelley, eds., *Valley of Challenge and Change: Roane*

County, Tennessee, 1860–1900 (Knoxville: East Tennessee Historical Society, 1986), 49–51.

16. The road was named for William Walton, a member of the board of commissioners of the Cumberland Turnpike Company.

17. Thomas P. Abernethy, *Frontier to Plantation in Tennessee: A Study in Frontier Democracy* (Chapel Hill: University of North Carolina Press, 1932), 155–58; Stanley J. Folmsbee, Robert E. Corlew, and Enoch L. Mitchell, *Tennessee: A Short History* (Knoxville: University of Tennessee Press, 1969), 241–44; Albert C. Holt, *The Economic and Social Beginnings of Tennessee* (Nashville: George Peabody College, 1923), 68–72.

18. A break-of-bulk point is a location at which there is a transfer of commodities from one mode of transportation to another. At this point in time, Kingston became a break-of-bulk point based on access to water and road transportation routes.

19. Holt, *Economic and Social Beginnings,* 70–71.

20. *Knoxville Daily Register,* March 4, 1828.

21. Gilbert E. Govan and James W. Livingood, *Chattanooga Country 1540–1951: From Tomahawks to TVA* (New York: E. P. Dutton & Company, 1952), 121–22.

22. Edwin P. Patton, "Transportation Development" in Lucille Deadrick, ed., *Heart of the Valley: A History of Knoxville, Tennessee* (Knoxville: East Tennessee Historical Society, 1976), 179–81; Mary U. Rothrock, ed., *The French Broad–Holston Country: A History of Knox County, Tennessee* (Knoxville: East Tennessee Historical Society, 1946), 96–100.

23. In 1838 a state appropriation was made to improve navigation on selected tributaries of the Tennessee River. As a result of this, keelboat transport of produce on tributaries such as the Holston, Clinch, and Emory Rivers increased, and these agricultural areas were connected with steamboat travel on the Tennessee River.

24. Ted B. Clark, "The Changing Central Place Function of Loudon, Tennessee" (master's thesis, University of Tennessee, 1968), 6–8.

25. Rothrock, *French Broad–Holston Country,* 104–7; Folmsbee et al., *Tennessee—A Short History,* 261–62.

26. Rothrock, *French Broad–Holston Country,* 105.

27. *Goodspeed's History of Tennessee: Containing Historical and Biographical Sketches of Thirty East Tennessee Counties* (Nashville: reprinted from Goodspeed's History of Tennessee 1887 by Elder Booksellers, 1972), 826–27.

28. Patton, "Transportation Development," 193–95.

29. James W. Fertig, *The Secession and Reconstruction of Tennessee* (Chicago: University of Chicago Press, 1898), 28–32; Folmsbee, Corlew, and Mitchell, *Tennessee: A Short History,* 324–25.

30. Jack McInnis and William Jamborsky, "A County in Time of Turmoil," in Jere Hall and Jack B. Shelley, eds., *Valley of Challenge and Change: Roane County, Ten-*

nessee, 1860–1900 (Knoxville: East Tennessee Historical Society, 1986), 8–12; Fertig, *Unionism and Reconstruction in Tennessee*, 68–72.

Chapter 2

1. Harry Braverman, *Labor Monopoly and Capital: The Degradation of Work in the Twentieth Century* (New York: Monthly Review Press, 1974).

2. Martin J. Sklar, *The Corporate Reconstruction of American Capitalism* (Cambridge: Cambridge University Press, 1988).

3. Olivier Zunz, *Making America Corporate: 1870–1920* (Chicago: University of Chicago Press, 1990).

4. John Gaventa, *Power and Powerlessness: Quiescence and Rebellion in an Appalachian Valley* (Urbana: University of Illinois Press, 1980), 58–61; Eller, *Miners, Millhands, and Mountaineers*, 48.

5. Eller, *Miners, Millhands, and Mountaineers*, 56.

6. Braverman, *Labor Monopoly and Capital*, 63–67.

7. Daniel Nelson, *Managers and Workers: Origins of the New Factory System in the United States, 1880–1920* (Madison: University of Wisconsin Press, 1975), 90–95.

8. Crandall A. Shifflett, *Coal Towns: Life, Work, and Culture in Company Towns of Southern Appalachia, 1880–1960* (Knoxville: University of Tennessee Press, 1991), 33–38; Margaret M. Mulrooney, *A Legacy of Coal: The Coal Company Towns of Southwestern Pennsylvania* (Washington: National Park Service, 1989), 9–11.

9. Fertig, *Unionism and Reconstruction in Tennessee*, 34–59. Only men who took an oath of loyalty to the Union were allowed to vote for civil state government positions. This was the reason for Brownlow's easy victory.

10. Constantine G. Belissary, "The Rise of Industry and the Industrial Spirit in Tennessee, 1865–1885," *Journal of Southern History* 19 (May 1953): 193–215.

11. Quoted from the Knoxville Whig and Rebel Ventilator, May 5, 1869, in W. B. Hesseltine, "Tennessee's Invitation to Carpet-baggers," *East Tennessee Historical Society's Publications* 4 (1932) 104.

12. Hesseltine, "Tennessee's Invitation to Carpet-baggers," 108–9; Belissary, "The Rise of the Industrial Spirit in Tennessee," 207–8.

13. Hermann Bokum, *The Tennessee Handbook and Immigrant's Guide* (Philadelphia, 1868), 3.

14. James E. Boyle, *Cotton and the New Orleans Cotton Exchange: A Century of Commercial Evolution* (Garden City, NY, 1934), 180–81.

15. James E. Boyle, *Chicago Wheat Prices for Eighty-One Years: Daily, Monthly, and Yearly Fluctuations and Their Causes* (Ithaca, NY, 1922), 15.

16. The distinction between Radicals and Conservatives began in the immediate postwar Reconstruction period. Radicals were identified as those who wanted to follow a harsh Reconstruction program for the South that included the

exclusion of former Confederates from such citizenship rights as voting and holding office. Conservatives in general followed the leadership of President Andrew Johnson and Washington Conservatives who wished to put into effect the Lincoln-Johnson plan of leniency in Reconstruction. Thus, with Conservatives in power after 1869, former Confederates began to return to positions of power within the state.

17. Redemption was a term applied to the restoration of Conservative rule by native southerners in southern states. Many southerners felt that they had been unjustly governed by Radical Republican outsiders during Reconstruction, and hailed the return of Conservative state administrations.

18. C. Vann Woodward, *Origins of the New South, 1877–1913* (Baton Rouge: Louisiana State University Press, 1951), 21–22.

19. Ibid., 3.

20. *Tenth Census, 1880: Manufactures* (Washington, D.C., 1883), xiv.

21. Peter Temin, *Iron and Steel in Nineteenth-Century America: An Economic Inquiry* (Cambridge, MA: MIT Press, 1964), 102–5.

22. Glenn Porter and Harold C. Livesay, *Merchants and Manufacturers: Studies in the Changing Structure of Nineteenth Century Marketing* (Baltimore: Johns Hopkins University Press, 1971).

23. Samuel C. Williams, *General John T. Wilder: Commander, The Lightning Brigade* (Bloomington, IN, 1936), 2.

24. Michael J. McDonald and William B. Wheeler, *Knoxville, Tennessee: Continuity and Change in an Appalachian City* (Knoxville: University of Tennessee Press, 1983), 21.

25. Office of the Register of Deeds, Roane County, TN, Deed Book O, 354–59. Office of the Register of Deeds will hereafter be cited as ORD.

26. Roane Iron Company, Board of Directors Minutes, June 8, 1867. Roane Iron Company will hereafter be cited as RIC. In previous studies of the Roane Iron Company, it was suggested that no records of the company were still in existence. However, I discovered through local citizens that a man named Tom Ward had salvaged the board of directors minutes when the rest of the records had been hauled off for scrap in the 1950s. Mr. Ward informed me that he had donated these records to the University of Tennessee in the early 1980s, and upon investigating this I found that the Special Collections Library at the university indeed had a microfilm copy of them.

27. Judge John Allison, ed., *Notable Men of Tennessee, Volume 2* (Atlanta: Southern Historical Association, 1905), 303–4; Snyder Roberts, "Roane County's Industrial Belt, 1868–1932," 11. This is a collection of historical essays written by Mr. Roberts and published by the *Roane County News* from December 30, 1981, to September 15, 1982.

28. *Acts of Tennessee*, 1867–68, chapter 27, 34–36.

29. ORD, Roane County, TN, Deed Book P, 566–67; RIC, Board of Directors Minutes, September 9, 1867.

30. Chamberlain, *A Brief History of the Pig Iron Industry in East Tennessee*, 2.

31. RIC, Board of Directors Minutes, December 18, 1868, June 2, 1869.

32. Shelley, Galloway, Wolfe, and Sneed, "Towns—Old and New," 60.

33. RIC, Board of Directors Minutes, June 2, 1869.

34. Temin, *Iron and Steel in Nineteenth-Century America*, 89, 201.

35. Chamberlain, *A Brief History of the Pig Iron Industry in East Tennessee*, 6.

36. Porter and Livesay, *Merchants and Manufacturers*, 41–43.

37. RIC, Board of Directors Minutes, April 22, 1870; May 12, 1870. The capital stock of the company was increased at this time to $600,000, presumably to reflect the new acquisition.

38. James F. Doster, "The Chattanooga Rolling Mill: An Industrial By-Product of the Civil War," *East Tennessee Historical Society's Publications* 36 (1964): 45–51.

39. Ibid., 53; R. O. Biggs, "The Cincinnati Southern Railway: A Municipal Enterprise," *East Tennessee Historical Society's Publications* 7 (1935): 81–102; RIC, Board of Directors Minutes, January 22, 1875.

40. RIC, Board of Directors Minutes, December 15, 1871.

41. Ibid., July 10, 1872.

42. The company struggled somewhat during the depression years of 1873 and 1874, but it continued to operate throughout the period.

43. Joseph G. Butler Jr., *Fifty Years of Iron and Steel* (Cleveland, OH: Penton Press Co., 1923), 56–60; Allan Nevins, *Abram S. Hewitt, with Some Account of Peter Cooper* (New York: Harper & Brothers, 1935), 246–50.

44. RIC, Board of Directors Minutes, July, 10, 1877. Alexander Holley was instrumental in the adoption of the Bessemer steelmaking process in the United States. He helped to develop the first successful Bessemer converter in the United States at Wyandotte, Michigan, in 1865 and was also involved in the construction of the Cambria Iron Company's Bessemer works at Johnstown, Pennsylvania, in 1867.

45. Ibid., April 17, 1878.

46. Leo F. Reinartz, "The Open Hearth Furnace—Part I" in *History of Iron and Steelmaking in the United States* (New York: American Institute of Mining, Metallurgical, and Petroleum Engineers, 1961), 75. The use of the regenerative furnace was patented by Sir William Siemans, a German-born English citizen, and the method of using scrap iron to dilute pig iron impurities was patented by the Martin Brothers of France shortly thereafter, hence the name Siemans-Martin process.

47. Nevins, *Abram S. Hewitt*, 241–42.

48. Temin, *Iron and Steel in Nineteenth-Century America*, 141.

49. Chamberlain, *A Brief History of the Pig Iron Industry,* 8.

50. Temin, *Iron and Steel in Nineteenth-Century America,* 141–42.

51. Doster, "The Chattanooga Rolling Mill," 53–54; Kenneth Warren, *The American Steel Industry, 1850–1970—A Geographical Interpretation* (Oxford: Clarendon Press, 1973), 182–84; RIC, Board of Directors Minutes, January 18, 1883.

52. RIC, Board of Directors Minutes, January 18, 1883.

53. Ibid., July 18, 1883.

54. William J. MacArthur Jr., "Charles McClung McGhee, Southern Financier" (Ph.D. diss., University of Tennessee, Knoxville, 1975), 199–200. MacArthur's dissertation provides a large volume of information on McGhee's financial and investment activity over his lifetime.

55. East Tennessee, Virginia & Georgia Railroad, Board of Directors Minutes, Railroad Manuscript Collection, Newman Library, Virginia Polytechnic University. East Tennessee, Virginia & Georgia Railroad will hereafter be cited as ETVG. The Newman Library at Virginia Polytechnic University administers the records of all of the railroad companies that were incorporated into the Southern Railway in 1895.

56. RIC, Board of Director's Minutes, April 19, 1882.

57. Chamberlain to McGhee, McGhee Papers, McClung Historical Collection, June 10, 1886, June 19, 1886, October 16, 1886, October 23, 1886. All letter references made in this chapter are to the McGhee Papers.

58. RIC, Board of Directors Minutes, January 19, 1887.

59. ETVG, Board of Directors Minutes.

60. Chamberlain to McGhee, October 25, 1887.

61. MacArthur, "Charles McClung McGhee," 201–4.

62. RIC, Board of Directors Minutes, October 16, 1889.

63. Warren, *The American Steel Industry, 1850–1970,* 182–84.

64. Chamberlain, *A Brief History of the Pig Iron Industry,* 8; Warren, *The American Steel Industry,* 184.

65. United States Congress, Senate, Committee on Education and Labor, *Report upon the Relations Between Labor and Capital,* 48th Congress, 1st Session, November 11–28, 1883, 5 Volumes, vol. 4, 129. Report upon the Relations Between Labor and Capital will hereafter be cited as Report upon Labor and Capital. Hiram S. Chamberlain, president of the Roane Iron Company, testified in 1883 and was cited in this report.

66. Rockwood *Times,* December 18, 1924.

67. RIC, Board of Directors Minutes, June, 2, 1869, May 20, 1870.

68. Ibid., December 18, 1868.

69. Structures at which coal was sorted and loaded into horse-drawn or railroad cars. Coal was sorted according to size in some instances, and excess rock was separated to be dumped in waste (culm) piles.

70. *Report upon Labor and Capital,* 129.

71. Ibid., 133.

72. These data were compiled from the 1870 U.S. Federal manuscript census data for Rockwood. The classification is based on a scheme developed by Olivier Zunz for his study of late-nineteenth- and early-twentieth-century Detroit. See Olivier Zunz, *The Changing Face of Inequality: Urbanization, Industrial Development, and Immigrants in Detroit, 1880–1920* (Chicago: University of Chicago Press, 1982), 420–33 (appendix 3).

73. U.S. Department of Congress, Bureau of the Census, *Ninth Census, 1870: Population Manuscripts,* Tennessee, Roane County; *Compendium of the Eleventh Census* (Government Printing Office, 1893), 507.

74. Nashville *Daily American,* May 15, 1875 cited in William H. Moore, "Rockwood: A Prototype of the New South" (master's thesis, University of Tennessee, Knoxville), 30.

75. *Report upon Labor and Capital,* 133.

76. RIC, Board of Directors Minutes, July 10, 1872 and numerous others. The Cincinnati Southern was a municipal railroad financed and constructed by the city of Cincinnati. The major objective of the city in building the road was to establish a direct rail connection to southern markets, increasing its ability to compete with river cities such as Louisville, Kentucky. For an in-depth discussion of the Cincinnati-Southern Railway and route selection, see Biggs, *The Cincinnati Southern Railway: A Municipal Enterprise.*

77. *Tenth Census, 1880: Population Manuscripts,* Tennessee, Roane County.

78. *Ninth Census, 1870: Population Manuscripts; Tenth Census, 1880: Population Manuscripts.* Because the population manuscripts of Rockwood for 1870 and 1880 do not include street names or house numbers, it is impossible to accurately map the residential locations of persons listed. Therefore, the only accurate spatial inferences that can be drawn from the manuscripts are relational ones.

79. This includes coal and iron miners, furnace workers, coke oven workers, and other occupations that could be linked to company operations. Unspecified laborers were also included, because there is an overwhelming probability that they worked for the Roane Iron Company in some capacity. Unspecified laborers were distinguished from farm laborers in both the 1870 and 1880 Census manuscripts, supporting this interpretation.

80. RIC, Board of Directors Minutes, October 22, 1874; January 22, 1885; January 15, 1886; January 17, 1889.

81. Ibid., April 19, 1877; January 26, 1880; March 12, 1890; January 14, 1874; October 16, 1889.

82. Ibid., July 18, 1883.

83. Some industrial companies, including the Roane Iron Company, offered scrip as an alternative to scheduled salary payments of U.S. currency. Scrip could be drawn at any time by an employee, and was subtracted from a person's regular

paycheck. Instances have been documented in which scrip was the sole method of payment in company towns, but this was not the case in Rockwood.

84. Ibid., January 15, 1886.

Chapter 3

1. Leslie Hannah, *The Rise of the Corporate Economy* (London: Methuen and Company, Ltd., 1983); and Zunz, *Making America Corporate*.

2. Thomas R. Navin and Marian V. Sears, "The Rise of a Market for Industrial Securities, 1887–1902," *Business History Review* 19 (June 1955): 105–38.

3. Zunz, *Making America Corporate*.

4. John F. Stover, *The Railroads of the South, 1865–1900: A Study in Finance and Control* (Chapel Hill: University of North Carolina Press, 1955); Burke Davis, *The Southern Railway—Road of the Innovators* (Chapel Hill: University of North Carolina Press, 1985).

5. Eller, *Miners, Millhands, and Mountaineers*, 65–85; Cobb, *Industrialization and Southern Society*, 17–20; Ronald L. Lewis, *Transforming the Appalachian Countryside: Railroads, Deforestation, and Social Change in Appalachia, 1880–1920* (Chapel Hill: University of North Carolina Press, 1998).

6. See Eller, *Miners, Millhands, and Mountaineers*; Cobb, *Industrialization and Southern Society*; Gaventa, *Power and Powerlessness*; and John Benhart Jr., "Capitalism, Regional Development, and Place Formation: An Analysis of the Upper Tennessee River Valley, 1860–1900" (Ph.D. diss., University of Tennessee, 1995).

7. Chandler, *The Visible Hand*, 91. According to Chandler, Philadelphia and Boston were the leading financial centers in the United States during the first four decades of the nineteenth century. New York became the major national financial center after the late 1840s, mainly because of a general capital shortfall among Boston lenders, which led to higher lending rates than were available in New York.

8. Ibid., 90–100; Navin and Sears, "The Rise of a Market for Industrial Securities."

9. Navin and Sears, "The Rise of a Market for Industrial Securities," 107; Chandler, *The Visible Hand*, 92–93.

10. *Goodspeed's History of Tennessee*, 821.

11. ETVG, Board of Directors Minutes, March 29, 1887, May 23, 1887.

12. Victor S. Clark, *The History of Manufactures in the United States* (New York, 1929), 211–20.

13. *Corporation Records, State of Tennessee*, April 21, 1889; March 18, 1890; April 12, 1890.

14. Walter T. Pulliam, *Harriman: The Town That Temperance Built* (Maryville, TN: Brazos Press, 1978), 19–23.

15. *Dictionary of American Biography* 6 (New York: Charles Scribner's Sons, 1931), 413–14. .

16. *Dictionary of American Biography* 7: 72–73; *The National Cyclopaedia of American Biography,* vol. 23 (New York: James T. White and Company, 1925), 44.

17. Pulliam, *Harriman,* 54; Chandler, *The Visible Hand,* 294.

18. Pulliam, *Harriman,* 47–60.

19. Ibid., 50; *Dictionary of American Biography* 7: 72–73.

20. *Prospectus of the East Tennessee Land Company* (New York: The South Publishing Company, 1890), 23.

21. Ibid.

22. Navin and Sears point out that some of the largest manufacturing concerns of the 1880s were either family owned or incorporated and closely held. Examples include the Singer Manufacturing Company, Carnegie Steel Company, and the McCormick Harvesting Machine Company. Although land companies were not industrials, they apparently were among the first American non-railroad companies to embrace the public ownership structure. See Navin and Sears, "The Rise of a Market for Industrial Securities," 109–10.

23. *Prospectus of the East Tennessee Land Company,* 44.

24. Ibid., 23.

25. *Two Years of Harriman, Tennessee* (New York: The South Publishing Company, 1892), 44–52.

26. Ibid., 64–69.

27. *Prospectus of the East Tennessee Land Company,* 43.

28. ORD, Roane County, TN, Deed Book B-2, 549, 553, 570; Deed Book C-2, 34, 201, 233; Deed Book D-2, 243, 247, 250, 395, 518.

29. *Harriman Daily Advance,* January 30, 1893; January 31, 1893; February 14, 1893.

30. Navin and Sears, "The Rise of a Market for Industrial Securities," 119; Chandler, *The Visible Hand,* 319–28; ETVG, Board of Directors Minutes, June 30, 1886; May 23, 1887. In the creation of a trust, a number of companies in a particular industry turned their stock certificates over to a board of trustees, receiving in turn trust certificates of equivalent value. Reasons for trust conversion in an industry were usually related to limiting competition and price fluctuations.

31. *Prospectus of the East Tennessee Land Company,* 25–26.

32. Ibid., 25.

33. *Two Years of Harriman,* 11–12.

34. *Cardiff Herald,* April 23, 1890; May 7, 1890; W. P. Rice to J. F. Randolph, December 20, 1890, Cardiff Coal & Iron Company Papers, Roane County Heritage Commission, Kingston, TN. Rice was the president of the Fort Payne Coal and Iron Company during the late 1880s and early 1890s.

35. *The Town of Cardiff, and Lands and Mines of the Cardiff Coal and Iron Company* (Cardiff Coal & Iron Company, 1890), unattached insert; *Cardiff Herald,* April 23, 1890.

36. Ibid.

37. *The Town of Cardiff,* 4–5.

38. *Cardiff Herald,* April 30, 1890.

39. *The Town of Cardiff,* 11–12.

40. *Cardiff Herald,* April 23, 1890.

41. *Haley & Ingram vs. Henry C. Young* (No Date), Complainant Report, Cardiff Coal & Iron Company Papers, Roane County Heritage Commission, Kingston, TN, 1–2.

42. *The Town of Cardiff,* 8.

43. Mary U. Rothrock, ed., *The French Broad–Holston Country: A History of Knox County, Tennessee* (Knoxville: East Tennessee Historical Society, 1946), 479–80.

44. Sanford and McGhee wrote to each other on a fairly steady basis during the late 1880s and early 1890s. A survey of these letters provides much useful information about businesses in Knoxville and East Tennessee during this period. See the McGhee Papers, preserved at the McClung Historical Collection in the Customs Building, Knoxville, Tennessee.

45. McGhee to Sanford, June 10, 1887; partially quoted in MacArthur, "Charles McClung McGhee," 227.

46. ETVG, Board of Directors Minutes, January 8, 1889, and numerous others.

47. *Dictionary of American Biography* 1:31–32.

48. Ibid., 7: 329–30; Chandler, *The Visible Hand,* 321–22.

49. Lenoir City Company, Board of Directors Minutes, May 20, 1890; Navin and Sears, "The Rise of a Market for Industrial Securities," 129. The board of directors minutes of the Lenoir City Company have been preserved and are available, as the company continues to maintain offices at Lenoir City, Tennessee.

50. *Prospectus of the Lenoir City Company* (Lenoir City Company, 1890), 4. C. M. McClung was McGhee's son-in-law, and E. T. Sanford was E. J. Sanford's son.

51. Ibid., 24–25.

52. Ibid., 23.

53. Ibid., 25.

54. Ibid., 8.

55. Ibid., 12.

56. MacArthur, "Charles McClung McGhee," 218–23.

57. *Prospectus of the Lenoir City Company* (Lenoir City Co., 1890), 11.

58. Ashley T. Hawn, "The Lenoir City Company, An Attempt In Community Development" (master's thesis, University of Tennessee, Knoxville, 1940), 7. In part because of this land grant, William Lenoir was an influential figure in western North Carolina and East Tennessee during the late 1700s and early 1800s. His vast landholdings were passed on to his sons at his death in 1839, and they in turn were important figures in these areas for the balance of the century. Hence, the name of the Lenoir City and the Lenoir City Company.

59. *Prospectus of the Lenoir City Company* (Lenoir City Company, 1890), 12.

60. Sam Bass Warner Jr., *The Urban Wilderness: A History of the American City* (New York: Harper and Row, 1972); Robert Ernst, "Immigrants and Tenements in

New York City, 1825–1863," in R. A. Mohl and N. Betten, eds., *Urban America in Historical Perspective* (New York: Weybright and Talley, 1970), 113–26.

61. Bender, *Toward an Urban Vision;* Boyer, *Urban Masses and Moral Order in America.*

62. Peterson, *The Birth of City Planning,* 29–54.

63. Joel A. Tarr, "The Evolution of Urban Infrastructure in the Nineteenth and Twentieth Centuries," in Royce Hanson, ed., *Perspectives on Urban Infrastructure* (Washington, D.C.: National Academy Press, 1984), 5–66; Ellis Armstrong et al., *History of Public Works in the United States, 1776–1976* (Chicago: American Public Works Association, 1976).

64. Robert L. Wrigley Jr., "The Plan of Chicago," in Donald A. Krueckeberg, ed., *Introduction to Planning History in the United States* (New Brunswick, NJ: The Center for Urban Policy Research, 1987), 58–72; Stanley K. Schultz, *Constructing Urban Culture: American Cities and City Planning, 1800–1920* (Philadelphia: Temple University Press, 1989), 129–49.

65. Walter L. Creese, *The Search for Environment, The Garden City: Before and After* (New Haven: Yale University Press, 1966); Anne E. Mosher, *Capital's Utopia—Vandergrift, Pennsylvania, 1855–1916* (Baltimore: Johns Hopkins University Press, 2004), 73–75.

66. Stanley Buder, *Pullman: An Experiment in Industrial Order and Community Planning, 1880–1930* (New York: Oxford University Press, 1967).

67. John S. Garner, *The Model Company Town: Urban Design Through Private Enterprise in Nineteenth Century New England* (Amherst: University of Massachusetts Press, 1984), 205–10; Buder, *Pullman: An Experiment in Industrial Order and Community Planning;* Mosher, *Capital's Utopia,* 73–75.

68. The distinction between these terms is made because the land companies did not retain ownership of land in the subject communities and did not rent property as a profit strategy (as is often assumed when the term *company town* is used).

69. The sanitary reform movement was based upon an empirically grounded explanation of the origin and spread of infectious diseases, often called the "filth theory" by medical historians. Reformers, for instance, pointed to filth as the cause of numerous scourges—among them yellow fever, cholera, typhoid, scarlet fever, and diphtheria. Filth, depending upon the disease and the observer, could encompass such conditions as odors arising from decomposing organic waste, stagnant water, sodden ground, and the absence of sunlight. See Jon A. Peterson, "The Impact of Sanitary Reform Upon American Urban Planning, 1840–1890," 13–39.

70. *Prospectus of the East Tennessee Land Company,* 35.

71. *Cardiff Herald,* April 23, 1890.

72. *Prospectus of the Lenoir City Company* (Lenoir City Company, 1890), 19–20.

73. *Prospectus of the East Tennessee Land Company,* quoted in Pulliam, *Harriman: The Town That Temperance Built,* 31.

74. *Cardiff Herald,* July 23, 1890.

75. Ibid., October 1, 1890.

76. *Two Years of Harriman,* 94.

77. *Prospectus of the Lenoir City Company,* 19.

78. *Two Years of Harriman,* 94.

79. Olmsted, Frederick Law, *Civilizing American Cities: A Selection of Frederick Law Olmsted's Writings on City Landscapes,* ed. S. B. Sutton (Cambridge: MIT Press, 1971). Olmsted felt that the suburb should provide a setting for domestic life free of the commotion, crowding, and physical chaos that characterized the central areas of industrial cities. His suburban designs usually featured curvilinear streets, large irregularly shaped lots, and public open spaces, as well as sewer and water systems.

80. Ibid., 32–42.

81. *Prospectus of the Lenoir City Company,* 21–22.

82. Pulliam, *The Town That Temperance Built,* 10.

83. *Harriman Daily Advance,* April 8, 1890.

84. *City Directory of Harriman, Tennessee, Volume 1, 1892* (Chattanooga: G. M. Connelly, 1892), 26.

85. Information on lot sale prices was obtained from the *Harriman Daily Advance,* April 8, 1890. This information was cross-checked against Roane County deed records.

86. *Two Years of Harriman,* 28.

87. F. R. Cordley to J. F. Randolph, August 23, 1890; F. R. Cordley to J. F. Randolph, September 3, 1890; F. R. Cordley to J. F. Randolph, September 10, 1890; F. R. Cordley to J. F. Randolph, September 15, 1890; F. R. Cordley to J. F. Randolph, September 22, 1890; H. H. French to J. F. Randolph, September 22, 1890; H. H. French to J. F. Randolph, September 24, 1890, Cardiff Coal & Iron Company Papers, Roane County Heritage Commission, Kingston, TN. John F. Randolph was an agent of the Cardiff Coal and Iron Company, and traveled widely in advertising the company's activities and soliciting investors. The letters cited above discussed Randolph's activities as agent and were mailed to him on the job in Boston, Ottawa, Toronto, and Detroit.

88. Ibid., April 30, 1890.

89. *Cardiff Herald,* April 23, 1890.

90. *Prospectus of the Lenoir City Company,* 24–25.

91. Sanborn fire insurance maps are very detailed maps of towns and cities that show street addresses, building materials, types of structures, thickness of walls, machinery (for example, in factories), and other infrastructure. The maps cover the period between 1867 and 1970 and were originally used by insurance underwriters to assess risk and determine premiums for insuring particular properties.

92. *Two Years of Harriman,* 23–26.

93. *City Directory of Harriman, Tennessee,* 30; *Harriman Advance,* March 1, 1890.

94. *Two Years of Harriman,* 48.

95. Ibid., 72–76.

96. The 1892 Harriman City Directory did not give exact street addresses for residents of Oak View Addition. It did, however, designate Oak View as a residence area for heads-of-household, which gave a general indication of a person's location.

97. See Olivier Zunz, *The Changing Face of Inequality: Urbanization, Industrial Development, and Immigrants in Detroit, 1880–1920* (Chicago: University of Chicago Press, 1982), 422–33.

98. Based on the timing of city directory and census data, it would not be feasible to cross-check city directory heads-of-households with the census manuscripts. The city directory was published in 1892. Harriman did not exist when the 1890 census was conducted, and it had changed very significantly (because of the Panic of 1893) by the time 1900 census data was collected. In order to geocode Harriman residents accurately, the city directory data were used to make conditional statements regarding geographic distribution.

99. Statements of over- or underrepresentation of class groups are made in reference to the number of given class group heads-of-households expected under an assumption of random proportional spatial distribution. This assumption is made when using the Chi-Square analysis.

100. C. Vann Woodward, *The Strange Career of Jim Crow* (New York: Oxford University Press, 1966), 17–21.

101. Ibid., 97–101. The first Jim Crow law in Tennessee, involving streetcars, was not enacted until 1903. Laws regarding residential race segregation were not initiated in the South until 1910.

Chapter 4

1. Gilbert C. Fite and Jim E. Reese, *An Economic History of the United States* (Boston: Houghton Mifflin Company, 1973), 271–72.

2. Joseph Wechsburg, *The Merchant Bankers* (Boston: Little, Brown & Company, 1966), 99–102.

3. Richard Kellett, *The Merchant Banking Arena* (New York: St. Martin's Press, 1967), 118–23.

4. Harry N. Scheiber, Harold G. Vatter, and Harold U. Faulkner, *American Economic History* (New York: Harper & Row, 1976), 307.

5. In 1873 the silver dollar was worth $1.02 in gold, and it was no longer profitable to coin it. Silver was scarce at this time, and very little had been presented to the mints for coining. Congress's action was not highly controversial at this time, and passage of the act was seen merely as legislative acknowledgment that silver dollars were not being coined.

6. At the close of the Civil War, the United States was benefiting from the effects of inflationary methods of war finance. Paper money had been issued in amounts exceeding $400 million, and in addition, a part of the war effort had been financed through the sale of government securities to national banks. In the early aftermath of the war, the general sentiment in Washington was that paper money should be retired by the federal government in order to permit a return to price and income levels of the prewar period.

7. Scheiber et al., *American Economic History,* 307.

8. Fite and Reese, *An Economic History of the United States,* 272.

9. Harold M. Somers, "The Performance of the American Economy, 1866–1918," in Harold F. Williamson, ed., *The Growth of the American Economy* (Englewood Cliffs, NJ: Prentice-Hall, 1951), 652–53.

10. Scheiber et al., *American Economic History,* 306–7; Fite and Reese, *An Economic History of the United States,* 272.

11. *Haley and Ingram vs. Henry C. Young,* Complainant Report, 12–13.

12. *Chattanooga Tradesman* 32 (1895): 116.

13. *Harriman Daily Advance,* January 27, 1893.

14. Louise Davis, "Town Built for Teetotalers," *The Tennesseean Magazine,* Sunday, November 19, 1972, 16–18.

15. Lenoir City Company, Board of Directors Minutes, June 1, 1892.

16. Ibid.

17. Ibid., November 12, 1892.

18. E. J. Sanford to C. M. McGhee, November 27, 1891.

19. Lenoir City Company, Board of Directors Minutes, March 13, 1893.

20. Manufacturing data were not reported by county in the 1910 Federal Census.

21. John H. White Jr., *The American Railroad Freight Car: From the Wood Era to the Coming of Steel* (Baltimore: Johns Hopkins University Press, 1993), 141–42.

22. Chamberlain to McGhee, October 25, 1887.

23. One of the major advantages of the Birmingham production site was the availability of large deposits of low-phosphorus iron ore, which was favorable for steel production.

24. William Howard Moore, "Rockwood: A Prototype of the New South" (master's thesis, University of Tennessee, Knoxville, 1965).

25. Walter T. Pulliam, *Harriman: The Town That Temperance Built* (Maryville, TN: Brazos Press, 1978), 499–501.

26. United States Department of Commerce and Labor, Bureau of the Census, *Thirteenth Census, 1910: Population Manuscripts, Tennessee, Loudon County.* In these manuscripts, the census taker specified the incorporated place (Lenoir City) that persons resided in.

27. Ibid.

Conclusion

1. Eller, *Miners, Millhands, and Mountaineers*, xxiv.

2. Stover, *The Railroads of the South, 1865–1900*, xiii.

3. *Prospectus of the East Tennessee Land Company*, 44.

4. Ibid., 23.

5. ORD, Roane County, TN, Deed Book O-1, pp. 354–55, 359.

6. Gaventa, *Power and Powerlessness*, 53–55; Eller, *Miners, Millhands, and Mountaineers*, 54–58.

7. ORD Roane County, Tennessee, numerous deed agreements Book A-2.

8. United States Department of Commerce, Bureau of the Census, *Thirteenth Census, 1910: Agriculture, Tennessee* (Loudon and Roane Counties).

9. *The Town of Cardiff and Lands and Mines of the Cardiff Coal and Iron Company*, 7; *Prospectus of the Lenoir City Company*, 13.

10. Alan Banks, "Class Formation in the Southeastern Kentucky Coalfields, 1890–1920," in *Appalachia in the Making*, ed. M. B. Pudup et al. (Chapel Hill: University of North Carolina Press, 1995), 330–33.

11. See Alan Banks, "Class Formation in the Southeastern Kentucky Coalfields, 1890–1920," 330–33; J. Fred Holly, "The Co-Operative Town Company of Tennessee. A Case Study of Planned Economic Development" *East Tennessee Historical Society's Publications;* Justin Fuller, "Boom Towns and Blast Furnaces: Town Promotion in Alabama, 1885–1893," *The Alabama Review*, January, 1976 36–48; John Hennen, "Benign Betrayal: Capitalist Intervention in Pocahontas County, West Virginia, 1890–1910," *West Virginia History*, vol. 50, 1991 46–62, Eller, *Miners, Millhands, and Mountaineers*, 82–84.

12. Folsom, *Urban Capitalists*, 145–47.

13. MacArthur, "Charles McClung McGhee," 80–83; Stover, *Railroads of the South, 1865–1900*, 114–16.

14. Eller, *Miners, Millhands, and Mountaineers*, 15.

15. Roane Iron Company, Board of Directors Minutes, May 20, 1870.

16. *Prospectus of the East Tennessee Land Company* (New York: The South Publishing Company, 1890), 23.

17. Buder, *Pullman: An Experiment in Industrial Order and Community Planning, 1880–1930;* Creese, *The Search for Environment, The Garden City: Before and After;* Garner, *The Model Company Town*.

18. Boyer, *Urban Masses and Moral Order in America*, 175.

19. Ibid., 181–82.

20. *Two Years of Harriman*, 94.

21. *Prospectus of the Lenoir City Company*, 19.

22. Schultz, *Constructing Urban Culture*, 113.

23. Boyer, *Urban Masses and Moral Order in America*, 221.

24. Peterson, "The Impact of Sanitary Reform," 13–39; Mosher, *Capital's Utopia*, 78–80.

25. *Prospectus of the East Tennessee Land Company*, quoted in Pulliam, *Harriman: The Town That Temperance Built*, 31.

26. *Cardiff Herald*, July 23, 1890.

27. *Prospectus of the Lenoir City Company* (Lenoir City Company, 1890), 19–20.

28. Schultz, *Constructing Urban Culture*, xiii.

29. William H. Wilson, *The City Beautiful Movement* (Baltimore: Johns Hopkins University Press, 1989); Edward Relph, *The Modern Urban Landscape* (Baltimore: Johns Hopkins University Press, 1987), 51–55; Schultz, *Constructing Urban Culture*, 211–13; Allison Isenberg, *Downtown America* (Chicago: University of Chicago Press, 2004), 14–20.

30. Howard N. Rabinowitz, "Continuity and Change: Southern Urban Development, 1860–1900," in *The City in Southern History: The Growth of Urban Civilization in the South*, ed. B. A. Brownell and D. R. Goldfield (Port Washington: Kennikat Press, 1977), 99–101; Goldfield, *Cotton Fields and Skyscrapers*, 111–12.

31. Doyle, *New Men, New Cities, New South*, 260–66.

32. For example, Rabinowitz "Continuity and Change," 100.

33. The major problem with documenting residential patterns of socioeconomic groups involves the issue of multiple household earners or families with income from other sources. If there were multiple earners within households, then the estimated earning level of a head-of-household's occupation does not provide an accurate depiction of the household's total earnings.

BIBLIOGRAPHY

Unpublished Primary Sources

Blacksburg, Virginia. Virginia Polytechnic Institute. Newman Library. Railroad Manuscript Collection. East Tennessee, Virginia & Georgia Railway Company, Board of Directors Minutes, November 1868–March 1892.

Kingston, Tennessee. Old Roane County Courthouse. Roane County Heritage Commission. Cardiff Coal and Iron Company Papers. n.d.

———. East Tennessee Land Company Papers. n.d.

———. Roane Iron Company Papers. n.d.

Kingston, Tennessee. Roane County Courthouse. Roane County Deed Register. 1866–91.

———. Roane County Register of Plans. Harriman, Tennessee, Property of the East Tennessee Land Company, 1890.

———. Map of the City of Cardiff, Roane County, Tennessee, 1890.

———. Roane Iron Company's Map of the Village of Rockwood, 1887.

Knoxville, Tennessee. Old Customs House Building. McClung Historical Collection. Charles McClung McGhee Papers. January, 1886–June, 1888.

———. Welcker Papers. March 1888–June 1892.

Knoxville, Tennessee. University of Tennessee. Hoskins Library. Special Collections. Roane Iron Company, Board of Directors Minutes. June 1865–July 1897.

Lenoir City, Tennessee. The Lenoir City Company. Lenoir City Company Stockholders and Board of Directors Minutes. May 1890–June 1904.

Loudon, Tennessee. Loudon County Courthouse. Loudon County Deed Register, 1889–94.

———. Loudon County Register of Plans. Map of Lenoir City, East Tennessee, 1890.

Nashville, Tennessee. Tennessee State Archives. Records, State of Tennessee. March, 1875–August, 1891.

———. Acts of Tennessee. 1867–68.

Published Primary Sources

Bokum, Hermann. *The Tennessee Handbook and Immigrant's Guide*. Philadelphia, PA, 1868.

Boyle, James E. *Chicago Wheat Prices for Eighty-One Years: Daily, Monthly and Yearly Fluctuations and Their Causes*. Ithaca, NY 1922.

————. *Cotton and the New Orleans Cotton Exchange: A Century of Commercial Evolution*. Garden City, NY, 1934.

Cardiff Coal and Iron Company. *The Town of Cardiff, and Lands and Mines of the Cardiff Coal and Iron Company*. Cardiff Coal and Iron Company, 1890.

The Cardiff Herald. 1890.

Chamberlain, Morrow. *A Brief History of the Pig Iron Industry in East Tennessee*. Chattanooga, TN: The author, 1942.

Chattanooga Tradesman. 1895.

Connelly, G. M. *City Directory of Harriman, Tennessee*. Chattanooga, TN: Times Printing Company, 1892.

Dictionary of American Biography. Volumes 6–7. New York: Charles Scribner's Sons, 1931.

————. Volume 1. New York: Charles Scribner's Sons, 1936.

East Tennessee Land Company. *Prospectus of the East Tennessee Land Company*. New York: The South Publishing Company, 1890.

————. *Two Years of Harriman, Tennessee*. New York: The South Publishing Company, 1892.

East Tennessee, Virginia & Georgia Railroad Company. *The Eighth Annual Report of the Officers to the Stockholders*. Knoxville, TN: Whig and Chronicle Printing Company, 1876.

————. *Local Time on the East Tennessee, Virginia & Georgia System*. Buffalo, NY: Matthews-Northrup Company, 1891.

Harriman Daily Advance. 1893.

Harriman Land Company. *The Southland*. Harriman, TN: Harriman Land Company, 1899.

Lenoir City Company. *Prospectus of the Lenoir City Company*. Lenoir City Company, 1890.

The National Cyclopaedia of American Biography. Volume 23. New York: James T. White and Company, 1925.

Roberts, Snyder. "Roane County's Industrial Belt, 1868–1932," n.p.: the author, 1982.

Rockwood Times. 1888–1924.

United States Congress. Senate. Committee on Education and Labor, *Report Upon the Relations Between Labor and Capital*. 48th Congress, 1st Session, November 11–28. Volume 4.

United States Department of Commerce. Bureau of the Census *Eighth Census: Agriculture, 1860*. Tennessee, Roane County.

————. *Eighth Census: Manufactures, 1860.* Tennessee, Roane County.

————. *Eighth Census: Manufactures of the United States in 1860.*

————. *Compendium of the Ninth Census, 1870.* Tennessee.

————. *Ninth Census: Agriculture, 1870.* Tennessee, Roane County.

————. *Ninth Census: Manufactures, 1870.* Tennessee, Roane County.

————. *Ninth Census, 1870: Population Manuscripts.* Tennessee, Roane County.

————. *Compendium of the Tenth Census, 1880.* Tennessee.

————. *Tenth Census: Agriculture, 1880.* Tennessee, Loudon County, Roane County.

————. *Tenth Census: Manufactures, 1880.* Tennessee, Loudon County, Roane County.

————. *Tenth Census: The Manufacture of Iron and Steel, 1880.* Tennessee, Loudon County, Roane County.

————. *Tenth Census, 1880: Population Manuscripts.* Tennessee, Roane County.

————. *Compendium of the Eleventh Census, 1890.* Tennessee.

————. *Eleventh Census: Agriculture, 1890.* Tennessee, Loudon County, Roane County.

————. *Eleventh Census: Manufactures, 1890.* Tennessee, Loudon County, Roane County.

————. *Compendium of the Twelfth Census, 1900.* Tennessee.

————. *Twelfth Census: Agriculture, 1900.* Tennessee, Loudon County, Roane County.

————. *Twelfth Census: Manufactures, 1900.* Tennessee, Loudon County, Roane County.

————. *Thirteenth Census: Agriculture, 1910.* Tennessee, Loudon County, Roane County.

————. *Compendium of the Fourteenth Census, 1920.* Tennessee.

————. *Fourteenth Census: Agriculture, 1920.* Tennessee, Loudon County, Roane County.

————. *Fourteenth Census: Manufactures, 1920.* Tennessee, Loudon County, Roane County.

Secondary Sources

Abernethy, Thomas P. *Frontier to Plantation in Tennessee: A Study in Frontier Democracy.* Chapel Hill: University of North Carolina Press, 1932.

Allison, Judge John, ed. *Notable Men of Tennessee, Volume 2.* Atlanta: Southern Historical Association, 1905.

American Institute of Mining, Metallurgical, and Petroleum Engineers. *History of Iron and Steelmaking in the United States.* New York, 1961.

Armstrong, Ellis. *History of Public Works in the United States, 1776–1976.* Chicago: American Public Works Association, 1976.

Bellissary, Constantine G. "The Rise of Industry and the Industrial Spirit in Tennessee, 1865–1885." *The Journal of Southern History* 19 (May 1953): 193–215.

Bender, Thomas. *Toward an Urban Vision: Ideas and Institutions in Nineteenth-Century America.* Lexington: University Press of Kentucky, 1975.

Biggs, R. O. "The Cincinnati Southern Railway: A Municipal Enterprise." *East Tennessee Historical Society's Publications* 7 (1935): 81–102.

Billings, Dwight B., Jr. *Planters and the Making of a New South: Class, Politics, and Development in North Carolina, 1865–1900.* Chapel Hill: University of North Carolina Press, 1979.

Black, Brian. *Petrolia—The Landscape of America's First Oil Boom.* Baltimore: Johns Hopkins University Press, 2000.

Boyer, Paul. *Urban Masses and Moral Order in America, 1820–1920.* Cambridge: Harvard University Press, 1978.

Braverman, Harry. *Labor and Monopoly Capital: The Degradation of Work in the Twentieth Century.* New York: Monthly Review Press, 1974.

Brownell, Blaine A., and David R. Goldfield, eds. *The City in Southern History.* Port Washington, NY: Kennikat Press, 1977.

Buckley, Geoffrey L. *Extracting Appalachia: Images of the Consolidation Coal Company, 1910–1945.* Athens: Ohio University Press, 2004.

Buder, Stanley. *Pullman: An Experiment in Industrial Order and Community Planning, 1880–1930.* New York: Oxford University Press, 1967.

Buder, Stanley. *Visionaries and Planners—The Garden City Movement and Modern Community.* Oxford: Oxford University Press, 1990.

Butler, Joseph G., Jr. *Fifty Years of Iron and Steel.* Cleveland: The Penton Press Co., 1923.

Byington, Margaret F. *Homestead: The Households of a Mill Town.* New York: Russell Sage, 1910.

Cash, Wilbur J. *Mind of the South.* New York: Alfred A. Knopf, 1941.

Chandler, Alfred D., Jr. "The Beginnings of 'Big Business' in American Industry." *Business History Review* 33 (Spring 1959): 1–31.

———. *The Visible Hand: The Managerial Revolution in American Business.* Cambridge: Harvard University Press, 1977.

Clark, Ted B. "The Changing Central Place Function of Loudon, Tennessee." Master's thesis, University of Tennessee, Knoxville, 1968.

Clark, Victor S. *The History of Manufactures in the United States.* New York, 1929.

Cobb, James C. *Industrialization and Southern Society, 1877–1984.* Lexington: University Press of Kentucky, 1984.

Conzen, Michael P. "The Maturing Urban System in the United States, 1840–1910." *Annals of the Association of American Geographers* 67 (1977): 88–108.

Couvares, Francis G. *The Remaking of Pittsburgh: Class and Culture in an Industrializing City, 1877–1919.* Albany: State University of New York Press, 1984.

Creese, Walter L. *The Search for Environment, The Garden City: Before and After.* New Haven: Yale University Press, 1966.

Davis, Burke. *The Southern Railway—The Road of the Innovators.* Chapel Hill: University of North Carolina Press, 1985.

Davis, Louise. "Town Built For Teetotalers." *The Tennessean Magazine,* 19 November 1972, 16–18.

Deadrick, Lucille, ed. *Heart of the Valley: A History of Knoxville, Tennessee*. Knoxville: East Tennessee Historical Society, 1976.

Doster, James F. "The Chattanooga Rolling Mill: An Industrial By-Product of the Civil War." *East Tennessee Historical Society's Publications* 36 (1964).

Doyle, Don H. *New Men, New Cities, New South—Atlanta, Nashville, Charleston, Mobile, 1860–1910*. Chapel Hill: University of North Carolina Press, 1990.

Dunaway, Wilma A. *The First American Frontier*. Chapel Hill: University of North Carolina Press, 1996.

Eller, Ronald D. *Miners, Millhands, and Mountaineers*. Knoxville: University of Tennessee Press, 1982.

Fertig, James W. *The Secession and Reconstruction of Tennessee*. Chicago: The University of Chicago Press, 1898.

Folmsbee, Stanley J., Robert E. Corlew, and Enoch L. Mitchell, eds. *History of Tennessee, Volume 2*. New York: Lewis Historical Publishing Co., 1960.

Folsom, Burton W., Jr. *Urban Capitalists*. Baltimore: Johns Hopkins University Press, 1981.

Francaviglia, Richard V. *Hard Places: Reading the Landscape of America's Historic Mining Districts*. Iowa City: University of Iowa Press, 1991.

Garner, John S. *The Model Company Town: Urban Design Through Private Enterprise in Nineteenth Century New England*. Amherst, MA: University of Massachusetts Press, 1984.

Gaventa, John. *Power and Powerlessness*. Urbana: University of Illinois Press, 1980.

Gillenwater, Mack H. "Cultural and Historical Geography of Mining Settlements in the Pocahontas Coal Field of Southern West Virginia, 1880–1910." Ph.D. dissertation, University of Tennessee, Knoxville, 1972.

Goldfield, David R. *Cotton Fields and Skyscrapers*. Baton Rouge: Louisiana State University Press, 1982.

Goodspeed, ed. *Goodspeed's General History of Tennessee*. Nashville: Goodspeed Publishing Company, 1887.

Govan, Gilbert E., and James W. Livingood. *The Chattanooga Country 1540–1951: From Tomahawks to TVA*. New York: E. P. Dutton, 1952.

Green, D. Brooks, ed. *Historical Geography: A Methodological Portrayal*. Savage, MD: Rowman & Littlefield, 1991.

Gregory, Derek, and John Urry, eds. *Social Relations and Spatial Structures*. London: Macmillan, 1985.

Griffin, Clyde. "Community Studies and the Investigation of Nineteenth-Century Social Relations." *Social Science History* 10 (1986): 315–38.

Hall, Jere, and Jack B. Shelley, eds. *Valley of Challenge and Change: Roane County, Tennessee, 1860–1900*. Knoxville: East Tennessee Historical Society, 1986.

Hannah, Leslie. *The Rise of the Corporate Economy*. London: Methuen, 1983.

Hart, John Fraser. "The Highest Form of the Geographer's Art." *Annals of the Association of American Geographers* 72, no. 4 (1982): 557–59.

Harvey, David. *Social Justice and the City.* London: Edward Arnold, 1973.

Hawn, Ashley T. "The Lenoir City Company, An Attempt In Community Development." Master's thesis, University of Tennessee, Knoxville.

Haydu, Jeffery. *Between Craft and Class: Skilled Workers and Factory Politics in the United States and Britain, 1890–1922.* Berkeley: University of California Press, 1988.

Haywood, John. *The Civil and Political History of the State of Tennessee from its Earliest Settlement up to the Year 1796.* Reprinted from 1823 Edition, Knoxville; Tenase Co., 1969.

Hennen, John C. *The Americanization of West Virginia: Creating a Modern Industrial State, 1916–1925.* Lexington: University Press of Kentucky, 1996.

Hesseltine, W. B. "Tennessee's Invitation to Carpet Baggers," *East Tennessee Historical Society's Publications* 4 (1932).

Hoerr, John P. *And the Wolf Finally Came: The Decline of the American Steel Industry.* Pittsburgh: University of Pittsburgh Press, 1988.

Holt, Albert C. *The Economic and Social Beginnings of Tennessee.* Nashville: George Peabody College, 1923.

Isenberg, Allison, *Downtown America.* Chicago: University of Chicago Press, 2004.

James, John A. *Money and Capital Markets in Postbellum America.* Princeton: Princeton University Press, 1978.

Jones, Peter d'A. *The Consumer Society: A History of American Capitalism.* Baltimore: Penguin Books, 1965.

Kellett, Richard. *The Merchant Banking Arena.* New York: St. Martins Press, 1967.

King, D., ed. *The Cherokee Indian Nation: A Troubled History.* Knoxville: University of Tennessee Press, 1979.

Kreckeberg, Donald. *Introduction to Planning History in the United States.* New Brunswick, NJ: Center for Urban Policy Research, 1987.

Lewis, Ronald. *Transforming the Appalachian Countryside: Railroads, Deforestation and Social Change in Appalachia, 1880–1920.* Chapel Hill: University of North Carolina Press, 1998.

Lewis, Thomas M. N., and Madeline Kneberg. *Tribes That Slumber: Indians of the Tennessee Region.* Knoxville: University of Tennessee Press, 1960.

MacArthur, William J., Jr. "Charles McClung McGhee, Southern Financier." Ph.D. dissertation, University of Tennessee, Knoxville, 1975.

Massey, Doreen. "In What Sense a Regional Problem?" *Regional Studies* 13 (1979).

———. "Regionalism: Some Current Issues," *Capital & Class* 6 (1978).

———. *Spatial Divisions of Labour: Social Structures and the Geography of Production.* London: Macmillan Publishers, 1985.

McDonald, Michael J., and William B. Wheeler, *Knoxville, Tennessee: Continuity and Change in an Appalachian City.* Knoxville: University of Tennessee Press, 1983.

Mitchell, Robert D., and Paul A. Groves, eds. *North America: The Historical Geography of a Changing Continent*. Savage, MD: Rowman & Littlefield,1990.

Mohl, R. A., and N. Betten, eds. *Urban America in Historical Perspective*. New York: Weybright and Talley, 1970.

Moore, William H. "Rockwood: A Prototype of the New South." Master's thesis, University of Tennessee, Knoxville, 1965.

Mosher, Anne E. *Capital's Utopia—Vandergrift, Pennsylvania, 1855–1916*. Baltimore: Johns Hopkins University Press, 2004.

Mulrooney, Margaret M. *A Legacy of Coal: The Coal Company Towns of Southwestern Pennsylvania*. Washington: National Park Service, 1989.

Navin, Thomas R., and Marian V. Sears. "The Rise of a Market for Industrial Securities, 1887–1902," *Business History Review* 19 (1955).

Nelson, Daniel. *Managers and Workers: Origins of the New Factory System in the United States, 1880–1920*. Madison: University of Wisconsin Press, 1975.

Nevins, Allan. *Abram S. Hewitt, With Some Account of Peter Cooper*. New York: Harper & Brothers, 1935.

Parker, William N. *Europe, America, and the Wider World: Essays on the Economic History of American Capitalism, Volume 2—America and the Wider World*. New York: Cambridge University Press, 1991.

Peet, Richard, and Nigel Thrift, eds. *New Models in Geography, Volume 1*. London: Unwin Hyman, 1989.

Peterson, Jon A. *The Birth of City Planning in the United States, 1840–1917*. Baltimore: Johns Hopkins University Press, 2003.

Pickel, Eugene M. "A History of Roane County, Tennessee to 1860." Master's thesis, University of Tennessee, Knoxville, 1971.

Porter, Glenn, and Harold C. Livesay. *Merchants and Manufacturers: Studies in the Changing Structure of Nineteenth Century Marketing*. Baltimore: Johns Hopkins University Press, 1971.

Pudup, Mary Beth, et al., eds. *Appalachia in the Making—The Mountain South in the Nineteenth Century*. Chapel Hill: University of North Carolina Press, 1995.

Pulliam, Walter T. *Harriman: The Town That Temperance Built*. Maryville, TN: Brazos Press, 1978.

Relph, Edward. *The Modern Urban Landscape*. Baltimore: Johns Hopkins University Press, 1987.

Rothrock, Mary U., ed., *The French Broad–Holston Country: A History of Knox County, Tennessee*. Knoxville: East Tennessee Historical Society, 1946.

Salstrom, Paul. *Appalachia's Path to Dependency*. Lexington: University Press of Kentucky, 1994.

Scheiber, Harry N., Harold G. Vetter, and Harold U. Faulkner. *American Economic History*. New York: Harper & Row, 1976.

Schmitt, Peter J. *Back to Nature—The Arcadian Myth in Urban America*. New York: Oxford University Press, 1969.

Schultz, Stanley K. *Constructing Urban Culture: American Cities and Urban Planning, 1800–1920*. Philadelphia: Temple University Press, 1989.

Scott, Alan J., and Michael Storper, eds. *Production, Work, Territory: The Geographical Anatomy of Industrial Capitalism*. Boston: Allen & Unwin, 1986.

Shifflett, Crandall A. *Coal Towns: Life, Work, and Culture in Company Towns of Southern Appalachia, 1880–1960*. Knoxville: University of Tennessee Press, 1991.

Sklar, Martin J. *The Corporate Reconstruction of American Capitalism, 1890–1916*. Cambridge: Cambridge University Press, 1988.

Stover, John F. *The Railroads of the South, 1865–1900*. Chapel Hill: University of North Carolina Press, 1955.

Temin, Peter. *Iron and Steel Industry in Nineteenth Century America: An Economic Inquiry*. Cambridge: Massachusetts Institute of Technology Press, 1964.

Temple, Oliver P. *East Tennessee and the Civil War*. Cincinnati: Robert Clarke Co., 1899.

Warner, Sam Bass, Jr. *The Urban Wilderness: The History of the American City*. New York: Harper & Row, 1972.

Warren, Kenneth. *The American Steel Industry, 1850–1970: A Geographical Interpretation*. Oxford: Clarendon Press, 1973.

Wechsburg, Joseph. *The Merchant Bankers*. Boston: Little, Brown, 1966.

White, John H., Jr. *The American Railroad Freight Car: From the Wood Era to the Coming of Steel*. Baltimore: Johns Hopkins University Press, 1993.

Wiener, Jonathan M. *Social Origins of the New South: Alabama, 1860–1885*. Baton Rouge: Louisiana State University Press, 1978.

Williams, Samuel C., *General John T. Wilder: Commander, The Lightning Brigade*. Bloomington, IN, 1936.

Williamson, Harold F., ed. *The Growth of the American Economy*. Englewood Cliffs, NJ: Prentice-Hall, 1951.

Willis, H. Parker, and Jules I. Bogan. *Investment Banking*. New York: Harper & Brothers, 1936.

Wilson, William H. *The City Beautiful Movement*. Baltimore: Johns Hopkins University Press, 1989.

Woodward, C. Vann. *Origins of the New South, 1877–1913*. Baton Rouge: Louisiana State University Press, 1951.

———. *The Strange Career of Jim Crow*. New York: Oxford University Press, 1966.

Zunz, Olivier. *Making America Corporate, 1870–1920*. Chicago: University of Chicago Press, 1990.

———. *The Changing Face of Inequality: Urbanization, Industrial Development, and Immigrants in Detroit, 1880–1920*. Chicago: University of Chicago Press, 1982.

INDEX

D

Decatur, AL, 23
Dalton, GA, 5, 24, 58, 126, 133
Diamond Match Company, 64
Draper Company, 82, 138

E

East Tennessee Land Company (ETLC)
1, 6, 7, 10, 63, **66**, 73, 77, 82, 83–
86, 91, 92–95, **96**, 98, 100–102,
104, 108–9, 115, 125, 128–30, 137,
147, 149–51; and residential segre-
gation, 141–42; structure of 64–70;
and urban reform, 137–39
East Tennessee & Georgia Railroad
(ET&G). *See* railroads
East Tennessee & Virginia Railroad
(ET&V). *See* railroads
East Tennessee, Virginia & Georgia
Railroad (ETV&G). *See* railroads
Edmonds, Richard, 10

F

Fisk, Clinton B., 64–65
Forsythe, Antrim R., 34
forts, locations of, 17, 19–20
Fort Loudon, 19–21
Fort Southwest Point, 20–21
Fort White, 20–21
Fort Payne, AL, 70, 131, 165
Funk, I. K., 64–65

G

Gates, Frederick, 64, 91, 149–50
Goodall, Ernest M., 65
Gould, Jay, 61
Grady, Henry, 10

H

Harriman, TN, 6–7, 11, **67**, **68**, 74–75,
94, **99–100**, 122, 131, 140, 141,
144, **147**–53; after 1893, 115–19;
as a model industrial real estate
venture, 82–85; development of,
69–70, 98–**101**; land sale, 92–96;
literal description of, 90–91; and
residential segregation, 141–42; site
and plan of, 86–87; urban-social
geography of, 101–9
Harriman, Walter C., Jr., 65, 70
Heald, T. H., 77
Heard, Carlos, 71
Hewitt, Abram S., 78
Hopedale, MA, 82, 85, 138
Hopewell, John, Jr., 65
Hopkins, Alphonso A., 65

I

iron production, 5, 13, 32, 44–45, 47,
51, 55, 78, 82, 114, 129, 134, 135–
36; by the Roane Iron Company,
33–37; explained, 32–33

J

James, Charles L., 71, 73

K

Kingston, TN, 8, 18, 26, 43, 50, 52, 75,
82, 117–18, 126, 158; business
leaders 76–77; establishment and
growth of, 22–24; Knoxville, TN,
xiii, xiv, 3, 5, 19, 22–25, 33, 34, 36,
40, 58, 61, 70, 74, 78, 79, 100, 116,
126, 134, 166
Knoxville Iron Company, 36, 122

L

land companies, 7, 9, 12, 57, 59, 80, 98,
109, 111, 118, 130, 135, 143, 165,
167; as capitalist strategies, 127–29;
and city plans, 86–90, 139–41;
development activities of, 63–64;
land company literature, 90–92;
and land sales, 92–97; and model
industrial real estate ventures,
82–85, 136–39; and Panic of 1893,

APPALACHIAN ASPIRATIONS was designed and typeset on a Macintosh OS 10.4 computer system using InDesign software. The body text is set in 10/13 Berkeley and display type is set in Bitstream Carmina. This book was designed and typeset by Stephanie Thompson and manufactured by Thomson-Shore, Inc.